Lecture Notes in Computer Science 12502

More information about this series at http://www.springer.com/series/7412

Jens Petersen · Raúl San José Estépar ·
Alexander Schmidt-Richberg ·
Sarah Gerard · Bianca Lassen-Schmidt ·
Colin Jacobs · Reinhard Beichel ·
Kensaku Mori (Eds.)

Thoracic Image Analysis

Second International Workshop, TIA 2020
Held in Conjunction with MICCAI 2020
Lima, Peru, October 8, 2020
Proceedings

 Springer

Editors
Jens Petersen
University of Copenhagen
Copenhagen, Denmark

Alexander Schmidt-Richberg ⓘ
Philips (Germany)
Hamburg, Hamburg, Germany

Bianca Lassen-Schmidt
Fraunhofer Institute for Medical Image
Computing
Bremen, Bremen, Germany

Reinhard Beichel
University of Iowa
Iowa City, IA, USA

Raúl San José Estépar ⓘ
Harvard Medical School
Boston, MA, USA

Sarah Gerard ⓘ
Harvard Medical School
Boston, MA, USA

Colin Jacobs ⓘ
Radiology and Nuclear Medicine
Radboud University Medical Center
Nijmegen, Gelderland, The Netherlands

Kensaku Mori ⓘ
Graduate School of Informatics
Nagoya University
Nagoya, Japan

ISSN 0302-9743   ISSN 1611-3349 (electronic)
Lecture Notes in Computer Science
ISBN 978-3-030-62468-2   ISBN 978-3-030-62469-9 (eBook)
https://doi.org/10.1007/978-3-030-62469-9

LNCS Sublibrary: SL6 – Image Processing, Computer Vision, Pattern Recognition, and Graphics

This Springer imprint is published by the registered company Springer Nature Switzerland AG
The registered company address is: Gewerbestrasse 11, 6330 Cham, Switzerland

Preface

The Second International Workshop on Thoracic Image Analysis (TIA 2020) was held as an entirely online satellite event of the Medical Image Computing and Computer-Assisted Intervention Conference (MICCAI 2020). Building on the history of the workshop and the Pulmonary Image Analysis workshop, a roughly biannual event at MICCAI going back more than 10 years, the workshop aimed to bring together medical image analysis researchers in the area of thoracic imaging to discuss recent advances in this rapidly developing field. The COVID-19 pandemic has brought much attention to lung imaging, and the role of CT imaging in the diagnostic workflow of COVID-19 and its clinical resolution has been an important research topic. In addition to that, cardiovascular disease, lung cancer, and chronic obstructive pulmonary disease, three diseases all visible on thoracic imaging, are among the top causes of death worldwide. Many imaging modalities are currently available to study the pulmonary and cardiac system, including X-ray, CT, PET, ultrasound, and MRI. We invited papers that dealt with all aspects of image analysis of thoracic data, including but not limited to: image acquisition and reconstruction, segmentation, registration, quantification, visualization, validation, population-based modeling, biophysical modeling (computational anatomy), deep learning, image analysis in small animals, outcome-based research, and novel infectious disease applications (e.g., COVID-19, TB, etc.). We particularly welcomed novel work focused around the need for new methodologies for predisposition, diagnosis, staging, and resolution assessment of COVID-19 infections as an emerging disease as well as good-sized independent validation studies on the use of deep learning models in the area of thoracic imaging, despite having possibly little technical novelty.

The 16 papers submitted to the workshop were reviewed in a double-blind manner with at least three reviewers per paper, whose affiliations and recent publications were checked to avoid conflicts of interest. The review process included a blind review followed by a meta-review done by consensus by three committee members that evaluated the reviews and the papers as a whole. All of the submitted papers were long format (8–12 pages). Out of the submitted papers, 15 were accepted for presentation; however, 1 paper was withdrawn after acceptance for inconsistencies in the reported results. The remaining papers were grouped into four topics, which are reflected in the structure of these proceedings – Image Segmentation (5), Computer-Aided Diagnosis and Localization (4), Image Translation and Inpainting (3), and Image registration (2). Deep learning techniques continue to expand with 15 out of the 16 submissions using some elements of deep learning. We were pleased to see that the workshop has helped bring focus to COVID-19 research with no less than three works covering the analysis and detection of this disease. The imaging modalities used were a good mixture of 2D X-ray, 3D CT, 4DCT, DECT, and MRI, demonstrating the complementary information brought together by different modalities used to study the thoracic system. We believe that thoracic image analysis keeps on playing a crucial role in the understanding of chronic and infectious diseases with high morbidity and mortality as reflected by the works submitted to this workshop.

We want to express our gratitude to all the authors for submitting papers to TIA 2020 and everyone involved in the organization and peer-review process.

September 2020   Jens Petersen
                                                                          Raúl San José Estépar

Organization

Organizing Committee

Kensaku Mori — Nagoya University, Japan
Raúl San José Estépar — Brigham and Women's Hospital, Harvard Medical School, USA
Sarah Gerard — Brigham and Women's Hospital, Harvard Medical School, USA
Reinhard Beichel — The University of Iowa, USA
Colin Jacobs — Radboud University Medical Center, The Netherlands
Alexander Schmidt-Richberg — Philips Research Laboratories, Germany
Bianca Lassen-Schmidt — Fraunhofer Institute for Digital Medicine MEVIS, Germany
Jens Petersen — University of Copenhagen, Denmark

Program Committee

Raúl San José Estépar — Brigham and Women's Hospital, Harvard Medical School, USA
Sarah Gerard — Brigham and Women's Hospital, Harvard Medical School, USA
Alexander Schmidt-Richberg — Philips Research Laboratories, Germany
Jens Petersen — University of Copenhagen, Denmark

Additional Reviewers

Abraham George Smith
Alexander Schmidt-Richberg
Christian Buerger
Colin Jacobs
Jens Petersen
Lasse Hansen
Matthias Wilms
Mattias Heinrich

Olivier Nempont
Pietro Nardelli
Raghavendra Selvan
Rene Werner
Sarah Gerard
Silas Ørting
Tobias Klinder

Contents

Image Segmentation

Two-Stage Mapping-Segmentation Framework for Delineating COVID-19 Infections from Heterogeneous CT Images

Tong Li[1,2], Zhuochen Wang[1,2], Yanbo Chen[2], Lichi Zhang[1], Yaozong Gao[2], Feng Shi[2], Dahong Qian[3], Qian Wang[1(✉)], and Dinggang Shen[2(✉)]

[1] School of Biomedical Engineering, Shanghai Jiao Tong University, Shanghai, China
`wang.qian@sjtu.edu.cn`
[2] Shanghai United Imaging Intelligence Co., Ltd., Shanghai, China
`Dinggang.Shen@gmail.com`
[3] Institute of Medical Robotics, Shanghai Jiao Tong University, Shanghai, China

Abstract. Infection segmentation is essential for quantitative assessment in computer-aided management of COVID-19. However, clinical CT images are usually heterogeneous, which are reconstructed by different protocols with varying appearance and voxel spacing due to radiologist preference. Most existing infection segmentation models are only trained using specific types of CT images, which would undermine the performance when applied to other types of CT images. Therefore, it is highly desirable to construct a model that could be applied to heterogeneous CT images in the urgent COVID-19 applications. In this paper, we present a two-stage mapping-segmentation framework for delineating COVID-19 infections from CT images. To compensate for heterogeneity of CT images obtained from different imaging centers, we develop an image-level domain-adaptive process to transform all kinds of images into a target type, and then segment COVID-19 infections accordingly. Experiments show that the infection delineation performance based on our proposed method is superior to the model trained jointly using mixture of all types of images, and is also comparable to those models supervised by using only specific types of images (if applicable).

Keywords: COVID-19 · Domain-adaption · Image segmentation

1 Introduction

The mass dissemination of Coronavirus Disease 2019 (COVID-19) catches everyone's attention since the end of 2019 [1]. Chest CT imaging provides an essential approach, as an important complement to the reverse-transcription polymerase chain reaction (RT-PCR) tests [2], to facilitate the assessment and management of COVID-19. A study shows that the sensitivity of CT images for COVID-19

T. Li and Z. Wang—Contributed equally.

© Springer Nature Switzerland AG 2020
J. Petersen et al. (Eds.): TIA 2020, LNCS 12502, pp. 3–13, 2020.
https://doi.org/10.1007/978-3-030-62469-9_1

infection is higher than that of RT-PCR [3]. The clinicians can also evaluate the severity of patients from chest CT based on the appearance and sizes of the lesions [5].

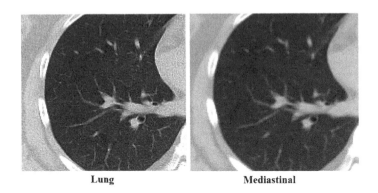

Lung   Mediastinal

Fig. 1. Examples of two types of thick-slice lung CT images. Left: Image produced by lung reconstrution algorithm has higher quality and contrast; Right: Image produced by mediastinal reconstruction algorithm can show GGO (Ground Glass Opacity) better.

However, due to the varying acquisition parameters and user preferences in different clinical facilities, the obtained CT images are often heterogeneous. Basically, two reconstruction algorithms, i.e., lung reconstruction algorithm and mediastinal reconstruction algorithm, are often used, corresponding to lung kernel and soft-tissue kernel, respectively. Note that the use of lung kernel may produce sharper images with higher spatial resolution [6], implying higher image quality yet longer time expense in reconstruction. On the contrary, the images produced by mediastinal reconstruction algorithm have lower quality yet faster speed to reconstruct. In clinical emergency such as COVID-19, acquiring thick-slice CT images with large voxel spacing is often the first choice, since it takes too long time to acquire thin-slice CT images. Typical examples of thick-slice CT images are shown in Fig. 1.

Segmentation of COVID-19 infections can be used to assist clinicians in diagnosis and treatment [20]. While it is often needed to quantify the infection area and extract visual features accordingly, deep learning methods contribute a lot particularly to segmenting the infections and generating the contours. There are some segmentation frameworks designed for lung CT images. Zheng et al. [7] incorporated U-Net to develop a weakly supervised software to detect COVID-19 infection. Shan et al. [4] adopted a human-in-the-loop strategy to accelerate the manual delineation of CT images for VB-Net training [13]. Besides, Jin et al. [8] proposed a two-stage pipeline for screening COVID-19 in CT images, in which the whole lung region is firstly detected to assist the segmentation of infection by an UNet++ extended network.

The above-mentioned works didn't take heterogeneity of data from different reconstruction methods and the possible domain gap into consideration. Due to the limited time and equipment, the scanning settings vary depending on different institutes and situations. Therefore, it is difficult to train a single network for all segmentation tasks in clinical practice, since a good performance of neural networks usually requires a well-normalized data distribution [9]. Some previous works indicate that directly mixing various types of data for model training only brings marginal improvements, or even worse performance, if the heterogeneity is significant [11].

There are attempts made to remedy the above issue. For example, Liu et al. [10] proposed to leverage annotations from one modality to be useful in other modalities. Mauricio et al. [14] introduced a novel method to adapt from one source domain to several target domains by a consistency loss combined with adversarial learning. Judy et al. [15] formed a linear transformation that mapped features from the target (test) domain to the source (training) domain as part of training the classifier. Yan et al. [16] proposed a new image fusion method based on principal component analysis and dual-tree complex wavelet transform. Liu et al. [11] proposed a novel multi-site network (MS-Net) for improving prostate segmentation by learning robust representations, leveraging multiple sources of data, and accepting a single image to test.

In this paper, we attempt to build a unified model for various CT images from different clinical facilities to solve the urgent need of infection segmentation of COVID-19. In order to avoid performance drop caused by heterogeneity of different data, we aim to map all images into consistent data distribution and improve the segmentation performance. In our proposed method, the training data of our model is thus a mixture of three types of CT images. As in clinical emergency such as COVID-19, the capability of using all available data for training a model is crucial. Particularly, apart from common thick-slice images, the available thin-slice images could also be used for training. We demonstrate in experiments that the performance in segmenting thick-slice images is comparable to results of separate training, regardless whether the corresponding training images are available.

2   Method

The proposed method aims to take input from heterogeneous CT images with arbitrary reconstruction algorithm and voxel spacing for the COVID-19 infection segmentation task, where thin-slice CT images are used to assist segmentation of thick-slice images. In the urgent fight with COVID-19, one may acquire thick-slice images fast, yet suffer from lacking of manual delineation for training a segmentation model. To this end, we develop a two-stage mapping-segmentation solution. First, multi-type domain adaption is used to transform heterogeneous data into the same type. Second, we train a single 3D segmentation network to obtain COVID-19 infectious areas on the unified domain. The overall structure of our pipeline is illustrated in Fig. 2.

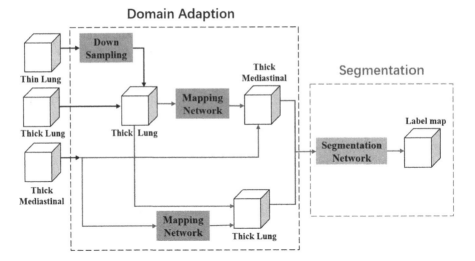

Fig. 2. The overall architecture of our model. It consists of two stages: multi-type domain adaption and segmentation on mapped dataset. We design two specific mapping strategies in domain adaptation, transforming diverse images into thick mediastinal (blue arrow) and thick lung (green arrow), respectively, to facilitate subsequent segmentation. All available images including thin-slice images could be used to assist segmentation of thick-slice images. (Color figure online)

2.1 Multi-type Domain Adaption

In this stage, we use image-level domain adaptation to normalize all types of CT images into the unified domain. As previously mentioned, three image types are included in this work: thin lung, thick lung, and thick mediastinal. Heterogeneity in these three types of CT images collected by different clinical criteria hinders the application of the single 3D segmentation model, which usually results in a performance drop when validated on other types. Image-level domain adaptation can directly convert all image types into unified appearance for subsequent segmentation.

To deal with the difference from reconstruction algorithms, we employ a mapping network to transform CT images reconstructed by different algorithms into the same type. The lung algorithm reconstructed images (lung images) have high contrast and sharp texture. Meanwhile, the mediastinal algorithm reconstructed images (mediastinal images) have low contrast and blurry texture. We evaluate the results of two domain adaptation strategies: mapping all various images to thick mediastinal images, or thick lung images (c.f., Fig. 2). To add thin-slice images into training, we use tri-linear interpolation to down-sample them to match thick-slice images, and use nearest-neighbor interpolation to down-sample the label maps.

Our image-level mapping network is illustrated in Fig. 3. We use contiguous three slices as 2.5D input. The network contains three sub-networks: image gener-

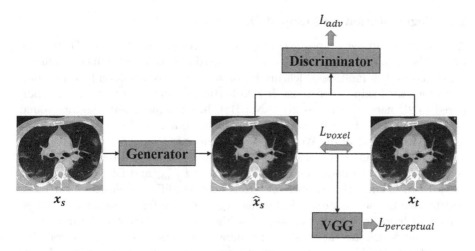

Fig. 3. The structure of the mapping network in image-level domain adaption. Here we take the mapping from thick-lung image to thick-mediastinal image for example.

ator, pre-trained VGG-16 network and discriminator. When used in the testing stage, only image generator is needed. The generator G adopts the encoding-decoding framework. We denote the input of generator as x_s, and the output as $\hat{x}_t$. As the training data is paired, we have the real image x_t as ground truth. Here, the voxel-wise loss (L_1) can be defined between $\hat{x}_t$ and x_t. Besides intensity values, we also need to constrain the structures of the images and consider the relationship among voxels. The discriminator D and pretrained VGG-16 network V are used to keep the output consistent with the real image in structure. The discriminator contains five convolution layers, and computes the adversarial loss [17] between generated image and real image. The VGG-16 network pre-trained on ImageNet extracts high-level feature representations of images. We define perceptual loss [12] to assure the synthetic image and the real image to share the same high-level features from V. It could measure image similarities more robustly than voxel losses.

The total loss for the mapping network can be defined as:

$$L_{total} = \alpha * L_{voxel} + \beta * L_{adv} + \gamma * L_{perceptual} \tag{1}$$

$$L_{voxel} = ||G(x_s) - x_t||_{L_1} \tag{2}$$

$$\min_{D} L_{adv} = \mathbb{E}_{x \sim x_s}(D(G(x)))^2 + \mathbb{E}_{x \sim x_t}(D(x) - 1)^2 \tag{3}$$

$$\min_{G} L_{adv} = \mathbb{E}_{x \sim x_s}(D(G(x)) - 1)^2 \tag{4}$$

$$L_{perceptual} = ||V(G(x_s)) - V(x_t)||_{L_1} \tag{5}$$

2.2   Segmentation on Mapped Datasets

After unifying all data types, we adopt V-Net to segment the COVID-19 infections. The segmentation network can learn spatial features with 3D convolution layer, accomplish multi-level feature fusion and preserve low-level feature representations with skip-connections. It gets better segmentation performance compared to 2D network such as 2D U-Net [18]. In our experiment, the foreground segmentation area includes not only pneumonia but also the normal lung area as the pathological prior. We suppose that the infectious area can not appear out of the lung, and segmenting the normal lung area would be helpful for the segmentation of the pneumonia area. Focal loss L_{focal} and Dice loss L_{dice} [19] are used to balance the numbers of voxels between different classes. Dice loss is widely used in volumetric medical image segmentation for its robustness against class imbalance. α_i is the loss weight of the class i. C denotes the number of classes and N denotes the total pixel number of a single image. Tunable focusing parameter γ decides the rate by which easy examples are down-weighted. The final loss function for segmentation can be formulated as:

$$L_{seg} = L_{dice} + L_{focal}$$
$$= \sum_{i=0}^{C} \sum_{j=1}^{N} \alpha_i (1 - p_{ij})^{\gamma} log(p_{ij}) + \sum_{i=1}^{C} \sum_{j=1}^{N} \alpha_i (1 - \frac{2\sum_{j=1}^{N} p_{ij} g_{ij}}{\sum_{j=1}^{N} (p_{ij} + g_{ij})}) \quad (6)$$

3   Experiment

3.1   Data

We collect a private dataset of multi-type chest CT images to evaluate the performance. It includes thin-slice and thick-slice images reconstructed from lung algorithm and thick-slice reconstructed from mediastinal algorithm, respectively. Voxel spacing of thin-slice images is approximately $0.685 \times 0.685 \times 1 \, mm^3$ and that of thick-slice images is $0.68 \times 0.685 \times 5 \, mm^3$. It contains 159 subjects diagnosed as COVID-19, and each case contains all three types of images (thin lung, thick lung, thick mediastinal). The pneumonia infection is manually annotated by radiologists. The dataset is split into training set (119 cases), and test set (40 cases) randomly.

3.2   Analysis of Inter-type Heterogeneity

It is essential to quantitatively analyze the inter-type heterogeneity of multi-type CT images. We conduct cross-type validation among the three-type images. We train a segmentation network named as the separate model for each type and evaluate performance within and across types. The Dice coefficient is used to measure the pixel-wise consistency between the predicted label map and ground truth.

As shown in Table 1, the model independently trained on its own type of data is named as separate model. When evaluated within its own training type,

Table 1. Cross-type validation of separate trained model. Dice score (%) is used for evaluation of COVID-19 infection segmentation.

Model	Thick Lung	Thick Mediastinal	Thin Lung
M(Thin Lung)	69.29	56.65	**86.46**
M(Thick Lung)	**82.87**	80.96	79.92
M(Thick Mediastinal)	25.39	**82.64**	12.16

it usually gets a high Dice score. When evaluated on other types of images, every separate model would see a severe performance drop. It's obvious that the demanding image quality requirement of the thin lung model can undermine the performance on the thick-slice dataset. As lung and mediastinal CT images show different texture, sharpness and blurness respectively, models based on two kinds of texture show irreversible adaptation. The Dice score of thick mediastinal dataset test on thick lung model has dropped 2–3%. It should be noted that the thick mediastinal model can cause significant performance drop on the thick lung images. These results have revealed a sensible discrepancy among different types of CT images.

3.3   Experiments on the Multi-type Domain Adaptation

Considering that a single segmentation model is needed to handle various data and the inter-type heterogeneity matters for segmentation, we train a mapping model on paired thick-slice data to normalize the different styles caused by two reconstruction algorithms.

In our experiment, we set the weight of pixel-wise loss, adversarial loss and perceptual loss α, β, γ as 100, 1, and 100. Results from two mapping strategies are evaluated in Table 2: mapping from lung images with sharp texture to mediastinal images with blur texture denoted as Thick Lung-Mediastinal, and mapping mediastinal images into lung images denoted as Thick Mediastinal-Lung. Common measures include peak signal-to-noise ratio (PSNR) and structure similarity index (SSIM) are used to evaluate the quality of synthetic images. As shown in Table 2, Thick Lung-Mediastinal model achieves higher PSNR and SSIM than Thick Mediastinal-Lung model. It has proved that mapping from sharp texture to blur texture is easier to realize, as it's comparable to an operation of smoothing filtering. And mapping from blur images to sharp images needs to complement high-frequency features and can be more complex. The mapping visualization is shown in Fig. 4.

Table 2. Evaluation of synthetic image quality by mapping model.

Model	PSNR	SSIM
Thick Mediastinal-Lung	35.705	0.930
Thick Lung-Mediastinal	**45.020**	**0.975**

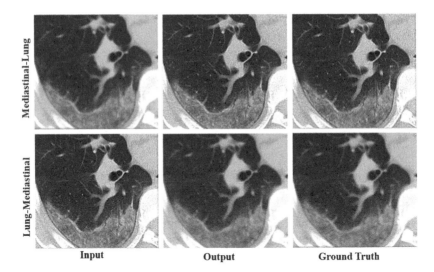

Fig. 4. The results of two mapping strategies. The first row: mapping from images produced by mediastinal reconstruction algorithm to images produced by lung reconstruction algorithm (Mediastinal-Lung). The second row: mapping from images produced by lung reconstruction algorithm to images produced by mediastinal reconstruction algorithm (Lung-Mediastinal).

3.4   Experiments of Segmentation on Mapped Dataset

These two data mapping strategies, specifically mapping into thick lung data or thick mediastinal data, are evaluated for segmentation. Every type of data has been processed by its pipeline into the target type. We input all target types for segmentation training. We also concern about whether the inter-type discrepancy is still significant when incorporating all original data for network training as a baseline, which is named as joint model.

Table 3. Performance on COVID-19 pneumonia infection segmentation from separate, joint and models based on two mapping strategies. We use Dice score (%) for evaluation.

Model	Thick Lung	Thick Mdiastinal	Thin Lung
Separate	82.87	82.64	**86.46**
Joint	80.69	79.64	83.61
Mapping Mediastinal	82.32	**82.67**	83.78
Mapping Lung	**83.29**	**82.67**	85.32

The results are shown in Table 3. Generally, training on the separate model for each type gets the best results. However, the Dice score of joint V-Net training is still 2–3% lower than the separate model. It shows that joint training

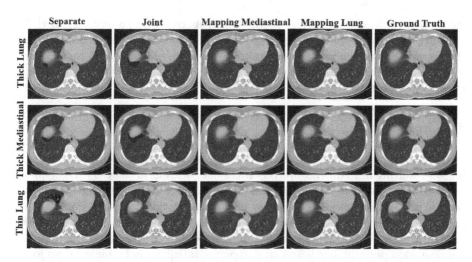

Fig. 5. Result of segmentation results of thick lung (the first row), thick mediastina (the second row), thin lung (the third row) CT images from models named as Seperate (the first column), Joint (the second column), Mapping Mediastina (the third column), Mapping Lung (the fourth column). And the last column shows ground truth. The red area represents normal lung area and the green parts represent COVID-19 infection. (Color figure online)

is helpful but insufficient to reduce the inter-type heterogeneity. This may be because the representation learned by joint learning only could reach an equilibrium optimum for all types rather than the real optimum for each type. It is worthy to note that the performance of segmentation based on two mapping strategies in our proposed method outperforms the joint model and can be comparable to the separate model on thick-slice images. As illustrated in Sect. 3.1, Lung-Mediastinal mapping strategy gets higher performance on the synthesis of mediastinal algorithm reconstructed images. However, segmentation on unified lung algorithm reconstructed images based on Mediastinal-Lung mapping strategy (Mapping Lung) gets a higher Dice score than segmentation on unified mediastinal algorithm reconstructed images (Mapping Mediastinal). It is indicated that blur texture in thick mediastinal images loses high-frequency features and reduces segmentation performance. Sharp texture in thick lung images can preserve the features of the infectious area, and lead to higher accuracy for subsequent segmentation task. The performance on thin-slice separate model achieves the highest Dice score as the down-sampling applied in other compared methods would ruin its own spatial representation. We mainly focus on improving the performance on thick-slice images which are commonly used in clinical emergency such as COVID-19. In addition, the down-sampled thin-slice images also provide extra information for thick-slice training and enlarge usable dataset.

Figure 5 shows examples of segmentation results. We can see that both separate model and joint model misjudge the boundary of lung and wrongly predict as COVID-19 infection. After mapping into the unified domain, in lung or mediastina images, these wrong prediction areas could be largely corrected. It indicates that the segmentation based on similar image context acquired from the network mapping operation reduces false positives of segmentation and keeps results consistent among different kinds of images. The validity of mapping network for segmentation has been proved.

4   Conclusion

In this paper, we propose a method to tackle the inter-type heterogeneity of CT images resulting from different reconstruction algorithms in the COVID-19 infection segmentation task. Our main idea is to map all data into target type using domain adaptation networks for subsequent segmentation tasks. We evaluate the segmentation performance of two mapping strategies and compare our proposed method with the separate and joint training models. Experiments show that the segmentation performance based on mapping strategies can be higher than joint training. Especially, the results of the model trained on the type of thick lung images could be superior to that on separate model. The proposed method has enabled the unified segmentation model applicable to various types of thick-slice images collected in COVID-19 pneumonia diagnosis, and gets relatively equivalent segmentation performance compared with individually trained models. The proposed method can be practical for the complicated clinical application scenarios.

References

1. Wang, C., Horby, P.W., Hayden, F.G., Gao, G.F.: A novel coronavirus outbreak of global health concern. Lancet **395**(10223), 470–473 (2020)
2. Ai, T et al.: Correlation of chest CT and RT-PCR testing in coronavirus disease 2019 (COVID-19) in China: a report of 1014 cases. Radiology, p. 200642 (2020)
3. Fang, Y., Zhang, H., Xie. J., Lin, M.: Sensitivity of chest CT for COVID-19: comparison to RT-PCR. Radiology, p. 200432 (2020)
4. Shan, F., Gao, Y., Wang, J.: Lung infection quantification of COVID-19 in CT images with deep learning (2020). arXiv preprint arXiv:2003.04655
5. Bernheim, A., Mei, X., Huang, M.: Chest CT findings in coronavirus disease-19 (COVID-19): relationship to duration of infection. Radiology **26**(1), 200463 (2020)
6. Dalrymple, N.C., Prasad, S.R., Freckleton, M.W.: Introduction to the language of three-dimensional imaging with multidetector CT. Radiographics **25**(5), 1409–1428 (2005)
7. Zheng, C., Deng, X., Fu, Q.: Deep learning-based detection for COVID-19 from chest CT using weak label. medRxiv (2020)
8. Jin, S., Wang, B., Xu., H.: AI-assisted CT imaging analysis for COVID-19 screening: Building and deploying a medical AI system in four weeks. medRxiv (2020)
9. Wang, X., Cai, Z., Gao, D.: Towards universal object detection by domain attention. In: CVPR (2019)
10. Liu, Y., et al.: Cross-modality knowledge transfer for prostate segmentation from CT scans. In: Wang, Q. (ed.) DART/MIL3ID -2019. LNCS, vol. 11795, pp. 63–71. Springer, Cham (2019). https://doi.org/10.1007/978-3-030-33391-1_8

11. Liu, Q., Dou, Q., Yu, L., Heng, P.A.: MS-net: multi-site network for improving prostate segmentation with heterogeneous MRI data. IEEE Trans. Med. Imaging **39**(9), 2713–2724 (2020)
12. Dar, S.U., Yurt, M., Karacan, L., Erdem, A.: Image synthesis in multi-contrast MRI with conditional generative adversarial networks. IEEE Trans. Med. Imaging **38**(10), 2375–2388 (2020)
13. Mu, G., Lin, Z., Han, M.: Segmentation of kidney tumor by multi-resolution VB-nets (2019)
14. Orbes-Arteaga, M., et al.: Multi-domain adaptation in brain MRI through paired consistency and adversarial learning. In: Wang, Q. (ed.) DART/MIL3ID -2019. LNCS, vol. 11795, pp. 54–62. Springer, Cham (2019). https://doi.org/10.1007/978-3-030-33391-1_7
15. Hoffman, J., Rodner, E., Donahue, J.: Efficient learning of domain-invariant image representations (2013). arXiv preprint arXiv:1301.3224
16. Yan, Y.H., Yang, Y.Z.: Image fusion based on principal component analysis in dual-tree complex wavelet transform domain. In: 2012 International Conference on Wavelet Active Media Technology and Information Processing (ICWAMTIP), pp. 70–73 (2012)
17. Goodfellow, L., Pouget-Abadie, J., Mirza, M.: Generative adversarial nets. In: Advances in neural information processing systems, pp. 2672–2680 (2014)
18. Ronneberger, O., Fischer, P., Brox, T.: U-Net: convolutional networks for biomedical image segmentation. In: Navab, N., Hornegger, J., Wells, W.M., Frangi, A.F. (eds.) MICCAI 2015. LNCS, vol. 9351, pp. 234–241. Springer, Cham (2015). https://doi.org/10.1007/978-3-319-24574-4_28
19. Milletari, F., Navab, N., Ahmad, S.A.: V-net: fully convolutional neural networks for volumetric medical image segmentation. In: Fourth International Conference on 3D vision (3DV) (2016)
20. Shi, F., Wang, J., Shi, J., Wu, Z.: Review of artificial intelligence techniques in imaging data acquisition, segmentation and diagnosis for COVID-19. IEEE Reviews in Biomedical Engineering, p. 1 (2016)

Multi-cavity Heart Segmentation in Non-contrast Non-ECG Gated CT Scans with F-CNN

Rafael Moreta-Martínez[1,2], Gonzalo Vegas Sánchez-Ferrero[2], Lasse Andresen[2], Jakob Qvortrup Holsting[2], and Raúl San José Estépar[2(✉)]

[1] Departamento de Bioingeniería E Ingeniería Aeroespacial, Universidad Carlos III de Madrid, Madrid, Spain
[2] Applied Chest Imaging Laboratory, Department of Radiology, Brigham and Women's Hospital, Boston, MA, USA
rsanjose@bwh.harvard.edu

Abstract. The anatomical delineation of heart cavities in CT scans is a well-known problem with extended applications in cardiopulmonary diseases. A common approach to provide multi-cavity segmentations is the use of atlas-based statistical shape models. This methodology is of particular interest when just non-contrast and non-gated scans are available since the non-observable internal structures of the heart can be inferred from the fitting of the pericardium provided by the shape model. These inferred cavities have shown predictive power in clinical studies when compared to reference standards. However, although promising, the shape model is limited to the fitting of the pericardium and cannot take advantage of the geometrical inter-relations of internal cavities. This leads to inaccurate segmentations of the smaller structures such as the atria and wrong estimations of the internal cavities. In this work, we study the potential of CNNs to learn the inter-relations of a multicavity active shape model to provide accurate estimations of the internal cavities in non-gated and non-contrast CT scans. We propose an architecture that is able to learn the appearance model of the heart from an inaccurate training dataset. Results demonstrate that our segmentation method improves the correlation of ventricular volume estimations when compared against a semiautomatic active shape approach using cardiac MRI as the reference standard.

Keywords: Heart segmentation · Deep learning · Active shape model · CT

1 Introduction

The analysis of cardiac structure and function have proven to be a key element in the diagnosis and follow-up of patients suffering from cardiopulmonary diseases.

This work has been partially funded by the National Institutes of Health NHLBI awards R01HL116473 and R01HL149877. We gratefully acknowledge the support of NVIDIA Corporation with the donation of the GPU used for this research.

J. Petersen et al. (Eds.): TIA 2020, LNCS 12502, pp. 14–23, 2020.
https://doi.org/10.1007/978-3-030-62469-9_2

Although echocardiography and cardiac MRI are often used to study cardiac structure and function, these are not systematically deployed in every thoracic exploration. In contrast, computed tomographic (CT) imaging of the chest is broadly used in clinical care and is increasingly used for lung cancer screening in high-risk smokers [1]. For this reason, there is an increasing interest in the community in the use of CT scans to identify patients at higher risk of developing cardiac dysfunction. Delineating the structures of the heart in chest CT scans is a challenging task, especially when non-contrast-enhanced and non-gated acquisitions are available. A promising approach was presented in [2], where the authors apply a multi-cavity active shape model (ASM) to provide estimates of the internal cavities (ventricles and atria) by fitting the outer walls to the pericardium. The estimations have shown correlation with MRI volume measures and can be used to predict the reduction in exacerbation frequency in cardiopulmonary diseases [3], as well as describe the complex lung-heart interplay in obstructive lung disease [4,5].

Although the use of the ASM can provide a proper delineation of the pericardium, the complex shape of chambers –especially the atria– usually causes overlapping with other structures such as the aorta or the lungs. Additionally, the lack of internal references contributes to internal inconsistencies in the estimated sizes of chambers

In this work, we study the potential of convolutional neural networks (CNNs) to learn the geometrical relationship between the outer shape of the heart provided by the segmentation with the internal geometry of chambers provided by the active shape model. This way, we join the anatomically consistent relationship given by the ASM with the powerful segmentation schemes provided by the recent advances in CNNs.

2 Method

The method we propose is inspired by the most recent advances in semantic segmentation. We adopt and encoder-decoder style architecture that allows recovering resolution information into the encoder (skip-connections) likewise the celebrated U-Net [6]. However, to take advantage of the information between layers, we increase shorter connections between layers by setting feed-forward connections among them, as proposed with the DenseNet in [7].

On the other hand, as we are interested in avoiding representational bottlenecks, we adopt the philosophy proposed in [8] in their Efficient-Net (ENet), where authors suggest not to use a maxpooling layer or strided convolution separately but to combine both non-linear transformations of the same input. This way, the efficiency is increased since the same information is combined in a lower amount of parameters.

The combination of all these ideas give rise to our proposal: the Dense Volumetric Network (DeVoNet). The DeVoNet architecture with all its parameters is represented in Fig. 1. Note that DeVoNet is built around the same philosophy as the FC-DenseNet [9]: the input is being propagated through the network

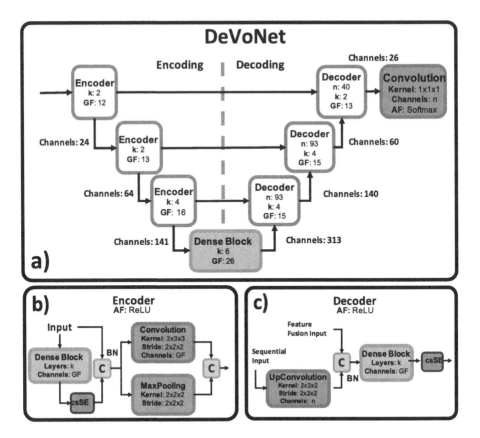

Fig. 1. a) DeVoNet architecture design, where k is the number of layers defined as a batch normalization, convolution and activation. GF: Growth factor, i.e. number of filters per convolutional layer. n: number of filters in the upConvolution layer. BN: batch normalization. b) Design of the encoder. c) Design of the decoder.

via dense connections while channels are appended across the network. To avoid representational bottlenecks by balancing network parameters though width and depth, we reduced the number of layers and increased their width. This was achieved by changing the structure of the encoder similarly to an ENet style. In our case, the max pooling serves as a way of passing the most prominent features of the input and the strided convolution adds them to the number of features.

Additionally, rather than keeping a constant growth factor throughout the network like FC-DenseNet, we increased it gradually as we reduce the spatial resolution. On the other hand, we decrease the number of channels to reach computationally feasible parameters without performing excessive information compression. The filters to use for the up-convolution layer in the decoder block were computed as 2/3 of the input channels.

Finally, we included a spatial and channel squeeze and excitation (scSE) [10] module in each decoder and encoder block. This module helps to recalibrate feature maps along channels and space dimensions, which results in an enhancement of relevant features while suppressing weak ones.

Table 1. Dice similarity coefficient over 66 supervised subjects. C: cavity, W: wall.

		Loss function			
		CE	WCE	Dice	Dice*
U-Net-3D	C	0.861 ± 0.059	0.839 ± 0.073	0.861 ± 0.055	**0.864 ± 0.053**
	W	0.392 ± 0.257	0.437 ± 0.204	0.524 ± 0.169	**0.525 ± 0.172**
FC-DenseNet	C	0.843 ± 0.066	0.821 ± 0.087	0.855 ± 0.059	**0.857 ± 0.066**
	W	0.320 ± 0.278	0.387 ± 0.224	**0.510 ± 0.173**	0.506 ± 0.177
DeVoNet	C	0.846 ± 0.083	0.807 ± 0.102	0.845 ± 0.067	**0.850 ± 0.059**
	W	0.355 ± 0.283	0.384 ± 0.218	0.475 ± 0.197	**0.508 ± 0.159**

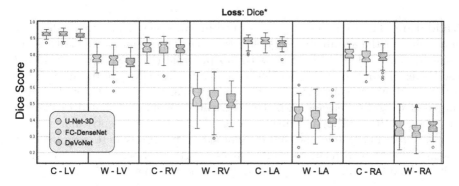

Fig. 2. BoxPlot of Dice scores for 8 heart structures compared along each architecture using Dice coefficient loss with lung as class. L: left, R: right, V: ventricle, A: atrium.

Training Data Generation. The training labels were generated by segmenting the heart using the Active Shape Model proposed in [11] and publicly available[1]. This ASM comprises 50 modes of variation to describe the geometry of the different cavities of the heart. The segmentation process is the one proposed in [2] which comprises the following steps: i) the model is located in the center of the ROI. ii) the shape is iteratively aligned in cycles of two stages: 1) Affine transformations to contain blood inside the cavities until it becomes stable. 2) Elastic deformation. When the elastic deformation becomes stable, the segmentation process stops. A set of 9 classes were considered in each architecture: left and right ventricles, left and right atria, their respective walls, and the background

---

[1] http://www.cistib.org.

class. It is important to note that these labels are a reference and can be inaccurate due to inconsistent such as the misclassification of lung parenchyma as heart tissue.

Losses. In order to test the effect of different learning metrics in the final solution, we defined several loss functions, namely, cross-entropy (CE), weighted cross entropy (WCE) [8], and Dice coefficient to train each architecture. Given that the reference standard was generated without taking into account the restrictions of surrounding structures like the lung, we decided to test an alternative solution that included an extra output class for the lung to model this external constrained. The label for the lung is trivially obtained by a simple threshold of the CT image for values below –500 HU. We just considered the Dice loss function in the method with the lung class, that we denote as Dice*.

Training. Our experiment was implemented with Tensorflow backend of Keras framework. The learning rate was initially set to 0.0001 and decreased by 0.1 after 2 epochs. The minibatch size was of 1. Adam was used for optimization. Once validation loss converged training was finished. All experiments were performed on a NVIDIA Titan X or/and NVIDIA GeForce GTX 108 GPU with 64 GB RAM.

Validation. The validation was performed in two stages. First, we studied the suitability for the architectures and losses in the description of the multi-cavity segmentation of the heart. Along with our proposal (DeVoNet), we considered the U-Net-3D and the FC-DenseNet as representative CNNs of the state of the art. Second, we compared the estimated ventricular volumes obtained from the proposed F-CNNs methods with the ventricular volumes calculated by experts in cardiac MRI (cMRI) imaging —the gold standard for ventricular volume calculation— in diastole and systole. Volume comparisons were performed by means of Pearson correlations and by assessing the bias between the estimated volume from CT and the diastolic and systolic cMRI volumes.

3   Experiments and Results

Data. The validation of the performance of the F-CNN architectures and the loss functions is performed in a dataset consisting of 4,186 high-resolution chest CT images from smokers with and without COPD from the COPDGene study. The dimensions of the CT scans are $512 \times 512 \times z$ where z varies roughly between 500 and 700 depending on the subject (with a pixel size of $\sim 0.65 \times 0.65 \times 0.75$ mm). To reduce the computational burden of the validation, we considered a region of interest (ROI) of dimensions $256 \times 256 \times 96$ centered in the heart. The images were re-sampled to $128 \times 128 \times 96$. The dataset was randomly divided into a training set (4000 scans), a validation set (100 scans), and a testing set (86 scans).

To provide a figure of merit without misclassified labels, an expert selected a subset of 66 scans from the testing set from which the ASM segmentation showed an excellent segmentation according to the anatomical localization of

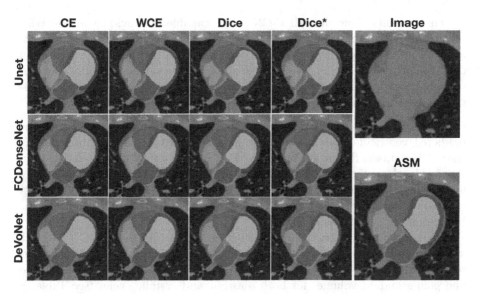

Fig. 3. Visual examination of multi-cavity heart segmentation. The F-CNN architectures are able to provide a multi-cavity segmentation of the heart similar to the ASM.

chambers with respect pulmonary artery and veins, Aorta and vena cava. It is worth noting that the training was performed in the dataset that was not reviewed by an expert and therefore contains noisy labels.

The correlation with the gold standard is performed in a subset of the testing set (20 subjects) for which the ventricular volumes were calculated in cardiac MRI (cMRI). The cMRI images were acquired using a 1.5 T scanner with resolution of ∼1.5 × 1.5 mm and 8 mm slice thickness. The available measures include the endocardial end diastolic and end systolic volumes of left and right ventricles. We calculated the same features from the segmentations given by the ASM and the CNNs and correlated them to those provided from the cMRI data.

Accuracy Validation. In Table 1, we show the average dice similarity coefficient obtained for the 66 supervised scans for cavities and walls. The results show high similarity with respect to the shape model, being the Dice loss the one that achieves the best values. Interestingly, the inclusion of the lung class in the architectures (denoted as Dice*) provide an subtle but noticeable improvement. This is probably a consequence of identifying the lung tissue as a non-cardiac structure, since the supervised segmentations have no misclassification of lung tissue. Note that the results obtained for the walls are lower when compared to the cavities. This is because the volume of walls is remarkably lower and, therefore, the Dice measures are much more variable. To illustrate this behavior, we show in Fig. 2 the detailed behavior of the testing group for the architecture considering the lung class (Dice*) for all cavities and walls.

These results show that all F-CNNs are capable of providing multi-cavity segmentations that are consistent with an active shape model. This is a significant result since the F-CNNs are not constrained to the modes of variation of the ASM or its topology and yet they are able to provide anatomically coherent segmentations of multiple chambers. Figure 3 shows an example of the segmentations achieved with the F-CNNs architectures.

cMRI Validation. In Table 2 we show the correlation coefficient between the predicted ventricular volumes and the gold standard measures obtained from the cMRI dataset. Result evidence that F-CNNs have a better correlation than the ASM, where there is a significant improvement in all measurements. If we look along all the different architectures and losses, DeVoNet obtains the best correlation coefficients for diastolic measures, whereas U-Net-3D achieves the best results in systolic measures.

Given that we are performing the segmentation from non-ECG gated CT scans, we analyzed in more detail the influence of the heart cycle with the correlation results of Table 2. We calculated the difference between the predicted and gold standard volumes for both diastolic and systolic cycles (see Table 3). Results show that the bias is lower for the proposed architecture, DeVoNet, for almost all the cases, with the exception of the systolic volume of the right ventricle, where U-Net-3D achieves a lower but similar bias. For the best results, the diastolic bias was smaller than the systolic. This is consistent with the fact that the diastolic phase is longer than the systolic during the cardiac cycle; therefore, the mediastinal region during CT acquisition was likely scanned closer to the diastolic phase.

Table 2. Pearson correlation coefficient of right ventricular (RV) and left ventricular (LV) volumes in both diastole (Dis) and systole (Sys) of 20 subjects between the gold standard (cardiac MRI calculated volumes), the ASM approach used a reference for training and the three architectures studied.

		ASM	U-Net-3D				FC-DenseNet				DeVoNet			
		Ref.	CE	WCE	Dice	Dice*	CE	WCE	Dice	Dice*	CE	WCE	Dice	Dice*
Cavity	Dis RV	0.607	0.716	0.735	0.682	0.708	0.613	0.600	0.667	0.685	0.675	0.683	0.703	**0.746**
	Dis LV	0.674	0.711	0.708	0.731	0.746	0.736	0.728	0.746	0.726	0.752	0.729	**0.761**	0.735
	Sys RV	0.430	0.599	**0.609**	0.532	0.567	0.547	0.475	0.524	0.546	0.578	0.515	0.563	0.589
	Sys LV	0.742	0.738	0.733	**0.758**	0.749	0.703	0.706	0.698	0.719	0.695	0.707	0.704	0.712

Table 3. Average absolute difference between the predicted and gold standard volumes for both diastolic (Dis) and systolic (Sys) cycles.

		ASM	U-Net-3D				FC-DenseNet				DeVoNet			
		Ref.	CE	WCE	Dice	Dice*	CE	WCE	Dice	Dice*	CE	WCE	Dice	Dice*
Cavity	Sys RV	34.3	37.7	43.7	**26.4**	23.6	34.9	46.5	29.7	29.9	38.6	50.6	**26.9**	28.5
	Dis RV	30.5	27.1	21.2	38.5	41.2	29.9	18.4	35.2	34.9	26.3	**14.3**	38.0	36.3
	Sys LV	87.6	86.4	86.4	80.5	81.8	84.6	77.7	**73.0**	76.6	84.3	77.0	**73.6**	85.5
	Dis LV	19.4	18.1	18.1	12.3	13.5	16.4	9.4	**4.8**	8.3	16.1	8.7	**5.4**	17.2

Finally, Fig. 4 shows an illustration of the method performance for five subjects randomly selected from our testing set with an increasing degree of pulmonary impairment defined by the GOLD guidelines using the DeVoNet trained with a Dice loss. It is worth noting that the overall segmentation is robust for all the subjects despite the anatomical variation. In general, the ventricles are better defined than the atria, and the different chamber walls are well-circumscribed within the pericardial space.

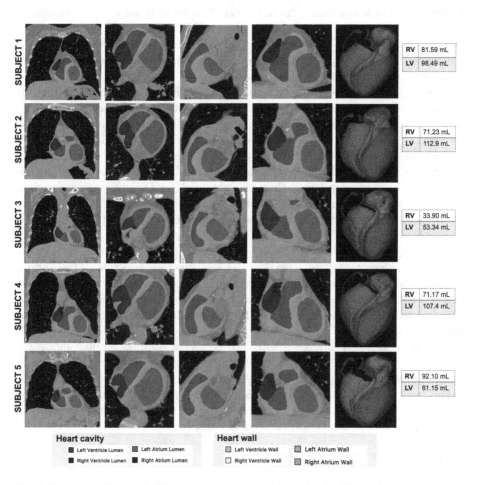

Fig. 4. Heart cavities and walls segmentation overlays using DeVoNet for five subjects from our testing set corresponding to smokers with different degrees of obstructive disease from top to bottom. From left to right, full coronal view from the CT at the ventricles' level, axial, sagittal, and coronal close-up views and 3D mesh rendering (walls semitransparent). For each subject, the estimated chamber ventricular volumes are also shown.

4 Conclusion

This work studies the potential of convolutional neural networks to segment multi-cavity structures of the heart learned from segmentations in non-contrast non-ECG gated chest CT scans. The training labels can be considered as noisy labels due to the limitations of the model-based approach that we used as reference. We also propose a new CNN architecture (DeVoNet) that provides a balance between the number of parameters and the depth of the network to avoid representational bottlenecks. The validation in a set of 66 supervised segmentations showed that the approaches based on CNNs (U-Net-3D, FC-DenseNet, DeVoNet) can provide multi-cavity segmentations with coherent anatomical structures. Additionally, the inclusion of a lung class within the architectures increases the performance of the segmentations.

The analysis of correlation with measures acquired in cMRI showed that all the approaches based on CNNs improve the results with respect to the reference standard. More specifically, our proposed architecture provides the highest correlation with cMRI for the diastolic measures for both ventricles (from 0.60 to 0.75 for right ventricle; from 0.67 to 0.76 for left ventricle). The U-Net-3D architecture achieves the best correlation for systolic cMRI measures, although it exhibits a lower correlation than the obtained for Diastolic measures with DeVoNet. The consistent improvement in correlations implies that F-CNN has an intrinsic ability to capture the heart's appearance model with noisy samples. This robustness of the learning process is a remarkable feature.

Although our results are encouraging, the methods show different performance for different cavities based on the loss function selection. This finding suggests that alternative loss functions that show consistent improvements for all the cavities could be sought. We believe that further improvements could be achieved by learning the optimal loss function within a Generative Adversarial framework, and we will be considered in future extensions of this work.

Finally, Chest CT images are by no means an optimal cardiac modality; however, this is one of the most used imaging modalities with more than 24 million scans per year in the US [12]. Automated methods as the one presented in this work to quantify heart dysfunction given by abnormal ventricular volumes could serve as an invaluable screening tool during regular CT explorations, for example, within the lung cancer screening context.

References

1. Jemal, A., Fedewa, S.A.: Lung cancer screening with low-dose computed tomography in the United States–2010 to 2015 lung cancer screening with low-dose computed Tomography letters. JAMA Oncol. **3**(9), 1278–1281 (2017)
2. Rahaghi, F.N., et al.: Ventricular geometry from non-contrast non-ECG-gated CT scans: an imaging marker of cardiopulmonary disease in smokers. Academic radiology **24**(5), 594–602 (2017)
3. Bhatt, S.P., et al.: Cardiac morphometry on computed Tomography and exacerbation reduction with β-blocker therapy in chronic obstructive pulmonary disease. Am. J. Respir. Crit. Care Med. **196**(11), 1484–1488 (2017)

4. Washko, G.R., et al.: Arterial vascular pruning, right ventricular size, and clinical outcomes in chronic obstructive pulmonary disease. A longitudinal observational study. Am. J. Respir. Crit. Care Med. **200**(4), 454–461 (2019)
5. Washko, G.R., et al.: Smaller left ventricle size at noncontrast CT is associated with lower mortality in COPDGene participants. Radiology **296**(1), 208–215 (2020)
6. Ronneberger, O., Fischer, P., Brox, T.: U-Net: convolutional networks for biomedical image segmentation. In: Navab, N., Hornegger, J., Wells, W.M., Frangi, A.F. (eds.) MICCAI 2015. LNCS, vol. 9351, pp. 234–241. Springer, Cham (2015). https://doi.org/10.1007/978-3-319-24574-4_28
7. Huang, G., Liu, Z., van der Maaten, L., Weinberger, K.Q.: Densely connected convolutional networks. In: 2017 IEEE Conference on Computer Vision and Pattern Recognition (CVPR), pp. 2261–2269 (2017)
8. Paszke, A., Chaurasia, A., Kim, S., Culurciello, E.: ENet: A Deep Neural Network Architecture for Real-Time Semantic Segmentation (2016)
9. Jégou, S., Drozdzal, M., Vazquez, D., Romero, A., Bengio, Y.: The one hundred layers tiramisu: fully convolutional densenets for semantic segmentation. In: 2017 IEEE Conference on Computer Vision and Pattern Recognition Workshops (CVPRW), pp. 1175–1183 (July 2017)
10. Roy, A.G., Navab, N., Wachinger, C.: Concurrent spatial and channel 'squeeze & excitation' in fully convolutional networks. In: Frangi, A.F., Schnabel, J.A., Davatzikos, C., Alberola-López, C., Fichtinger, G. (eds.) MICCAI 2018. LNCS, vol. 11070, pp. 421–429. Springer, Cham (2018). https://doi.org/10.1007/978-3-030-00928-1_48
11. Hoogendoorn, C., et al.: A high-resolution atlas and statistical model of the human heart from multislice CT. IEEE Trans. Med. Imaging **32**(1), 28–44 (2013)
12. Kamel, S.I., Levin, D.C., Parker, L., Rao, V.M.: Utilization trends in noncardiac thoracic imaging, 2002–2014. J. Am. Coll. Radiol. **14**(3), 337–342 (2017)

3D Deep Convolutional Neural Network-Based Ventilated Lung Segmentation Using Multi-nuclear Hyperpolarized Gas MRI

Joshua R. Astley[1,2] ⓘ, Alberto M. Biancardi[1], Paul J. C. Hughes[1], Laurie J. Smith[1], Helen Marshall[1], James Eaden[1], Jody Bray[1], Nicholas D. Weatherley[1], Guilhem J. Collier[1], Jim M. Wild[1], and Bilal A. Tahir[1,2(✉)] ⓘ

[1] POLARIS, Department of Infection, Immunity and Cardiovascular Disease, The University of Sheffield, Sheffield, UK
b.tahir@sheffield.ac.uk
[2] Department of Oncology and Metabolism, University of Sheffield, Sheffield, UK

Abstract. Hyperpolarized gas MRI enables visualization of regional lung ventilation with high spatial resolution. Segmentation of the ventilated lung is required to calculate clinically relevant biomarkers. Recent research in deep learning (DL) has shown promising results for numerous segmentation problems. In this work, we evaluate a 3D V-Net to segment ventilated lung regions on hyperpolarized gas MRI scans. The dataset consists of 743 helium-3 (^{3}He) or xenon-129 (^{129}Xe) volumetric scans and corresponding expert segmentations from 326 healthy subjects and patients with a wide range of pathologies. We evaluated segmentation performance for several DL experimental methods via overlap, distance and error metrics and compared them to conventional segmentation methods, namely, spatial fuzzy c-means (SFCM) and K-means clustering. We observed that training on combined ^{3}He and ^{129}Xe MRI scans outperformed other DL methods, achieving a mean $\pm$ SD Dice of 0.958 $\pm$ 0.022, average boundary Hausdorff distance of 2.22 $\pm$ 2.16 mm, Hausdorff 95th percentile of 8.53 $\pm$ 12.98 mm and relative error of 0.087 $\pm$ 0.049. Moreover, no difference in performance was observed between ^{129}Xe and ^{3}He scans in the testing set. Combined training on ^{129}Xe and ^{3}He yielded statistically significant improvements over the conventional methods ($p < 0.0001$). The DL approach evaluated provides accurate, robust and rapid segmentations of ventilated lung regions and successfully excludes non-lung regions such as the airways and noise artifacts and is expected to eliminate the need for, or significantly reduce, subsequent time-consuming manual editing.

Keywords: Functional lung imaging · Hyperpolarized gas MRI · Deep learning · Convolutional neural network · Lung segmentation

1 Introduction

Hyperpolarized gas MRI enables visualization of regional lung ventilation with high spatial resolution [1]. Quantitative biomarkers derived from this modality, including

© Springer Nature Switzerland AG 2020
J. Petersen et al. (Eds.): TIA 2020, LNCS 12502, pp. 24–35, 2020.
https://doi.org/10.1007/978-3-030-62469-9_3

the ventilated defect percentage, provide further insights into pulmonary pathologies currently not possible with alternative techniques [2]. To facilitate the computation of such biomarkers, segmentation of ventilated regions of the lung is required [3].

Conventional approaches for hyperpolarized gas MRI ventilation segmentation employ classical image processing and machine learning techniques, such as hierarchical K-means clustering [4] and spatial fuzzy c-means (SFCM) with tuned bilateral filtering and clustering [5]. However, as these methods are based on voxel intensities and thresholding, they provide only semi-automatic segmentations; as such, they are prone to errors that often require significant time to manually correct such as the removal of non-ventilated lung voxels and non-lung regions, including the airways and artifacts.

Recent research in image segmentation has focused on the use of deep learning (DL) and has been applied to numerous problems, showing promising results [6, 7]. Convolutional neural networks (CNN) have become the most common DL network used for image segmentation, enhanced by the adoption of transfer learning to cope with limited datasets [8, 9]. Tustison et al. employed a 2D CNN with a U-Net architecture using 113 hyperpolarized gas MRI scans, obtaining impressive results [10]. However, application of DL on a more extensive database with a broader range of pathologies is required for clinical adoption.

In this work, we evaluate a 3D volumetric V-Net CNN to accurately, robustly and rapidly segment ventilated lungs on hyperpolarized gas MRI scans using a large, diverse dataset with both helium-3 (^{3}He) and xenon-129 (^{129}Xe) scans and corresponding expert segmentations. We evaluate several DL methods for training a neural network and use a diverse set of evaluation metrics for comparison. We then compare the best performing DL method to conventional approaches used for hyperpolarized gas MRI segmentation. We also investigate the effect of the noble gas on DL performance.

2 Materials and Methods

2.1 Hyperpolarized Gas MRI Acquisition

All subjects underwent 3D volumetric ^{3}He [11] and ^{129}Xe [12] hyperpolarized gas MRI with full lung coverage at 1.5T. Flexible quadrature radiofrequency coils were employed for transmission and reception of MR signals at the Larmor frequencies of ^{3}He and ^{129}Xe. In-plane (x-y) resolution of scans for both gases was 4×4 mm^2. ^{129}Xe scans ranged from 16–34 slices with a mean of 23 slices and slice thickness of 10 mm. ^{3}He scans ranged from 34–56 slices with a mean of 45 slices and slice thickness of 5 mm.

2.2 Dataset

The imaging dataset used in this study was collected retrospectively from several clinical observational studies and patients referred for clinical scans. The dataset consisted of 743 volumetric hyperpolarized gas MRI scans (22890 slices), with either ^{3}He (248 scans, 11370 slices) or ^{129}Xe (495 scans, 11520 slices), from 326 subjects. The slices are distributed approximately 50:50 between ^{3}He and ^{129}Xe. The subjects included healthy individuals and patients with various pulmonary pathologies and are summarized in Table 1. Examples of ^{3}He and ^{129}Xe images for a range of pathologies are shown in Fig. 1.

Table 1. Dataset information and disease breakdown.

	Number of scans	Hyperpolarized gas
Healthy	41	^{129}Xe
Lung cancer	22	^{3}He or ^{129}Xe
Chronic obstructive pulmonary disease (COPD)	54	^{3}He or ^{129}Xe
Cystic fibrosis (CF)	223	^{3}He or ^{129}Xe
Premature children	50	^{3}He or ^{129}Xe
Interstitial lung disease (ILD)*	127	^{3}He or ^{129}Xe
Patients referred for clinical scans**	245	^{3}He or ^{129}Xe

*Contains idiopathic pulmonary fibrosis (IPF), connective tissue disease associated ILD (CTD-ILD), hypersensitivity pneumonitis (HP) and drug induced ILD (DI-ILD).
**Clinical referral cases include patients with asthma, COPD, bronchiectasis, cystic fibrosis, collapsed lung and primary ciliary dyskinesia (PCD).

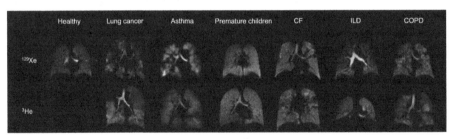

Fig. 1. Example coronal slices from the dataset. ^{3}He MRI scans for healthy subjects were unavailable.

Each scan has a corresponding manually-edited ground truth segmentation representing the ventilated region of the lung. These segmentations were generated by multiple expert observers and reviewed by an independent imaging scientist to ensure quality and identify potential errors; errors such as the inclusion of the trachea or background noise were manually corrected.

2.3 Parameterization

Several experiments were conducted to assess the effect of varying network architecture, loss function and pre-processing technique using a subset of the data comprising of 431 hyperpolarized gas MRI scans, with either ^{3}He (n = 173) or ^{129}Xe (n = 258), from healthy subjects and patients with pulmonary pathologies. 29 scans were used as a parameterization testing set and 40 scans used for internal validation.

Table 2 displays the results of these investigations showing mean performance on the parameterization testing set. The V-Net architecture with cross-entropy loss function exhibited improved performance in terms of Dice similarity coefficient (DSC), average Hausdorff distance at the boundary (Avg HD) and Hausdorff 95th percentile distance at the boundary (HD95). The impact of two commonly used pre-processing techniques for hyperpolarized gas MRI, namely, normalization and denoising [10], were evaluated. Due to the lack of substantial improvements, no pre-processing was implemented on the larger dataset used to evaluate DL methods in this work.

Table 2. Mean results on the parameterization testing set shown for three experiments investigating the effect of varying network architecture, loss function and pre-processing technique. The highest DSC values are shown in bold.

Experimental methods		Evaluation metrics		
		DSC	Avg HD (mm)	HD95 (mm)
Network architecture	**V-Net**	**0.956**	**1.68**	**5.61**
	Dense V-Net	0.952	2.03	7.30
	HighResNet	0.927	5.46	19.32
Loss function	**Cross entropy**	**0.956**	**1.68**	**5.61**
	Dice	0.947	2.86	10.98
Pre-processing	**None**	**0.956**	**1.68**	**5.61**
	Denoising	**0.956**	1.93	6.83
	Normalization	**0.956**	2.02	6.79

Further derived from the above investigations, 25000 iterations were selected as the appropriate number of training iterations, as they represent the optimal balance between segmentation performance and training time.

Conducting these experiments on a subset of the total data allows for optimization of parameters without introducing potential biases to a specific training and testing set. The following section describes the data split and DL parameters, informed by the above investigations, used in the remainder of this work.

2.4 Convolutional Neural Network

We used the V-Net fully convolutional neural network which processes 3D scans using volumetric convolutions [13]. The network is trained end-to-end using hyperpolarized gas MRI volumetric scans. The network utilizes a non-linear PReLu activation function [14] and is optimized using a binary cross-entropy (BCE) loss function defined below:

$$BCE(PR, GT) = -\frac{1}{N} \sum_{i=1}^{N} [gt_i \log(pr_i) + (1 - gt_i) \log(1 - pr_i)] \qquad (1)$$

where $GT = \{gt_i \in GT\}$ denotes the manually-edited ground truth segmentation, $PR = \{pr_i \in PR\}$ the predicted segmentation by the network and i represents the voxel location within the image, which is assumed to have N number of voxels.

Parameters. ADAM optimization was used to train the CNN [15]. The spatial window size was set to [96, 96, 24] with a batch size of 10. A learning rate of 1×10^{-5} was used for initial training and 0.5×10^{-5} for fine-tuning methods.

Data Split. The dataset was split into training, validation and testing sets. The training set contained 232 ^{3}He scans (10686 slices) and 437 ^{129}Xe scans (10212 slices) from a total of 252 subjects. 74 scans, each from a different subject, were selected for the testing set (^{3}He: 16 scans; ^{129}Xe: 58 scans). 10% of the training set was randomly selected as a validation dataset. Repeat or longitudinal scans from multiple visits for the same patient were contained in the training set; however, no subject was present in both the training/validation and testing sets, with the testing set containing only one scan from each patient. The range of diseases in the testing set is representative of the dataset as a whole.

Computation. The networks were trained using the medical imaging DL framework NiftyNet 0.6.0 [16] on top of TensorFlow 1.14 [17]. Training and inference were performed on an NVIDIA Tesla V100 GPU with 16 GB of RAM.

2.5 DL Experimental Methods

Five DL experimental methods were performed to train the network:

(1) The model was trained on 232 ^{3}He scans for 25000 iterations.
(2) The model was trained on 437 ^{129}Xe scans for 25000 iterations.
(3) The model was trained on 232 ^{3}He scans for 20000 iterations; these weights were used to initialize a model trained on 437 ^{129}Xe scans for 5000 iterations.
(4) The model was trained on 437 ^{129}Xe scans for 20000 iterations; these weights were used to initialize a model trained on 232 ^{3}He scans for 5000 iterations.
(5) The model was trained on 669 ^{129}Xe and ^{3}He scans for 25000 iterations.

The five experimental methods were applied to the data split defined in Sect. 2.4 using the same testing set for each method, facilitating comparison between the five methods to identify the best performing training process on multiple metrics.

2.6 Comparison to Conventional Methods

For further benchmarking of the CNN methods, the best-performing DL method was compared against other conventional machine learning methods for hyperpolarized gas MRI segmentation. The methods used are briefly described as follows:

(1) Hierarchical K-means segmentation algorithm: A high number of iterations and centroid sorting were used to improve robustness [4].
(2) SFCM algorithm: The method uses bilateral filtering tuned to ^{3}He or ^{129}Xe and 19 clusters to assign membership before thresholding produces a binary segmentation (adaption of [5]).

2.7 Evaluation Metrics

The testing set results for each of the five DL experimental methods and two conventional methods were evaluated using several metrics. The DSC was used to assess overlap between the ground truth and predicted segmentations [18]. Two distance metrics, Avg HD (mm) and HD95 (mm) were used [19]. The Avg HD reduces sensitivity to outliers and is regarded as a stable metric for segmentation evaluation [20]. Furthermore, a relative error metric (XOR) was used to evaluate segmentation error [21].

2.8 Statistical Analysis

Paired t-tests were used to assess the statistical significance of differences between experimental methods. A Mann-Whitney U test was used to compare differences between ^{3}He and ^{129}Xe segmentations to assess the effect of the gas. The best performing experimental method was compared to other segmentation methods using paired t-tests. Statistical analysis was performed using Prism 8.4 (GraphPad, San Diego, CA).

3 Results

Table 3 shows a comparison of segmentation performance for the five DL experimental methods and the two conventional segmentation methods.

Table 3. Comparison of segmentation performance of DL methods and conventional methods for a testing set of 74 scans. Means are given; the best result for each metric is in bold.

Experimental methods	Evaluation metrics			
	DSC	Avg HD (mm)	HD95 (mm)	XOR
Train on ^{3}He	0.948	3.92	16.64	0.109
Train on ^{129}Xe	0.954	**1.84**	**6.32**	0.091
Train on ^{3}He, fine-tuned on ^{129}Xe	0.955	2.47	9.12	0.091
Train on ^{129}Xe, fine-tuned on ^{3}He	0.946	4.37	17.94	0.120
Combined ^{3}He and ^{129}Xe training	**0.958**	2.22	8.53	**0.087**
K-means	0.610	37.28	98.79	1.604
SFCM	0.907	5.61	23.06	0.242

P-values are shown in a 5 × 5 matrix in Table 4 using both the DSC and Avg HD evaluation metrics for the five DL experimental methods.

Figure 2 shows distributions of the DSC and Avg HD values for each method. Statistical significance was assessed using paired t-tests for the DSC and Avg HD metrics comparing the combined ^{3}He and ^{129}Xe method to other DL methods. The combined ^{3}He and ^{129}Xe method yielded statistically significant improvements over all DL methods using DSC (mean DSC = 0.958, p < 0.05). Using Avg HD, the combined ^{3}He and ^{129}Xe method generated statistically significant improvements over two DL methods (p < 0.05); no significant difference between the other methods was observed (p > 0.05).

Table 4. P-values from paired t-tests comparing DL experimental methods in Table 3 for DSC (blue) and Avg HD (green) evaluation metrics.

DSC Avg HD	Train on [3]He	Train on [129]Xe	Train on [3]He, fine tune on [129]Xe	Train on [129]Xe, fine tune on [3]He	Train on combined [129]Xe and [3]He
Train on [3]He		0.11	0.004*	0.28	<0.0001*
Train on [129]Xe	0.0072*		0.44	0.13	0.032*
Train on [3]He, fine tune on [129]Xe	<0.0001*	0.31		0.036*	0.0007*
Train on [129]Xe, fine tune on [3]He	0.53	0.0004*	0.0093*		0.0075*
Train on combined [129]Xe and [3]He	0.0005*	0.069	0.097	0.0003*	

*significant P-values (p < 0.05)

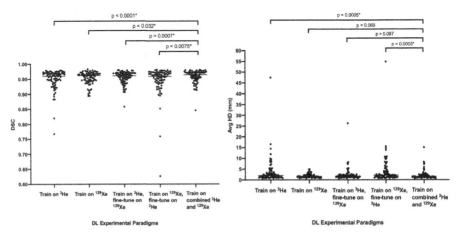

Fig. 2. Comparison on 74 testing scans for five DL experimental methods using DSC (left) and Avg HD (right). P-values are displayed for paired t-tests comparing the combined [3]He and [129]Xe DL method to the other DL methods.

Figure 3 shows examples of segmentation quality for a healthy subject and patients with six different pathologies across the five DL experimental methods using [3]He and [129]Xe, representing a wide range of hyperpolarized gas MRI scans. The original scans and ground truth segmentations are included to facilitate comparison. It can be observed that there are negligible voxels outside the lung parenchyma classed as ventilated and that the CNN accurately excluded ventilation defects, as shown in the examples of the CF and lung cancer patients. Table 5 stratifies results based on disease and shows that, for the majority of diseases, the combined [3]He and [129]Xe method is the best performing method.

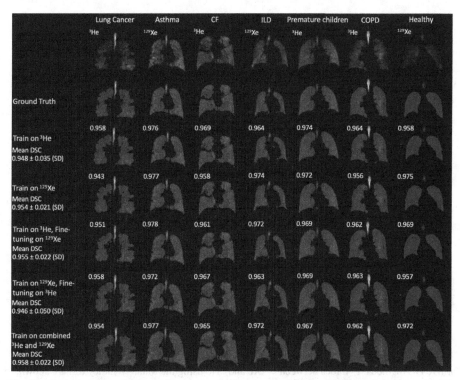

Fig. 3. Example coronal slices for seven subjects with different pathologies for each DL experimental method. Individual, and mean ± SD, DSC values are displayed.

Table 5. Comparison of segmentation performance of DL methods stratified by disease for 74 testing scans. Mean DSCs are given; the best result for each disease is shown in bold.

Disease	N	DL experimental methods				
		Train on ^{129}Xe	Train on ^{3}He	Train on ^{129}Xe, fine-tuned on ^{3}He	Train on ^{3}He, fine-tuned on ^{129}Xe	Train on combined ^{3}He and ^{129}Xe
Healthy	5	**0.952**	0.936	0.928	0.947	0.949
Lung cancer	3	0.932	0.951	**0.955**	0.943	0.951
COPD	3	0.949	0.967	**0.968**	0.959	**0.968**
CF	3	0.951	0.941	0.937	0.954	**0.956**
Premature children	7	0.927	0.917	0.919	0.929	**0.932**
ILD	8	0.959	0.959	0.962	0.961	**0.964**
Clinical referrals	45	0.959	0.952	0.947	0.959	**0.961**

Figure 4 shows the segmentation performance for the testing set between noble gases (^{129}Xe and ^{3}He) using the DSC and Avg HD metrics. Only the 'Train on ^{129}Xe, fine-tune on ^{3}He' method exhibits a significant difference in terms of both the DSC (p = 0.011) and Avg HD (p = 0.0002) metrics. The combined ^{3}He and ^{129}Xe method shows no statistically significant differences between gases using DSC and Avg HD metrics.

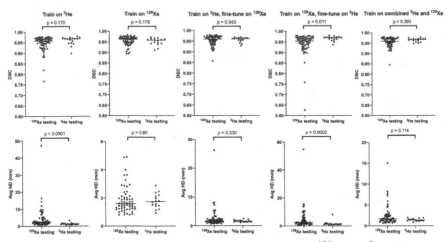

Fig. 4. Comparison of DSC (top) and Avg HD (bottom) values for ^{129}Xe and ^{3}He testing scans for five DL methods. P-values between ^{129}Xe and ^{3}He using the Mann-Whitney test are shown.

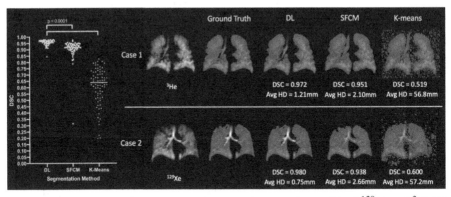

Fig. 5. Comparison of performance on testing scans between the combined ^{129}Xe and ^{3}He DL method and conventional segmentation methods (SFCM and K-means) with P-values from paired t-tests. Individual DSC and Avg HD values for each method are displayed for two cases. Case 1 is a COPD patient and case 2 is a clinical referral patient.

Combined ^{3}He and ^{129}Xe training was identified as the most accurate DL ventilated lung segmentation method due to statistically significant improvements over all other methods using DSC and XOR metrics. Figure 5 shows a comparison using the combined DL method and two conventional segmentation methods, K-means and SFCM. The

DL segmentation method exhibits significant improvements (p < 0.0001), accurately excluding low-level noise as well as non-lung regions such as the trachea and bronchi.

4 Discussion and Conclusion

DL segmentation methods produced highly accurate segmentations across a range of evaluation metrics on the dataset used. To the best of the authors' knowledge, the hyperpolarized gas MRI dataset used here is the largest used to date for ventilated lung segmentation and contains over 743 scans from patients with a wide range of lung pathologies. This is advantageous for preserving generalizability as it enables the algorithm to learn features present in a range of diseases and multiple hyperpolarized gases (^{3}He and ^{129}Xe), producing robust and accurate segmentations across numerous cases.

The CNN produced more accurate segmentations than the two conventional approaches investigated for all evaluation metrics used in this study. In particular, the CNN was able to deal with images containing background noise and artifacts, as well as successfully excluding ventilation defects and airways. In comparison, the SFCM method is unable to distinguish airways or artifacts and segments these areas erroneously. As such, it is highly probable that the CNN eliminates or dramatically reduces the manual-editing time required after automatic segmentation. Tustison et al. used a 2D U-Net for hyperpolarized gas MRI segmentation and achieved a mean DSC of 0.94 [10]. In comparison, our combined ^{3}He and ^{129}Xe method trained via a 3D V-Net yielded a mean DSC value of 0.96. The 3D CNN allows the model to treat the segmentation as a 3D volume and learn features which are present across multiple slices.

The combined ^{3}He and ^{129}Xe method shows statistically significant improvements over all other methods using the DSC metric; however, using the Avg HD metric, there is no significant difference between the combined and ^{129}Xe-only methods. In terms of mean values, the ^{129}Xe-only method generates a reduced Avg HD; this is likely due to the ability of the ^{129}Xe-only method to accurately segment an outlier testing scan that was segmented relatively poorly by the other methods. In addition, the testing set is imbalanced in favor of ^{129}Xe, introducing a possible bias into the analysis. No statistically significant differences were observed in performance when comparing ^{3}He and ^{129}Xe testing set scans, indicating that for a given ^{3}He or ^{129}Xe scan, neither the combined nor the ^{129}Xe-only methods are biased towards a specific hyperpolarized gas.

The training algorithm was implemented on a single GPU and required 12 days to reach 25000 iterations. Inference was also implemented on a single GPU, taking 27 s per ^{129}Xe scan and 35 s per ^{3}He scan, corresponding to approximately one second per slice for both gases.

A limitation of the study is the presence of only one expert segmentation per scan which limits the ability to evaluate inter- and intra-observer variability. However, the wide range of expert observers to generate the expert segmentations lead to significant variability in the training and testing sets. Hence, the CNN can learn a robust segmentation method across ground truth segmentations with multiple expert observers. In future work, multiple ground truth segmentations may be used to train the algorithm and allow evaluation of inter-observer variability.

The variation in the number of repeat or longitudinal scans and slice thickness between ^{3}He and ^{129}Xe scans impeded us from achieving a training and testing set split equally between both gases. Although multiple scans from the same patient were included in the training set to increase dataset numbers, to increase the robustness of the evaluation, no scan of the same patient was present both in the training and testing sets. In doing so, the testing set suffers from an imbalance in hyperpolarized gases in favor of ^{129}Xe. As such, the comparison of DL methods may have been subject to bias.

Although the effect of several CNN architectures was investigated, a more robust study of network architectures, such as 2D and 3D networks, is required; in future work, further comparisons between common network architectures will be conducted to assess whether superior performance can be achieved. Furthermore, hyper-parameterization and additional loss functions need to be investigated.

For the evaluation of clinically relevant metrics such as ventilated defect percentage [2], the whole-lung cavity volume is required in addition to ventilated lung volumes, most commonly computed from a whole-lung segmentation generated from a structural proton MRI scan. Accurate automatic segmentation of both ventilated and structural images will lead to significant improvements in the clinical workflow, including reduced segmentation generation time and manual editing time.

In conclusion, we evaluated a 3D fully-connected CNN using the V-Net architecture that is capable of producing accurate, robust and rapid hyperpolarized gas MRI segmentations on a large, diverse dataset. We compared five experimental DL methods and observed that combining ^{3}He and ^{129}Xe scans in the training set produces the most accurate segmentations with multiple evaluation metrics. This CNN-based method also significantly outperforms two conventional segmentation methods.

Acknowledgements. This work was supported by Yorkshire Cancer Research (S406BT), Weston Park Cancer Charity, National Institute of Health Research, the Medical Research Council and GlaxoSmithKline (BIDS3000032592). The authors also acknowledge access to high-performance computing equipment available via an Engineering and Physical Sciences Research Council Equipment Grant (EP/P020275/1; Joint Academic Data Science Endeavour) and support provided for this equipment grant via Research Software Engineering Sheffield.

References

1. Fain, S.B., Korosec, F.R., Holmes, J.H., O'Halloran, R., Sorkness, R.L., Grist, T.M.: Functional lung imaging using hyperpolarized gas MRI. J. Magn. Reson. Imaging: Off. J. Int. Soc. Magn. Reson. Med. **25**, 910–923 (2007)
2. Woodhouse, N., et al.: Combined helium-3/proton magnetic resonance imaging measurement of ventilated lung volumes in smokers compared to never-smokers. J. Magn. Reson. Imaging **21**, 365–369 (2005)
3. Tustison, N.J., et al.: Ventilation-based segmentation of the lungs using hyperpolarized (3)He MRI. J. Magn. Reson. Imaging **34**, 831–841 (2011)
4. Kirby, M., et al.: Hyperpolarized He-3 magnetic resonance functional imaging semiautomated segmentation. Acad. Radiol. **19**, 141–152 (2011)
5. Hughes, P.J.C., Horn, F.C., Collier, G.J., Biancardi, A., Marshall, H., Wild, J.M.: Spatial fuzzy c-means thresholding for semiautomated calculation of percentage lung ventilated volume from hyperpolarized gas and (1)H MRI. J. Magn. Reson. Imaging **47**, 640–646 (2018)
6. Bakator, M., Radosav, D.: Deep learning and medical diagnosis: a review of literature. Multimodal Technol. Interact. **2**, 47 (2018)

7. Lundervold, A.S., Lundervold, A.: An overview of deep learning in medical imaging focusing on MRI. Zeitschrift für Medizinische Physik **29**, 102–127 (2019)

8. Tajbakhsh, N., et al.: Convolutional neural networks for medical image analysis: full training or fine tuning? IEEE Trans. Med. Imaging **35**, 1299–1312 (2016)

9. Zha, W., Fain, S.B., Schiebler, M.L., Evans, M.D., Nagle, S.K., Liu, F.: Deep convolutional neural networks with multiplane consensus labeling for lung function quantification using UTE proton MRI. J. Magn. Reson. Imaging **50**, 1169–1181 (2019)

10. Tustison, N.J., et al.: Convolutional neural networks with template-based data augmentation for functional lung image quantification. Acad. Radiol. **26**, 412–423 (2019)

11. Horn, F.C., et al.: Lung ventilation volumetry with same-breath acquisition of hyperpolarized gas and proton MRI. NMR Biomed. **27**, 1461–1467 (2014)

12. Stewart, N.J., Norquay, G., Griffiths, P.D., Wild, J.M.: Feasibility of human lung ventilation imaging using highly polarized naturally abundant xenon and optimized three-dimensional steady-state free precession. Magn. Reson. Med. **74**, 346–352 (2015)

13. Milletari, F., Navab, N., Ahmadi, S.A.: V-Net: fully convolutional neural networks for volumetric medical image segmentation. In: Proceedings of 2016 Fourth International Conference on 3D Vision, pp. 565–571 (2016)

14. He, K., Zhang, X., Ren, S., Sun, J.: Delving deep into rectifiers: surpassing human-level performance on ImageNet classification. In: IEEE International Conference on Computer Vision (ICCV 2015), vol. 1502 (2015)

15. Kingma, D., Ba, J.: Adam: a method for stochastic optimization. In: International Conference on Learning Representations (2014)

16. Gibson, E., et al.: NiftyNet: a deep-learning platform for medical imaging. Comput. Methods Programs Biomed. **158**, 113–122 (2018)

17. Abadi, M., et al.: Tensorflow: large-scale machine learning on heterogeneous distributed systems. arXiv preprint arXiv:1603.04467 (2016)

18. Dice, L.R.: Measures of the amount of ecologic association between species. Ecology **26**, 297–302 (1945)

19. Beauchemin, M., Thomson, K.P.B., Edwards, G.: On the hausdorff distance used for the evaluation of segmentation results. Can. J. Remote. Sens. **24**, 3–8 (1998)

20. Shapiro, M.D., Blaschko, M.B.: On hausdorff distance measures. Computer Vision Laboratory University of Massachusetts, Amherst, vol. 1003 (2004)

21. Biancardi, A.M., Wild, J.M.: New disagreement metrics incorporating spatial detail – applications to lung imaging. In: Valdés Hernández, M., González-Castro, V. (eds.) MIUA 2017. CCIS, vol. 723, pp. 804–814. Springer, Cham (2017). https://doi.org/10.1007/978-3-319-60964-5_70

Lung Cancer Tumor Region Segmentation Using Recurrent 3D-DenseUNet

Uday Kamal[1], Abdul Muntakim Rafi[2], Rakibul Hoque[1], Jonathan Wu[2], and Md. Kamrul Hasan[1(✉)]

[1] Bangladesh University of Engineering and Technology, Dhaka 1205, Bangladesh
udday2014@gmail.com, khasan@eee.buet.ac.bd
[2] University of Windsor, 401 Sunset Avenue, Windsor, ON N9B 3P4, Canada
{rafi11,jwu}@uwindsor.ca

Abstract. The performance of a computer-aided automated diagnosis system of lung cancer from Computed Tomography (CT) volumetric images greatly depends on the accurate detection and segmentation of tumor regions. In this paper, we present Recurrent 3D-DenseUNet, a novel deep learning based architecture for volumetric lung tumor segmentation from CT scans. The proposed architecture consists of a 3D encoder block that learns to extract fine-grained spatial and coarse-grained temporal features, a recurrent block of multiple Convolutional Long Short-Term Memory (ConvLSTM) layers to extract fine-grained spatio-temporal information, and finally a 3D decoder block to reconstruct the desired volume segmentation masks from the latent feature space. The encoder and decoder blocks consist of several 3D-convolutional layers that are densely connected among themselves so that necessary feature aggregation can occur throughout the network. During prediction, we apply selective thresholding followed by morphological operation, on top of the network prediction, to better differentiate between tumorous and non-tumorous image-slices, which shows more promise than only thresholding-based approaches. We train and test our network on the NSCLC-Radiomics dataset of 300 patients, provided by The Cancer Imaging Archive (TCIA) for the 2018 IEEE VIP Cup. Moreover, we perform an extensive ablation study of different loss functions in practice for this task. The proposed network outperforms other state-of-the-art 3D segmentation architectures with an average dice score of 0.7228.

Keywords: Lung tumor · CT scan · Segmentation · U-Net · Convolutional LSTM · Recurrent neural network

1 Introduction

Lung cancer, also known as *lung carcinoma*, is a malignant lung tumor characterized by uncontrolled cell growth in tissues of the lung. The abnormal cells

---

Source code available at https://github.com/muntakimrafi/TIA2020-Recurrent-3D-DenseUNet.

© Springer Nature Switzerland AG 2020
J. Petersen et al. (Eds.): TIA 2020, LNCS 12502, pp. 36–47, 2020.
https://doi.org/10.1007/978-3-030-62469-9_4

do not develop into healthy lung tissue. Instead, they divide rapidly and form tumors. Researchers have found that it takes a series of DNA mutations to create a lung cancer cell. It can be caused by the normal aging process or environmental factors, such as cigarette smoke, breathing in asbestos fibers, and exposure to radon gas [23]. There are two principal types of primary lung cancer, non-small cell lung cancer (NSCLC) and small cell lung cancer (SCLC). These two types are quite different in their behavior and response to treatments. The most common form among these is the NSCLC [26], which accounts for about 85% of all lung cancers.

The primary diagnosis of lung cancer is performed using different non-invasive screening procedures, such as CT scan or Magnetic Resonance Imaging (MRI). A radiologist confirms the existence of malicious cancer cells or tumors from the scanned images before conducting a more formal biopsy test. He extracts and analyzes several features (e.g., attenuation, shape, size, and location) from the medical images. For this purpose, CT scan is a more affordable choice than the MRI. However, it is a daunting task to detect lung tumors from CT scans, and they can often be overlooked [5]. Moreover, the developing and undeveloped countries face a scarcity of expert radiologists, and lung cancers are detected at the final stages in most cases [18]. In this regard, computer-aided diagnosis (CAD) tools have become a necessity to assist the radiologists in making decisions from the raw data of a CT scan quickly with better accuracy.

Several methods have been proposed in the literature to complete the task of lung tumor segmentation. Uzelaltinbulata and Ugur [26] have proposed an image processing based technique to segment the lung tumor in CT images. They have used morphological operations, filtering, seeding, thresholding, and image residue to develop a system that automatically segments lung tumors. Aerts et al. [1] present a radiomic analysis of 440 features that quantify tumor image intensity, shape, and texture, extracted from CT data. In [13], the authors have discussed different statistical approaches to analyze CT data and the associated challenges. Besides lung tumor, a lung image contains many other components, or structures, such as clavicles and lungs. Therefore, detection of a lung tumor can be easily misguided by techniques that solely depend on the image processing technique, where pixel intensity and thresholding are heavily utilized to differentiate the tumor region. Towards this end, researchers are now more focused on machine learning based methods such as Deep Neural Networks(DNN) to solve medical image segmentation problems. These data-driven approaches have radically improved the performance of tumor detection compared to the complete image processing based techniques.

In [19], the authors have introduced V-Net, a fully convolutional neural network (CNN), as well as a unique objective function to conduct volumetric segmentation from MRI [19]. Cicek et al. [4] perform volumetric segmentation through a successful adaptation of U-Net [24] by replacing all the 2D operations with their 3D counterparts. In [3], the authors propose a deep voxel-wise neural network 'VoxResNet,' where they explore residual learning for a 3D volumetric segmentation task. Liao et al. [15] have demonstrated the application of a stacked independent subspace analysis (ISA) network to perform 3D prostate segmentation. Another interesting work is the proposition of a novel Hybrid-DenseUNet [14], where the authors utilize the sophisticated connectivity of DenseNet [11] in the U-Net architecture. The dense connections convey associated input features into the deeper levels of the U-Net architecture, which may otherwise suffer from being diminished during the forward propagation. Hossain et al. [10] propose 3D LungNet for performing lung tumor segmentation, where they incorporate a hybrid training method to train their network. In [21], the authors adopt a transfer learning strategy for performing segmentation to alleviate the noisy pixel-level label interruption. Pang et al. [22] propose a unique adversarial learning framework for segmentation. Despite the breadth of works done in the field of volumetric tumor segmentation, none of these approaches have considered the end-to-end recurrent features inherent to the volume CT-scan data. Most of these works heavily rely on the 3D convolutional layers that extract coarse-grained temporal features by utilizing only the neighboring frames instead of the complete volume.

In this paper, we propose a novel Recurrent 3D-DenseUNet architecture for volumetric lung tumor segmentation from CT scans. The core structure of our network is inspired by the widely popular U-Net architecture [24] that consists of a traditional encoder-decoder structure. We modify the network by replacing the 2D convolution operations with their 3D counterparts, except for the pooling layers. Instead of the conventional spatio-temporal pooling operation followed by 3D convolution, we adopt spatial-only pooling layers in order to better preserve the temporal features across slices. We also incorporate the dense connectivity proposed in [11] within our architecture to enable more fine-grained and aggregated feature propagation. In order to transform the coarse-grained output of the 3D encoder into a richer and fine-grained spatio-temporal feature space, we incorporate a recurrent block consisting of several convolutional long short-term memory (ConvLSTM) layers [9] in between the encoder-decoder structure. In addition, the encoder-decoder blocks are interconnected by a hierarchical set of skip connections so that any necessary features lost through the encoding operation can be regenerated during the reconstruction procedure performed by the decoder. The final binary segmentation mask is generated by thresholding the model output followed by dilation, a morphological operation, to reduce the pixel-level anomaly present in the prediction for better representation of the tumor region.

The rest of the paper is organized as follows. Section 2 provides a detailed description of our proposed network. We offer a detailed description of our training procedures, evaluation criteria, experimental results, and ablation study in Sect. 3. We conclude in Sect. 4.

2   Proposed Network Architecture

In this work, we propose a novel architecture that harnesses the core essence of three fundamental networks: DenseNet [11], U-Net [24], and Convolutional

Recurrent Network. Our proposed model is illustrated in Fig. 1 and the outline of the architecture is presented in Table 1.

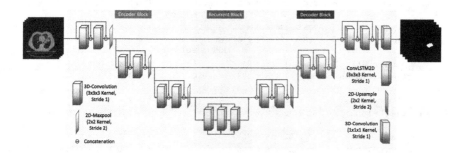

Fig. 1. The architecture of our proposed Recurrent 3D-DenseUNet model.

U-Net [24] is a very popular and well-established network for medical image segmentation and classification problems. Therefore, it is an obvious choice for us to experiment with U-Net for lung tumor segmentation. Thus, in this architecture, we have adopted the U-Net as the core skeleton of our network. Overall, our network consists of three major parts: Encoder, Recurrent block, and a Decoder. The details of each block are as follows:

Encoder Block. The encoder of our network comes with several convolutional blocks, each consisting of two subsequent 3D-Convolutional layers with kernel size $(3 \times 3 \times 3)$, a Batch-Normalization layer, ReLU as an Activation layer and 2D-Maxpooling operation with a kernel size of (2×2). The main reason for not using a 3D-pooling operation is to preserve temporal information as much as possible. A spatial dropout layer with a dropout rate of 10% has also been used at the end of every convolutional block in order to prevent overfitting on the training dataset. Since we are interested in pixel-level segmentation, the feature space we are more interested in needs to contain as much high-level information as possible. However, degradation of features strength due to forward propagation of the input data is unavoidable in any feedforward neural network unless the skip connection technique is applied. As shown in [11], dense-blocks, which are the building blocks of DenseNet, are interconnected with each other in the network and thereby prevent loss of acute statistical features due to forward propagation. Inspired by this idea, each convolutional block in the encoder is designed to perform as pseudo-dense-block, which establish inter-connectivity between the input and middle layers of the block.

Recurrent Block. The main intuition of using volume data is to capture the inter-slice continuity of the tumor as a solid object. For this purpose, we have used a recurrent block consisting of several ConvLSTM layers [27] within the

Table 1. The outline of our proposed Recurrent 3D-DenseUNet model

Block	Sub-block/layer	Output size	Details (layer and activation)	Kernels
Encoder block	Convolutional block	256 × 256 × 8 × 32	[Conv3D, BN, ReLU, SD] × 2	F = 32, k = 3 × 3 × 3, S = 1
	Maxpool2D	128 × 128 × 8 × 32	—	k = 2 × 2, S = 2
	Convolutional block	128 × 128 × 8 × 64	[Conv3D, BN, ReLU, SD] × 2	F = 64, k = 3 × 3 × 3, S = 1
	Maxpool2D	64 × 64 × 8 × 64	—	k = 2 × 2, S = 2
	Convolutional block	64 × 64 × 8 × 128	[Conv3D, BN, ReLU, SD] × 2	F = 128, k = 3 × 3 × 3, S = 1
	Maxpool2D	32 × 32 × 8 × 128	—	k = 2 × 2, S = 2
Recurrent block	ConvLSTM2D	32 × 32 × 8 × 256	—	F = 256, k = 3 × 3, S = 1
	ConvLSTM2D	32 × 32 × 8 × 256	—	F = 256, k = 3 × 3, S = 1
	ConvLSTM2D	32 × 32 × 8 × 256	—	F = 256, k = 3 × 3, S = 1
Decoder block	Convolutional block	32 × 32 × 8 × 128	[Conv3D, BN, ReLU] × 2	F = 128, k = 3 × 3, S = 1
	Upsampling2D	64 × 64 × 8 × 128	—	k = 2 × 2, S = 2
	Convolutional block	64 × 64 × 8 × 64	[Conv3D, BN, ReLU] × 2	F = 64, k = 3 × 3, S = 1
	Upsampling2D	128 × 128 × 8 × 64	—	k = 2 × 2, S = 2
	Convolutional block	128 × 128 × 8 × 32	[Conv3D, BN, ReLU] × 2	F = 32, k = 3 × 3, S = 1
	Upsampling2D	256 × 256 × 8 × 32	—	k = 2 × 2, S = 2
	Conv3D	256 × 256 × 8 × 1	Sigmoid	F = 1, k = 1 × 1, S = 1

transition section from the encoder to the decoder. With the increase in depth of convolutional layers, higher and higher level features are extracted from the input. To capture the interdependencies at the highest level of our network, we have used the recurrent block at the transition section of encoder and decoder, which helps the network to capture more fine-grained spatio-temporal features and inter-dependencies among the output features of the encoder. Each ConvL-STM layer is comprised of 2D-convolutional layers with kernel size $(3 \times 3 \times 3)$.

Decoder Block. The decoder block is the final part of the network that takes the high-level spatio-temporal features captured by the recurrent block as input and generates the volumetric segmentation mask as output. The decoder has a similar architectural structure of the encoder, except the spatial pooling layer is replaced by a spatial Upsample layer that performs the brings the latent feature space to the original input resolution. At decoder block output, a skip connect is established with the corresponding previous encoder block. Finally, a pointwise 3D convolution layer with Sigmoid activation is used to bring the volume mask back to its original input dimension.

3 Experimental Analysis

We perform several experiments to demonstrate the efficacy of our proposed method. In this section, we discuss those experimental procedures and results in detail. All of the experiments regarding training and implementation of the model are performed in hardware environments, which included Intel Core-i7 8700K, 3.70 GHz CPU, and Nvidia GeForce GTX 1080 Ti (11 GB Memory) GPU. The necessary codes are written in Python and, the neural network models are implemented by using the Keras API with Tensorflow-GPU in the backend.

3.1   Description of the Dataset

The dataset we use in our paper consists of 300 patients from the NSCLC-Radiomics dataset [6]. The contour-level annotations for these 300 patients have been prepared for the IEEE VIP Cup 2018 with the help of an expert radiologist [20]. The dataset contains scanned 3D volumes of the chest region for each patient. It is provided in DICOM format with slices of 512×512 size. We divide the dataset into two sets- train (260) and test (40), the same way as [10]. We use 10% of the training data as our validation set. The distribution of the tumorous and non-tumorous slices are provided in Table 2.

Table 2. Number of different types of CT scan slices in our dataset

Data	Number of patients	Tumor	Without tumor
Train	260	4296	26951
Test	40	848	3630

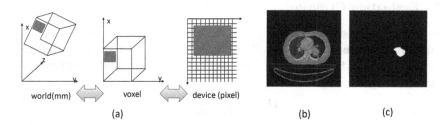

(a)   (b)   (c)

Fig. 2. Data generation steps from a DICOM file. **(a)** Conversion of DICOM files into pixel images. **(b)** A sample 2D-grayscale image of size 512×512 extracted from the DICOM files. **(c)** A binary mask of tumor for the image presented in *(b)*.

We convert the DICOM data to 2D gray-scale images using the Pydicom [17] Library and extract their respective binary masks from corresponding RTconstruct files. We resize the images from (512×512) to (256×256) to cope with the memory limitation of GPU. Afterward, we create patches of *eight* by concatenating eight consecutive images. We can observe in Table 2 that the dataset suffers from severe class imbalance. A large percentage of the CT scan slices do not contain any tumorous region. Moreover, the larger portion of slices containing tumors has non-tumorous regions, as shown in Fig. 2. Therefore, during training, we only use the patches (256 × 256 × 8) that contain at least one slice with a tumor. Here, the number of slices in a patch is also limited by the computational memory of the GPU. Also, it reduces the training parameters of the network.

3.2   Training Procedure

We have used several augmentation schemes to show different data to our neural network in each epoch during training. It helps to prevent the network from overfitting on the training data [25]. The augmentations we use are as follows: random rotation, random cropping, random global shifting, random global scaling, random noise addition, random noise multiplication, horizontal flip, and blurring. They are applied online randomly during training.

We have trained our Recurrent 3D-DenseUNet model using an initial learning rate of 10^{-4} and batch size of 2. We do not use a greater batch size number as the computational memory of the GPU limits it. The weights of the different layers are initialized randomly with the uniform distribution proposed by Glorot and Bengio [7]. We use binary cross-entropy as the loss function and Adam [12] as the optimizer with the exponential decay rate factors $\beta_1 = 0.9$ and $\beta_2 = 0.999$. We decrease the learning rate by a factor of 0.5 if the validation dice coefficient does not increase in three successive epochs. We train our network for a maximum number of 30 epochs and select the model with the highest validation dice coefficient.

3.3   Evaluation Criteria

We use dice coefficient as our evaluation criterion to compare between generated mask and the ground truth for all test images. Dice coefficient is a measure of relative overlap, where 1 represents perfect agreement and 0 represents no overlap.

$$D = \frac{2(|X| \cap |Y|)}{|X| + |Y|} \tag{1}$$

In (1), $\cap$ denotes the intersection operator, X and Y are the predicted binary mask and ground truth. It should be noted that the dice coefficient (D) has a restricted range of $[0, 1]$. The following two conventions are considered in the computation of Dice coefficient: (i) For True-Negative (i.e., there is no tumor, and the processing algorithm correctly detected the absence of the tumor), the dice coefficient would be 1, and; (ii) For False-Positive (i.e., there is no tumor, but the processing algorithm mistakenly segmented the tumor), the dice coefficient would be 0.

3.4   Results

During testing, we create overlapping patches of ($256 \times 256 \times 8$) from all the CT scan slices of a single patient with stride 1. Then we use our Recurrent 3D-DenseUNet network to generate volumetric prediction maps. For the masks that belong to multiple patches, we average over multiple predictions. The final binary segmentation mask is generated by thresholding the model output followed by dilation, a morphological operation. The hyperparameters, associated with the post-processing operations, are chosen based on the performance on the validation data. We use a 0.7 threshold to convert the network prediction to binary masks. Afterward, we apply dilation using a (7×7) circular kernel to improve the IOU (Intersection over Union) value. It reduces the pixel-level anomaly present in the prediction and provides a better representation of the tumor region. We compare our proposed method with several state-of-the-art methods available in the literature for performing segmentation tasks. The performance of the different methods is shown in Table 3. Our proposed method outperforms other approaches by a significant margin. A few predictions from the test set are shown in Fig. 3.

Table 3. Dice coefficient for different methods in lung tumor segmentation task

Model	Mean dice coefficient	Median dice coefficient
2D-UNet [24]	0.5848	0.6229
2D-LungNet [2]	0.6267	0.6678
3D-LungNet [10]	0.6577	0.7039
Proposed method	0.7228	0.7556

3.5   Ablation Study

In this subsection, we perform an ablation study of our proposed methodology and see how different architectural, training, and testing design choices affect our performance. First, we compare the performances of different variants of our network architecture (see Table 4).

A suitable cost function is equally important in training neural networks. The performance is determined by a combination of both the network and the loss function. Moreover, the dice coefficient may not always be the best indicator of a segmentation network's performance. The number of false positives and false negatives also play a vital role in determining the robustness of a model. Towards this end, we train and test our network with different loss functions and explore how they affect the performance of our network (see Table 5). We see that binary crossentropy outperforms the other loss functions we compare with. Also, the

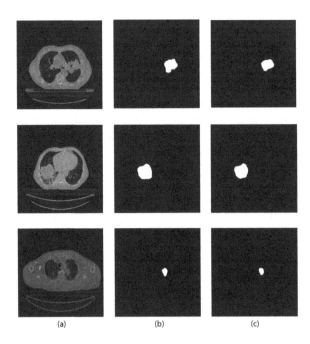

(a)   (b)   (c)

Fig. 3. Comparison between ground truth and binary masks predicted by our proposed method. (a) lung image, (b) ground truth, and (c) predicted mask.

tversky loss function provides an opportunity to reduce the number of false positives or false negatives by changing its parameter α [8]. It should be noted that we enable the proposed post-processing operations for the experiments shown in Table 5.

Lastly, we empirically validate the significance of our thresholding and morphological operation. From Table 6, we can see how the performance deteriorates without any thresholding or morphological operations. It can also be noticed that there is a trade-off among the dice coefficient, false positives, and false negatives for different thresholds. The optimum performance can be achieved with a threshold of 0.7 and dilation post-processing operation.

Table 4. Dice coefficient for different architectures similar to ours in lung tumor segmentation task

Model	Mean dice coefficient	Median dice coefficient
3D-UNet	0.6961	0.7326
3D-DenseUNet	0.6884	0.7188
3D-DenseUNet with recurrent block	0.7049	0.7646
Our proposed network	0.7228	0.7556

Table 5. Performance of our proposed method for different loss functions

Model	Mean dice coefficient	Median dice coefficient	False positives	False negatives
tversky loss ($\alpha = 0.1$)	0.6244	0.6637	786	221
tversky loss ($\alpha = 0.3$)	0.6933	0.7195	453	272
tversky loss ($\alpha = 0.5$) [Dice loss]	0.6963	0.7372	375	287
tversky loss ($\alpha = 0.7$)	0.7056	0.7282	417	324
tversky loss ($\alpha = 0.9$)	0.7125	0.7462	243	396
Focal loss [16]	0.7159	0.7493	498	349
IOU loss	0.6981	0.726	437	296
Binary crossentropy	0.7228	0.7556	321	331

Table 6. Performance of our proposed method for different thresholds and without morphological post-processing

Model	Mean dice coefficient	Median dice coefficient	False positives	False negatives
0.5 threshold	0.7169	0.7296	446	280
0.6 threshold	0.7174	0.7383	372	297
0.7 threshold	0.7228	0.7556	321	331
0.8 threshold	0.7368	0.7685	261	361
0.9 threshold	0.7278	0.7763	208	403
No threshold	0.6685	0.7624	120	789
No dilation with 0.7 threshold	0.6604	0.7147	321	332
No dilation with 0.8 threshold	0.6626	0.6859	261	362

4   Conclusion

In this paper, we have proposed Recurrent 3D-DenseUNet, a novel 3D Recurrent encoder-decoder based Convolutional Neural Network architecture for accurately detecting and segmenting lung tumors from volumetric CT scan data. We adopt spatial-only pooling layers in our architecture, instead of the conventional spatio-temporal pooling operation to better preserve the temporal features. We also use a recurrent block consisting of several ConvLSTM layers between the encoder-decoder structure to capture the inter-slice correlation at the high-level feature space. We have also incorporated short intra-block skip connections between the input and latter layers of every encoder and decoder block throughout the network to reduce the loss of any important feature during forward propagation. We train this model using 3D volume data of size $(256 \times 256 \times 8)$ and utilize various types of data augmentations to prevent overfitting during training. Finally, we apply a threshold on top of the network prediction to create binary masks and enhance it with dilation operation. This methodology has enabled us to achieve a better dice score in lung tumor segmentation tasks and reduce the overall number of false positives and false negatives. In our future works, we want to further modify and improve the model architecture, and explore how it performs on other medical imaging tasks.

References

1. Aerts, H.J., et al.: Decoding tumour phenotype by noninvasive imaging using a quantitative radiomics approach. Nat. Commun. **5**(1), 1–9 (2014)
2. Anthimopoulos, M., Christodoulidis, S., Ebner, L., Geiser, T., Christe, A., Mougiakakou, S.: Semantic segmentation of pathological lung tissue with dilated fully convolutional networks. IEEE J. Biomed. Health Inform. **23**(2), 714–722 (2018)
3. Chen, H., Dou, Q., Yu, L., Heng, P.A.: VoxResNet: deep voxelwise residual networks for volumetric brain segmentation. arXiv preprint arXiv:1608.05895 (2016)
4. Çiçek, Ö., Abdulkadir, A., Lienkamp, S.S., Brox, T., Ronneberger, O.: 3D U-Net: learning dense volumetric segmentation from sparse annotation. In: Ourselin, S., Joskowicz, L., Sabuncu, M.R., Unal, G., Wells, W. (eds.) MICCAI 2016. LNCS, vol. 9901, pp. 424–432. Springer, Cham (2016). https://doi.org/10.1007/978-3-319-46723-8_49
5. del Ciello, A., Franchi, P., Contegiacomo, A., Cicchetti, G., Bonomo, L., Larici, A.R.: Missed lung cancer: when, where, and why? Diagn. Interv. Radiol. **23**(2), 118 (2017)
6. Clark, K., et al.: The cancer imaging archive (TCIA): maintaining and operating a public information repository. J. Digit. Imaging **26**(6), 1045–1057 (2013)
7. Glorot, X., Bengio, Y.: Understanding the difficulty of training deep feedforward neural networks. In: Proceedings of the Thirteenth International Conference on Artificial Intelligence and Statistics, pp. 249–256 (2010)
8. Hashemi, S.R., Salehi, S.S.M., Erdogmus, D., Prabhu, S.P., Warfield, S.K., Gholipour, A.: Tversky as a loss function for highly unbalanced image segmentation using 3D fully convolutional deep networks. arXiv preprint arXiv:1803.11078 (2018)
9. Hochreiter, S., Schmidhuber, J.: Long short-term memory. Neural Comput. **9**(8), 1735–1780 (1997)
10. Hossain, S., Najeeb, S., Shahriyar, A., Abdullah, Z.R., Haque, M.A.: A pipeline for lung tumor detection and segmentation from CT scans using dilated convolutional neural networks. In: ICASSP 2019–2019 IEEE International Conference on Acoustics, Speech and Signal Processing (ICASSP), pp. 1348–1352. IEEE (2019)
11. Huang, G., Liu, Z., Van Der Maaten, L., Weinberger, K.Q.: Densely connected convolutional networks. In: CVPR, vol. 1, p. 3 (2017)
12. Kingma, D.P., Ba, J.: Adam: a method for stochastic optimization. arXiv preprint arXiv:1412.6980 (2014)

13. Lambin, P., et al.: Radiomics: extracting more information from medical images using advanced feature analysis. Eur. J. Cancer **48**(4), 441–446 (2012)
14. Li, X., Chen, H., Qi, X., Dou, Q., Fu, C.W., Heng, P.A.: H-DenseUNet: hybrid densely connected UNet for liver and liver tumor segmentation from CT volumes. arXiv preprint arXiv:1709.07330 (2017)
15. Liao, S., Gao, Y., Oto, A., Shen, D.: Representation learning: a unified deep learning framework for automatic prostate MR segmentation. In: Mori, K., Sakuma, I., Sato, Y., Barillot, C., Navab, N. (eds.) MICCAI 2013. LNCS, vol. 8150, pp. 254–261. Springer, Heidelberg (2013). https://doi.org/10.1007/978-3-642-40763-5_32
16. Lin, T.Y., Goyal, P., Girshick, R., He, K., Dollár, P.: Focal loss for dense object detection. In: Proceedings of the IEEE International Conference on Computer Vision, pp. 2980–2988 (2017)
17. Mason, D.: Su-e-t-33: pydicom: an open source DICOM library. Med. Phys. **38**(6Part10), 3493–3493 (2011)
18. Midthun, D.E.: Early detection of lung cancer. F1000Research **5** (2016)
19. Milletari, F., Navab, N., Ahmadi, S.A.: V-net: fully convolutional neural networks for volumetric medical image segmentation. In: 2016 Fourth International Conference on 3D Vision (3DV), pp. 565–571. IEEE (2016)
20. Mohammadi, A., et al.: Lung cancer radiomics: highlights from the IEEE video and image processing cup 2018 student competition [sp competitions]. IEEE Signal Process. Mag. **36**(1), 164–173 (2018)
21. Pang, S., Du, A., He, X., Díez, J., Orgun, M.A.: Fast and accurate lung tumor spotting and segmentation for boundary delineation on CT slices in a coarse-to-fine framework. In: Gedeon, T., Wong, K.W., Lee, M. (eds.) ICONIP 2019. CCIS, vol. 1142, pp. 589–597. Springer, Cham (2019). https://doi.org/10.1007/978-3-030-36808-1_64
22. Pang, S., et al.: CTumorGAN: a unified framework for automatic computed tomography tumor segmentation. Eur. J. Nucl. Med. Mol. Imaging **47**, 1–21 (2020)
23. Pataer, A., et al.: Histopathologic response criteria predict survival of patients with resected lung cancer after neoadjuvant chemotherapy. J. Thorac. Oncol. **7**(5), 825–832 (2012)
24. Ronneberger, O., Fischer, P., Brox, T.: U-Net: convolutional networks for biomedical image segmentation. In: Navab, N., Hornegger, J., Wells, W.M., Frangi, A.F. (eds.) MICCAI 2015. LNCS, vol. 9351, pp. 234–241. Springer, Cham (2015). https://doi.org/10.1007/978-3-319-24574-4_28
25. Shorten, C., Khoshgoftaar, T.M.: A survey on image data augmentation for deep learning. J. Big Data **6**(1), 60 (2019)
26. Uzelaltinbulat, S., Ugur, B.: Lung tumor segmentation algorithm. Procedia Comput. Sci. **120**, 140–147 (2017)
27. Xingjian, S., Chen, Z., Wang, H., Yeung, D.Y., Wong, W.K., Woo, W.C.: Convolutional LSTM network: a machine learning approach for precipitation nowcasting. In: Advances in Neural Information Processing Systems, pp. 802–810 (2015)

3D Probabilistic Segmentation and Volumetry from 2D Projection Images

Athanasios Vlontzos$^{(\boxtimes)}$, Samuel Budd, Benjamin Hou, Daniel Rueckert, and Bernhard Kainz

Department of Computing, BioMedIA, Imperial College London, London, UK
athanasios.vlontzos14@imperial.ac.uk

Abstract. X-Ray imaging is quick, cheap and useful for front-line care assessment and intra-operative real-time imaging (e.g., C-Arm Fluoroscopy). However, it suffers from projective information loss and lacks vital volumetric information on which many essential diagnostic biomarkers are based on. In this paper we explore probabilistic methods to reconstruct 3D volumetric images from 2D imaging modalities and measure the models' performance and confidence. We show our models' performance on large connected structures and we test for limitations regarding fine structures and image domain sensitivity. We utilize fast end-to-end training of a 2D-3D convolutional networks, evaluate our method on 117 CT scans segmenting 3D structures from digitally reconstructed radiographs (DRRs) with a Dice score of 0.91 ± 0.0013. Source code will be made available by the time of the conference.

1 Introduction

Computed tomography (CT) scans provide detailed 3D information of patient anatomy that is vital to many clinical workflows. For many pathologies, accurate diagnosis relies heavily on information extracted from CT images and volumes [14], e.g. biomarkers derived from 3D lung segmentations are used to characterize and predict Tuberculosis progression [17]. CT scans, however, are both time-consuming and expensive to perform, and are not always available at the patients current location, resulting in delayed diagnosis and treatment. CT scans also present a higher risk to the patient due to increased radiation exposure over a typical Chest X-Ray (CXR). Meanwhile CXRs are routinely taken in the clinical practice at significantly decreased cost and radiation dosage while acquisition times are many orders of magnitude less than a CT scan.

Learning based methods have shown great potential for synthesizing structurally coherent information in applications where information is lost due to non-invertible image acquisition [8]. A primary example of such an application is CXR projection. As the human anatomy is locally well-constrained, a canonical representation can be adopted to learn the anatomical features and extrapolate a corresponding 3D volume from a 2D projection view. This can be achieved by

J. Petersen et al. (Eds.): TIA 2020, LNCS 12502, pp. 48–57, 2020.
https://doi.org/10.1007/978-3-030-62469-9_5

reflecting likely configurations, as they were observed in the training data, while inference is conducted by giving a sparse conditioning data sample, like a single projection.

Contribution: We show how probabilistic segmentation techniques [3, 4] can be extended with the ability to reconstruct 3D structure from projected 2D images. Our approach evaluates the potential of deep networks to invert projections, an unsolved problem of projective geometry and medical image analysis. We evaluate our method by reconstructing 3D lung segmentation masks and porcine rib-cages from 2D DRRs. We show that our approach works well for large, connected regions and test for limitations regarding fine, unconnected anatomical structures projected on varying anatomy and domain sensitivity across datasets. We further show how to adapt our methods to perform Unsupervised Domain Adaptation on NIH chest X-Rays. The proposed network is fast to train, converges within a few hours and predicts 3D shapes in real-time.

2   Related Work

Extracting 3D models from a single or multiple 2D views is a well-established topic in computer vision [13,15]. Earlier approaches included learning shape priors, and fitting the 3D shape model onto the 2D image. In [2,11], the authors attempt to reconstruct ribs by using, a priori known, statistical shape models. Both methods use a bi-planar approach as they utilize 2 orthogonal X-ray views. These methods do not generate a CT like image, as they only deform a solid rib-like template.

With the advances in deep learning, generative deep convolutional neural networks have been proposed to perform image generation in the context of medical imaging. In a recent work, parallel to ours, Ying et al. proposed X2CT-GAN [20] to synthesize full 3D CT volumes from 2D X-rays. Like [2,11], Ying et al. also use multiple views to create the 3D volume. However, instead of statistical shape models, Ying et al. uses generative adversarial networks (GANs) to synthesize 3D CT volumes from 2D X-rays. As GANs are trained to approximate the probabilistic distribution of the training dataset implicitly, they are known to hallucinate "plausible" features. This is detrimental in cases of fine structures, e.g., bronchi, blood vessels and small lesions. In the case of vessel-like structures which are almost random in construction, a GAN will hallucinate a plausible structure that is highly probable from images in the training dataset, instead of generating a structure that's extrapolated from the input. Hence the resulting structures are of poor quality, often disconnected and non realistic.

In [19] the authors reconstruct a 3D volume of an object from a 2D image of it. Contrary to X-Rays which can be thought of as the "shadow" of the object, [19] used as inputs 2D images of 3D structures, not their projections. Hence there was significantly less information loss than in the case of projections. [1] attempts a similar task to ours but aims at decomposing the provided X-Ray image rather than reconstructing the CT volume. More aligned to our work, Henzler et al. [8] creates 3D Volumes from 2D Cranial X-Rays. Their architecture is similar to ours, however, they only regress the 3D cranial structure, whereas we attempt to regress directly to CT Hounsfield units (HU). Furthermore we adopt a probabilistic technique while their model is fully deterministic.

3 Methodology

Adapting a known 2D or 3D architecture to be able to perform a task across dimensions is not a trivial task. Special consideration has to be given in the flow and augmentation of information. As projection is an information destroying process our methods have to be able to deduce the lost information in order to revert the process. This can be achieved through appropriate pathways of information through the network. It is impossible to be entirely certain that the restored information is correct as projection is a many to one operation, thus we believe that a probabilistic approach can offer reasonable confidence intervals. We extend two base architectures to perform this task as they our outlined in Fig. 1.

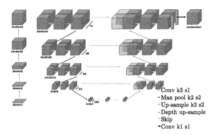 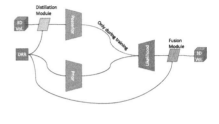

(a) 2D to 3D U-Net, Blue Blocks indicate 3D Convolutions; Orange Blocks indicate Dropout Layers, c.f. Sect. 3.1

(b) PhiSeg[3] with proposed augmentations, c.f. Sect. 3.2

Fig. 1. Two approaches for probabilistic 2D-3D un-projection. (Color figure online)

3.1 2D to 3D MC-Dropout-U-Net

Our first proposed method extends the work of [4]. Inputs will be first transformed into three dimensional objects using the structural reconstruction module and then passed through a 3D U-Net [5]. The U-Net is equipped with dropout layers on the decoding path, which are kept active during inference to mimic stochastic behavior. Figure 1a shows an overview over the proposed architecture.

Structural Reconstruction Module: 2D images can be considered as a 3D image with a "depth" of one. A series of five 3D transposed convolutional layers, with stride greater than 1 in the z-axis, is used to match the spatial dimensions of the volumetric 3D target. As opposed to bilinear up-sampling we propose to use transposed convolutions due to their theoretically better ability to learn more complex and non-linear image resizing functions [6]. The network at this stage contains a conceptual representation of the 3D properties of the object. As the 3D properties of the volume are yet to be fine-tuned by the subsequent 3D U-Net, the output of this layer does not hold human-understandable information of the 3D structure.

3D Segmentation: With the input data in correct spatial dimensions, segmentation can be performed using a 3D U-Net [5]. Similarly to its well known 2D counterpart, a 3D U-Net follows an encoding-decoding path with skip connections at each resolution. The network consists of four resolution layers; each consisting of two $3 \times 3 \times 3$ kernels with strides of $1 \times 1 \times 1$, followed by a $2 \times 2 \times 2$ max pooling with strides of $2 \times 2 \times 2$. Skip connections are used across the encoding and the decoding path, connecting same resolution levels, in order to propagate encoded features at each resolution. A dropout layer is added at the end of the decoder with a dropout probability of 0.6. These layers are kept active during inference as per the MC-Dropout methodology [7]. The network is then trained on 2D images with the respective 3D targets for segmentation and a binary cross-entropy loss.

3.2   2D to 3D PhiSeg

In [3] Baumgartner et al. introduce PhiSeg; a probabilistic segmentation algorithm able to capture uncertainty in medical image segmentations.

Phiseg is comprised of three modules; the prior, posterior and likelihood networks. The algorithm is modeled after a Conditional Variational Auto-Encoder where the posterior and prior networks operate as the encoders producing a series of latent variables z in different resolution levels. The likelihood network operates as the decoder utilizing the different resolution latent variables sampled from a normal distribution to produce segmentations. It is worth noting that the posterior network takes as input the ground truth segmentation and hence its only used during training. An auxiliary KL divergence loss between the distributions of the prior and the posterior is employed to steer the prior network to produce "good" latent variables.

We extend the previous method in three major ways aimed at controlling and augmenting the information contained in the DRR image.

1. Distillation Module: We propose a distillation module that performs the inverse operation of the Structural Reconstruction Module and we add it as a pre-processing step of the posterior network. The ground truth image is passed through a series of convolutional layers to distill its 3D information to a 2D representation. The resulting feature maps are concatenated with the input DRR image and passed through the posterior network. Contrary to the aforementioned 2D-3D U-Net PhiSeg is modeled after a VAE, hence the encoded latent distribution is highly susceptible to noisy inputs. In order to avoid the encoding of noise that would change the characteristics of our distribution we chose to work on 2 dimensions during the encoding phase rather than in 3. We would like to note that a fully 3D PhiSeg with a Structural Reconstruction Module as in the 2D-3D U-Net was evaluated but its training was unstable.

2. 3D Likelihood network: We extend the likelihood network to perform 3D reconstruction. The latent variables that the prior/posterior networks produce are transformed into 3D vectors and used as inputs for the likelihood network. We extend the latent vectors using vector operations rather than learning an augmentation to decrease the computational load of the the network. The series of latent variables are then passed through 3D decoder network, sharing the same architecture as the decoder path of the deterministic 3D U-Net.

3. Fusion Module: Our next extension of PhiSeg comes in form of a fusion module similar to [8] at the end of the likelihood module. Contrary to [8] our fusion method is fully learned by the model. Features extracted from the input DRR image x are concatenated to the output s of the likelihood network and convolved together to produce s' which serves as the final output of the network. The intuition behind this module lies with the assumption that PhiSeg will be able to reconstruct the overall structure but may lack details, thus the input DRR image is passed through a convolutional layer to extract relevant features which are then used in conjunction with the proposed segmentation s. We also note that the fusion module is not included in the 2D-3D U-Net as the direct skip connections of the model satisfy the flow of information that the fusion module aims at creating.

4. Unsupervised Domain Adaptation: Finally we propose a new augmentation of PhiSeg aimed at performing Unsupervised Domain Adaptation through self supervision. We chose the task of reconstruction as an auxiliary task in accordance with [16] since it is semantically close to our target segmentation task. To this end we make a new copy of the prior/posterior and likelihood networks that share the weights of the aforementioned modules. We train the resulting model for both segmentation and reconstruction in parallel. Hence the shared encoding paths learn to extract useful information from both domains. In Sect. 4 we exhibit results using this technique to segment lungs from NIH X-Rays.

4   Experiments and Results

For our experimentation we focus on two tasks, segmentation and volumetry. Two datasets have been used: 60 abdominal CT images of healthy human patients (*Exp1*), and 57 CT porcine livers [10] (*Exp2*). Both datasets are resampled to isotropic spacing of 1 mm × 1 mm × 1 mm. DRRs **p** were then generated by projecting the 3D volume on the DRR plane **p** = **Mf** according to:

$$p_{i,j} = \sum_{i,j,k} m(i,j,k) f(i,j,k)$$

where **f** is the voxel density vector and **M** is the projection matrix calculated using the Siddon-Jacob's Raytracing algorithm [9]. The synthetic X-ray images of the thorax and porcine abdomen are taken at a fixed distance of 2 m and 1 m respectively from the CT volume's isocenter, pixel spacing is 0.51 mm. Images contain 512 × 512 pixels, which in this particular configuration, aligns the DRR image and CT volume spatially in pixel space. Both images were then downsampled to 64×64 for network training, with the CT volume target centre cropped to preserve spatial alignment with respect to the DRR input. A third dataset (*Exp3*), obtained from the NIH Clinical Center, was used for a qualitative ablation study. 100 random chest X-ray images from the ChestX-ray8 [18] dataset were selected. No ground truth is present for this experiment.

Exp1: Compact Structures. The first experiment assess the network's ability to segment large connected regions. The thoracic CT dataset was used, with data split; 50 volumes for training and 10 for testing. Annotations were manually made to create ground truth masks for the lung structures. As the lungs appear much darker than other body structures, direct regression to the CT volume is a comparable ground truth target to the manual segmentation masks.

All networks are trained using the Adam-optimizer with an initial learning rate of 1×10^{-4} and a batch size of four. The resulting segmentations were post processed by thresholding based on their pixel intensity values followed by median filtering with a kernel size of 3×3 to eliminate sparse noise.

Table 1 shows the average Dice similarity coefficient (DSC) for the predicted volume compared to the target volume. Dice accuracy for both approaches give equivalent performance. Table 1 also exhibits the ratio between the predicted volume of the lungs and the ground truth. This is achieved by counting the pixels that lay inside the segmented volume. In terms of quantitative evaluation our deterministic model achieves high Dice score. Meanwhile our dropout and dropblock probabilistic approaches provide us with an on par or better performance to the deterministic method. The variance exhibited on a per sample basis is 0.02 on dice score and 0.03 on the ratio of lung capacity. The probabilistic method provides us with more informative lower and upper bound. As the process of projection inherently destroys information, it is our belief that providing an informed upper and lower bounds of our metrics is a more suitable approach.

Furthermore a version of Phi-Seg without our proposed fusion module was evaluated and noticed a significant increase in the variance of our measurements as well as degraded performance. This observation is in accordance with our hypothesis that the fusion model inserts high level details to our proposed segmentation. Qualitative examples are shown in Fig. 2(a).

Exp2: Fine Structures. In order to test for limitations and to evaluate the network's ability to segment fine structures we aim to segment the ribcage with the publicly available porcine CT dataset [10]. Porcine ribs are smaller and finer than human ribs and they project largely on different anatomy (stomach and liver). This data has higher resolution and anatomical focus than the dataset in *Exp 1*, which serves as additional robustness test. The dataset consists of 58 volumes and has been split into 48 volumes for training and 10 for testing. Automated thresholding via pixel intensity was used to provide a manual ground truth from the 3D volumes. Known Hounsfield units (HU) for bones in CT have been used to define this threshold ($+1800$ to $+1900$ HU). The network has been trained with a binary cross-entropy loss, using the Adam optimizer with an initial learning rate of 1×10^{-4} and a batch size of four. Similarly to *Exp1*, the

Table 1. Average Dice score and Volume Ratio ($\frac{Predicted}{True}$) of lung and porcine segmentations compared to manually generated 3D ground truth. Exp.2 shows the performance of our methods when the target task is to reconstruct fine 3D structures.

Method	Exp.1 Volume Ratio	Exp.1 Dice	Exp.2 Dice
Det. U-Net	0.96	0.86	0.41
2D-3D PhiSeg	0.92 ± 0.12	$\mathbf{0.91 \pm 0.01}$	0.46 ± 0.05
2D-3D PhiSeg w/o fusion	1.31 ± 0.22	0.81 ± 0.05	0.45 ± 0.07
2D-3D U-Net Dropout	0.91 ± 0.01	0.90 ± 0.01	$\mathbf{0.48 \pm 0.03}$
2D-3D U-Net Dropblock	$\mathbf{0.97 \pm 0.012}$	0.83 ± 0.007	0.36 ± 0.12

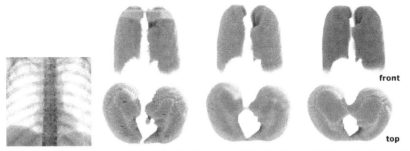

(a) Lung Segmentation with 2D-3D Unet; Left-Right: Input DRR; 3D Ground Truth; 3D Prediction 2D-3D-Unet; Prediction 2D-3D PhiSeg

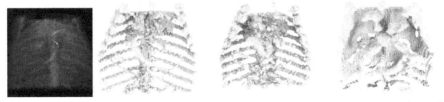

(b) Porcine Rib Cage Segmentation with 2D-3D Unet; Left-Right: Input DRR; 3D Ground Truth; 3D Prediction 2D-3D-Unet; Prediction 2D-3D PhiSeg

Fig. 2. Reconstructed Samples for Experiments 1,2. We use [12] to enhance depth perception in the 3D figures.

input to the network is a two dimensional DRR image while the segmentation target is the 3D segmentation mask.

The resulting segmentations achieved an average Dice score of 0.41 in the deterministic case. Meanwhile our probabilistic approaches were on par or better than the deterministic, achieving a Dice of 0.48 ± 0.03, while providing us with a more informed inference. We note that the difference between our PhiSeg model with and without the fusion module is smaller but still present. We believe this is due to the much harder task of segmenting fine structures across dimensions. Furthermore the Dice score is highly influenced by small outliers caused by noise and a blurry reconstruction of the spine as well as a slight misregistration between the predicted and ground truth volumes. Qualitative results are provided in Fig. 2(b). Note that small and fine structures as the tips of the ribs are reasonably well formed and shown in the predicted volume.

***Exp3*: Domain Adaptability.** In order to evaluate the nature of knowledge acquired by the network, and to test potentially limited domain invariance, the network that has been used and trained for *Exp1* was evaluated with chest X-ray images from the NIH chest X-Ray dataset [18]. In addition we evaluate our UDA method on the Montgomery Chest X-Ray dataset that is comprised of 2D chest X-Rays with corresponding 2D segmentations.

As it can be seen from Fig. 3(a), where the lungs are semi-occluded by a imaging artifact, our network produce the underlying 3D segmentation. This observation signifies that the network learns to reconstruct the anatomy rather than learning a mean lung segmentation. Without corresponding CT volumes, it is not possible to quantitatively evaluate the performance of the network. However, qualitative assessment of 91 subjects shows robust performance of our approach. In the Montgomery dataset the resulting 3D segmentation perimeters are unknown. Thus, we learn a projection to 2D and then compare to the ground truth, resulting in a dice score of **0.77** when we optimize towards the main DRR-CT task and **0.86** when we optimize towards the UDA. It is important to note that information is lost during the projection from 3D to 2D during the evaluation period, which explains the decreased performance. In Fig. 3(b) we show a selected example from the UDA algorithm.

(a) UDA on NIH Chest X-Ray Dataset; Left-Right: Input X-Ray; Mean of predicted volume across z-axis; 3D reconstruction of volume.

(b) UDA on the Montgomery X-Ray Thorax Dataset; Left-Right: Input X-Ray; 2D Ground Truth; 2D-3D PhiSeg volume projected onto 2D

Fig. 3. Examples from Experiment 3.

Discussion: As shown in *Exp1*, our proposed method achieves good Dice scores for 3D lung segmentation while providing informative uncertainty as lower and upper bounds of the volume and dice score. To the best of our knowledge, this is the first probabilistic methods to perform cross-modality 3D segmentation by unprojecting 2D X-ray images with acceptable performance. *Exp2* and *Exp3* have been designed to test expected limitations. In *Exp2* we observe that the prediction of fine structures can work, but with varying performance for either of the methods. *Exp3* shows that our method has promising domain adaptation properties. However, fine-tuning and calibration will be needed for applications.

5 Conclusion

In this paper we have introduced simple methods to perform probabilistic 3D segmentation from a projective 2D X-ray image. Our networks are data efficient as they have been trained with approximately 60 training DRR-CT pairs and time efficient as they converge within $\sim$2 h. In future work we will explore the capabilities of our approach for the reconstruction of vessel trees, e.g. coronary arteries from C-Arm Fluoroscopy. We expect that such reconstructions can be well suited to accurately initialize the registration of pre-operative scans.

Acknowledgments. Funding for this work was received by DoC of Imperial College London and the MAVEHA (EP/S013687/1) grant (A.V., D.R., B.K.). S.B. is supported by EP/S022104/1 and B.H. by the London Medical Imaging and AI Centre for Value Based Healthcare (19923). The authors would also like to thank NVIDIA corp for the donation of GPU resources.

References

1. Albarqouni, S., Fotouhi, J., Navab, N.: X-ray in-depth decomposition: revealing the latent structures. In: MICCAI (2017)
2. Aubert, B., Vergari, C., Ilharreborde, B., Courvoisier, A., Skalli, W.: 3D reconstruction of rib cage geometry from biplanar radiographs using a statistical parametric model approach. Comput. Methods Biomech. Biomed. Eng. Imag. Visual. 4(5), 281–295 (2016). https://doi.org/10.1080/21681163.2014.913990
3. Baumgartner, C.F.,et al.: PHiSeg: capturing uncertainty in medical image segmentation. In: MICCAI, pp. 1–14 (2019)
4. Budd, S., et al.: Confident head circumference measurement from ultrasound with real-time feedback for sonographers. In: MICCAI (2019)
5. Çiçek, Ö., Abdulkadir, A., Lienkamp, S.S., Brox, T., Ronneberger, O.: 3d u-net: learning dense volumetric segmentation from sparse annotation. In: Ourselin, S., et al. (eds.) MICCAI (2016)
6. Dumoulin, V., Visin, F.: A guide to convolution arithmetic for deep learning. arXiv preprint arXiv:1603.07285 (2016)
7. Gal, Y., Ghahramani, Z.: Dropout as a bayesian approximation: representing model uncertainty in deep learning. In: ICML (2016)
8. Henzler, P., Rasche, V., Ropinski, T., Ritschel, T.: Single-image tomography: 3d volumes from 2d cranial x-rays. Comput. Graph. Forum 37(2), 377–388 (2018). https://doi.org/10.1111/cgf.13369
9. Jian, W.: ITK-based implementation of two-projection 2D/3D registration method with an application in patient setup for external beam radiotherapy. In: Insight Journal (2010)
10. Kainz, B., Voglreiter, P., Sereinigg, M., et al.: High-Resolution Contrast Enhanced Multi-Phase Hepatic Computed Tomography Data from a Porcine Radio-Frequency Ablation Study (2014)
11. Koehler, C., Wischgoll, T.: Knowledge-assisted reconstruction of the human RIB cage and lungs. IEEE Comput. Graph. Appl. 30(1), 17–29 (2009)
12. Kroes, T., Post, F.H., Botha, C.P.: Exposure render: An interactive photo-realistic volume rendering framework. PLoS ONE 7(7), 75 (2012)

13. Lin, C.H., Kong, C., Lucey, S.: Learning efficient point cloud generation for dense 3d object reconstruction. In: Thirty-Second AAAI Conference on Artificial Intelligence (2018)
14. Rubin, G.D.: Computed tomography: revolutionizing the practice of medicine for 40 years. Radiology **273**(2S), S45–S74 (2014). https://doi.org/10.1148/radiol. 14141356, pMID: 25340438
15. Sun, X., et al.: Pix3d: dataset and methods for single-image 3d shape modeling. In: Proceedings of the IEEE Conference on Computer Vision and Pattern Recognition, pp. 2974–2983 (2018)
16. Sun, Y., Tzeng, E., Darrell, T., Efros, A.A.: Unsupervised domain adaptation through self-supervision (2019)
17. Van Dyck, P., Vanhoenacker, F.M., Van den Brande, P., De Schepper, A.M.: Imaging of pulmonary tuberculosis. In: European Radiology (2003)
18. Wang, X., Peng, Y., Lu, L., Lu, Z., Bagheri, M., Summers, R.M.: ChestX-ray8: Hospital-scale Chest X-ray Database and Benchmarks on Weakly-Supervised Classification and Localization of Common Thorax Diseases (2017)
19. Yan, X., Yang, J., Yumer, E., Guo, Y., Lee, H.: Perspective transformer nets: learning single-view 3D object reconstruction without 3d supervision. In: NeurIPS (2016)
20. Ying, X., Guo, H., Ma, K., Wu, J., Weng, Z., Zheng, Y.: X2ct-GAN: Reconstructing CT from biplanar x-rays with generative adversarial networks. In: The IEEE Conference on Computer Vision and Pattern Recognition (CVPR), June 2019

Computer-Aided Diagnosis
and Localization

CoviddDiagnosis: Deep Diagnosis of COVID-19 Patients Using Chest X-Rays

Kushagra Mahajan[1(✉)], Monika Sharma[1], Lovekesh Vig[1], Rishab Khincha[2],
Soundarya Krishnan[2], Adithya Niranjan[2], Tirtharaj Dash[2],
Ashwin Srinivasan[2], and Gautam Shroff[1]

[1] TCS Research, New Delhi, India
{kushagra.mahajan,monika.sharma1,lovekesh.vig,gautam.shroff}@tcs.com
[2] BITS Pilani, Sancoale, Goa, India
{f20160517,f20160472,f20160444,tirtharaj,ashwin}@goa.bits-pilani.ac.in

Abstract. As the COVID-19 pandemic threatens to overwhelm health-care systems across the world, there is a need for reducing the burden on medical staff via automated systems for patient screening. Given the limited availability of testing kits with long turn-around test times and the exponentially increasing number of COVID-19 positive cases, X-rays offer an additional cheap and fast modality for screening COVID-19 positive patients, especially for patients exhibiting respiratory symptoms. In this paper, we propose a solution based on a combination of deep learning and radiomic features for assisting radiologists during the diagnosis of COVID-19. The proposed system of *CovidDiagnosis* takes a chest X-ray image and passes it through a pipeline comprising of a model for lung isolation, followed by classification of the lung regions into four disease classes, namely Healthy, Pneumonia, Tuberculosis and COVID-19. To assist our classification framework, we employ embeddings of disease symptoms produced by the CheXNet network by creating an ensemble. The proposed approach gives remarkable classification results on publicly available datasets of chest X-rays. Additionally, the system produces visualization maps which highlight the symptoms responsible for producing the classification decisions. This provides trustworthy and interpretable decisions to radiologists for the clinical deployment of Covid-Diagnosis. Further, we calibrate our network using temperature scaling to give confidence scores which are representative of true correctness likelihood.

Keywords: COVID-19 · X-rays · Coronavirus · CovidDiagnosis · Radiomics

1 Introduction

The novel Coronavirus 2019 (COVID-19) originated in December, 2019 in China and soon spread across the entire world as a pandemic. Its spread has left a devastating mark on public health and global economy. The need of the hour is to

© Springer Nature Switzerland AG 2020
J. Petersen et al. (Eds.): TIA 2020, LNCS 12502, pp. 61–73, 2020.
https://doi.org/10.1007/978-3-030-62469-9_6

detect the COVID-19 positive cases as quickly as possible to stop further spread of the infection. The gold standard diagnostic criteria for COVID-19 is a real time reverse transcript polymerase chain reaction (RT-PCR) [7] test kit which is expensive, time-consuming and in short supply. In addition, these tests do suffer to produce false-negative and partial positive results at the onset of COVID-19 infection because they are unable to capture the minor viral infections in early stages [15,29]. Such patients when go undetected are a risk to other people. Several studies [4,17,20,31] published online claimed that Chest CT / X-rays can help in early screening of such suspected cases as they are cheaper and faster to test. While CT-Scans are more accurate, they are also more expensive, require more time and a more elaborate set up to ensure a contact free environment. X-rays, while not as sensitive as CT-Scans are able to perform with high accuracy in patients suffering from respiratory symptoms, which constitute the majority of patients visiting hospitals. Moreover, the X-ray technology is readily available in almost all parts of the world, and X-ray machines are already installed at public places like airports and railways stations and can be re-purposed to screen for characteristic COVID-19 radiomic features such as ground glass opacities and consolidations which are likely to have a peripheral distribution with bilateral, multi-focal lower lung involvement [13,16].

Radiologists are able to read X-rays and identify symptoms specific to COVID-19. However, manual diagnosis using X-rays is a time-consuming and effort-intensive task and there are not enough experienced medical professionals to cater to the exponentially increasing numbers of suspected cases around the world. This necessitates the automation of the COVID-19 diagnosis from Chest X-ray images using AI-based deep learning approaches which can facilitate quick identification of high risk COVID-19 patients who can then be further prescribed for RT-PCR tests. Meanwhile, such patients can be put into isolation wards to help reduce the spread of the coronavirus disease.

While there are burgeoning efforts on automation of COVID-19 diagnosis using Chest X-rays [3,8,18,24,27], we have contextualized our method to distinguish COVID-19 from commonly occurring respiratory problems in South-East Asia, such as Tuberculosis and Pneumonia. In this paper, we utilize Chest X-rays for classifying patients into four pathology categories namely, healthy, pneumonia, tuberculosis and COVID-19 positive. The proposed method first extracts the lung-region bounding boxes from the chest X-ray images using a trained Faster-RCNN [22] network. This step is performed to focus the subsequent classifiers attention on lung areas. Subsequently, an X-ray image containing only lung-regions is fed as input to a DenseNet-169 [10] network to yield a probability distribution over the four classes. Since, Chest X-rays contain several visually discernible symptoms such as ground glass opacities, consolidations, fibrosis, and pneumothorax which are distinctive features for detecting COVID-19 from other pathologies, we finetune the existing CheXNet model [21] on a combination of classes from the NIH dataset [28] and the Stanford CheXpert [11] dataset. We combine the embeddings from the second last layer of DenseNet-169 and fine-tuned CheXNet and then, train an MLP classifier to obtain the final output. To enhance trust in the model predictions, we isolate the lung regions and generate visualization maps using Grad-CAM [23] to highlight the affected lung regions in the X-ray image. We also calibrate our network using temperature scaling [9] to obtain accurate confidence scores for a prediction. A well calibrated model is critical for medical applications as it allows medical professionals identify and examine only those cases that are confusing for the model.

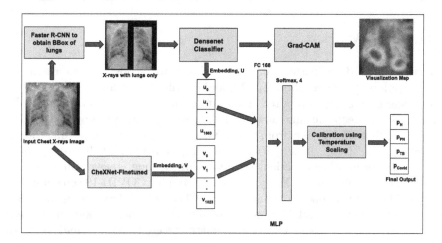

Fig. 1. Figure showing pipeline of our proposed method - CovidDiagnosis.

To summarize, we make following contributions in the paper:

- We propose a deep learning based automated method for COVID-19 diagnosis using Chest X-rays which is calibrated using temperature scaling [9] and outputs accurate and reliable confidence scores for predictions.
- We propose a diagnostic pipeline comprising first of lung isolation using Faster-RCNN network [22] allowing subsequent models to focus entirely on disease symptoms present in the lungs and not pay attention to other elements in the image.
- We finetune CheXNet [21] on classes from NIH and Stanford datasets, and further use this network's embeddings to capture information about visual disease symptoms useful for discriminating COVID-19 from diseases such as tuberculosis and pneumonia for making the final diagnosis. The final prediction is made by using a combined embedding from ChexNet and a DenseNet model proposed for classification.
- We also illustrate the effectiveness of our proposed approach by creating activation maps using Grad-CAM [23] to highlight affected regions of the lungs which can prove helpful to the radiologist to validate the model.
- We evaluate CovidDiagnosis on a publicly available Chest X-rays dataset and compare the performance against state-of-the-art networks such as Covid-Net [27] and CovidAID [18]. We show empirically that our pipeline outperforms competing approaches.

The remainder of the paper is organized as follows: Sect. 2 will describe the work previously done on COVID-19 diagnosis using X-ray images and how our approach is different from prior work. Next, we provide a description of our proposed method in Sect. 3. This is followed by brief detail on a Chest X-ray images dataset used for training and evaluation purposes. Subsequently, Sect. 5 provide details of the training, experiments conducted, their results and discussions on them. In the end, Sect. 6 will conclude the work with future avenues in this field.

2   Related Work

In recent times, deep learning has made significant strides in medical image classification and segmentation [1, 5, 19, 30] in addition to being applied to standard image processing, computer vision and natural language processing tasks. Several existing deep learning networks in literature have been proposed to identify various thoracic diseases from Chest X-rays like pneumonia, pneumothorax, fibrosis etc. [14, 21, 25]. Since, patients suffering from COVID-19 develop pneumonia and certain other infectious symptoms in the lung areas of Chest X-rays, it may be convenient to use X-rays for automation of COVID-19 screening.

With the sudden spike in the number of COVID-19 infected patients, there have been a number of publications addressing the problem of automatic diagnosis so as to quickly and effectively isolate infected patients and curb the spread of the virus. Authors in [27] proposed a deep neural network based Covid-Net to distinguish viral and bacteria pneumonia from COVID-19 patients and have also released their evaluation dataset COVIDx. Another paper utilized pre-trained CheXNet to finetune the network to classify X-ray images and named the network CovidAID [18]. Tulin et al. [24] developed a DarkNet based model to classify X-ray images into COVID-19, No-Findings and Pneumonia. Sanhita et al. [3] employ transfer learning based convolutional neural network for classification into four classes, e.g, normal, other disease, pneumonia and COVID-19. A slightly different approach was adopted by authors in [26] where they trained deep learning models like MobileNetV2, SqueezeNet on the created stacked dataset, and the features obtained by the models were processed using the Social Mimic optimization method. In the next step, efficient features were combined and classified using an SVM. A comparative study of the use of the recent deep learning models (VGG16, VGG19, DenseNet201, InceptionResNetV2, InceptionV3, Resnet50, and MobileNetV2) to deal with detection and classification of COVID-19 pneumonia is presented in paper [2].

We found that prior-art mostly consist of deep learning methods trying to distinguish COVID-19 from healthy cases and pneumonia in Chest X-rays. However, in our paper, we also propose to contextualize the solution to distinguish COVID-19 from commonly occurring respiratory problem in South-East Asia such as Tuberculosis. Moreover, the methods described above simply feed the Chest X-ray images into deep networks for classification and hence, it is uncertain if the prior networks are making decisions based on relevant information from Chest X-ray images and focusing on the right visual features. Therefore, we build a pipeline which first localizes the regions of interest (lungs) using a Faster-RCNN [22]. We also supplement our network with disease symptom embeddings obtained from CheXNet. Additionally, we have not seen any COVID-19 in the literature which is calibrated to give output probabilities with confidence scores representative of prediction correctness likelihood.

3 Proposed Approach: CovidDiagnosis

Figure 1 shows the overall architecture of the proposed CovidDiagnosis method for Chest X-rays. It consists of the following modules for processing X-ray images of patients to classify them into four classes - healthy, pneumonia, tuberculosis and COVID-19 positive:

- **Lung Isolation using Faster-RCNN:** As a first step, we train a Faster-RCNN [22] network for identifying bounding boxes (Bbox) of lungs present in Chest X-rays. The training data for the lungs Bbox is obtained by using Lung-Finder[1] which uses basic image processing features such as HAAR, LBP and HOG to detect the left and the right lungs from an X-ray image. The detections produced by HAAR features are better when compared with those produced by HOG determined through visual inspection, and hence we use bounding boxes from HAAR features for training the faster-rcnn. We manually verified the resultant Bboxes for having correct lung region and discarded those set of images for which lungs Bbox is not correct. We train a faster-rcnn on the lung Bboxes using VGG16 as the backbone network.
- **DenseNet Classifier:** DenseNet [10] is a convolutional network which has n layers and $n \times (n+1)/2$ direct connections. This means that each subsequent layer has feature maps of all preceding layers as input. DenseNets have fewer parameters to train and dense connections have a regularizing effect which reduces over-fitting on tasks with lesser training data. We use DenseNet-169 to train a classifier on a 3-channel input image comprising left and right isolated lung (channels 1 and 2) and a complete Chest X-ray image (channel 3). The underlying idea behind using lung-isolation is to explicitly enable the network to focus its attention on the lung regions for making a classification decision. The classifier is trained to classify input Chest X-ray images into one of four categories - healthy, pneumonia, tuberculosis and COVID-19 positive. We utilize the embeddings $U = (u_0, u_1, ..., u_{1663})$ from the second last layer of the trained DenseNet classifier for further processing.
- **CheXNet Finetuning for disease symptoms:** To enhance the discriminatory capabilities of our classifier, we propose to explicitly provide information about disease symptoms present in Chest X-rays such as opacities, consolidations, mass, fibrosis, pneumothorax etc. in the form of an embedding vector. This additional information assists the classifier by drawing correlations between our four disease classes and the disease symptoms displayed

---

[1] Lungs-Finder: https://github.com/xiaoyongzhu/lungs-finder.

by the X-ray. This, in turn, helps to ignore any bias present in the chest X-rays dataset obtained from different sources as is commonly the case when images for classes are gathered from different data sources. We use the NIH dataset consisting of 14 classes that represent visual disease symptoms present in chest X-rays. Since, the NIH dataset does not have 'opacities' as one of the classes which is an important COVID-19 positive feature, we include the samples of opacities class from Stanford CheXpert dataset and subsequently finetune the CheXNet [21] model for these 15 classes of disease symptoms. Further, the finetuned CheXNet is used to obtain second last layer embeddings $V = (v_0, v_1, ..., v_{1023})$ of Chest X-rays images which are used for processing in the next module.

- **MLP classifier:** The embeddings from DenseNet-169 and CheXNet are concatenated to train a 2-layer MLP for final classification of X-rays images into four classes - healthy, pneumonia, tuberculosis and COVID-19 positive. The MLP comprises of $(168, 4)$ hidden units, and is fed an input of 2688 dimensional vector $W = (u_0, u_1, ..., u_{1663}, v_0, v_1, ..., v_{023})$.

- **Calibration of Network:** We perform calibration of our proposed network so that radiologists can rely on output predictions of our network and the solution can be deployed for clinical use. The simplest way to visualize calibration is to plot the accuracy as a function of confidence and for a well-calibrated network, the plot should be an identity function. The reliability diagram of our proposed architecture is shown in Fig. 2. In order to calibrate the network, we have used Temperature scaling [9] which divides the logit vector obtained from the classification network by a learned scalar parameter T as follows:

$$P(\hat{y}) = \frac{e^{\mathbf{z}/T}}{\sum_j e^{z_j/T}} \quad (1)$$

where $\hat{y}$ and $\mathbf{z}$ is the output prediction and logit, respectively. The parameter T is learned on a validation set where T is chosen to minimize negative log-likelihood. In essence, the temperature scaling technique softens the network outputs, thereby making the network less confident and in turn, making the confidence scores reflect the true correctness probabilities.

- **Activation Maps Generation:** An extensive qualitative analysis is essential for determining whether our diagnostics approach is looking at the right portions of the image for determining the four disease classes. These correct regions were determined through consultations with a team of doctors. To obtain the regions of interest where our network is focusing its attention, we make use of Grad-CAM [23]. The activation maps highlight the regions where abnormalities such as consolidations and opacities etc. are present which can aid radiologists in deeper investigation of suspected cases.

4   Dataset

We utilize Chest X-rays of four classes - healthy, pneumonia, tuberculosis and COVID-19 from publicly available datasets for diagnosis of COVID-19. X-ray samples for COVID-19 positive patients are taken from the X-ray image database made available by Cohen JP et al. [6]. X-ray images for healthy and tuberculosis patients are obtained from Pulmonary Chest X-rays dataset [12]. The NIH dataset is used for pneumonia X-ray images. The dataset is divided into train (823), validation (181) and test sets (344) with number of samples for each class as follows: Train-set (COVID-19 - 153, Healthy - 240, Pneumonia - 190 and Tuberculosis - 240); Val-set (COVID-19 - 27, Healthy - 54, Pneumonia - 44 and Tuberculosis - 55); Test-set (COVID-19 - 46, Healthy - 110, Pneumonia - 88 and Tuberculosis - 100).

5 Experimental Results and Discussions

5.1 Training Details

The input to our classifier consists of 3 channels: the first channel is the left lung image (with the rest of the image blacked out), the second channel is the right lung image (with the rest of the image blacked out), and the third channel is the full image. We have experimented with images of size 224×224 and 448×448 for training CovidDiagnosis. We apply augmentations to all the above datasets by applying random transformations like rotation ($-20°$ to $+20°$), scaling (-10% to $+10\%$), normalization, and horizontal and vertical translation. The chest region is always present at the centre of the image and hence, the small translations do not push the important regions out of the image. We utilize DenseNet-169 pre-trained on ImageNet for finetuning on the four disease classes with SGD optimizer having an initial learning rate of 1e-3 and momentum of 0.9. We apply softmax activation function in the final layer of our DenseNet classifier to obtain the probabilities of predictions.

5.2 Baseline Networks

To show the effectiveness of our proposed CovidDiagnosis method, we compare its performance with two prior deep networks namely, Covid-Net [27] and CovidAID [18].

- **Covid-Net**: The architecture of Covid-Net is based on a residual projection-expansion-projection-extension (PEPX) design pattern and comprises of a mixture of convolutional layers with diverse kernel sizes and grouping configurations. We have used the original architecture and training configuration, as given by authors [27].
- **CovidAID**: Mangal et al. [18] proposed CovidAID which simply finetunes the CheXNet network for classifying Chest X-ray images into four classes - Normal, Bacterial Pneumonia, Viral Pneumonia and COVID-19 using a sigmoid activation. We used the same training configuration for comparison.

We trained all the three networks Covid-Net, CovidAID and CovidDiagnosis for 3-way classification of X-rays into healthy, pneumonia and COVID-19 positive from our Chest X-rays dataset, as mentioned in Sect. 4 for performance evaluation and comparison.

Table 1. Performance impact of different modules of CovidDiagnosis on AUC and Accuracy values of X-rays pathology classification

	Method	AUC	Acc
I(224 * 224)	Densenet	0.9699	0.8799
	Densenet + LungIsolation(LI)	0.9823	0.9040
I(448 * 448) w/ aug	Densenet	0.9798	0.8924
	Densenet + LungIsolation(LI)	**0.9885**	**0.9069**
	Densenet + LI + CheXNet + MLP	0.9694	**0.9157**
I(448 * 448) w/o aug	Densenet + LungIsolation(LI)	0.9462	0.8488
	Densenet + LI + CheXNet + MLP	0.9822	0.8895

5.3   Results and Discussion

First, we present the results of introducing different modules in our proposed method CovidDiagnosis in Table 1. Initially, we train the DenseNet-169 classifier for classifying the entire Chest X-rays image of size 224×224 as input and as can be seen in Table 1, we achieve an accuracy of 87.99% and AUC value of 0.9699. In the next experiment, we use lung isolation to explicitly enable DenseNet to focus on right areas in an X-ray image i.e., lungs to learn relevant discriminating features for classification. We can clearly see that lung isolation gives a boost in accuracy from 87.99% to 90.40%. Further, we use images of size 448×448 for training DenseNet with and without lung isolation and obtain an accuracy of 89.24% and 90.69%, and AUC of 0.9798 and 0.9885 respectively. As is evident from Table 1, lung isolation experiments for images of sizes 224×224 and 448×448 give almost equal performance. Thus, we can conclude that lung isolation is beneficial for getting good performance on low-resolution images as it helps the network narrow down its field of view, and allows it to focus its attention entirely on lung regions.

Table 2. Class-wise different performance measures for CovidDiagnosis (using DenseNet + LI + CheXNet + MLP) on image size 448×448. PN and TB represents pneumonia and tuberculosis, respectively

Confusion matrix	COVID	Healthy	PN	TB	Precision	Recall	F1-Score
COVID	45	0	1	0	0.98	0.98	0.98
Healthy	0	102	0	8	0.88	0.93	0.90
PN	1	0	84	3	0.97	0.95	0.96
TB	0	14	2	84	0.88	0.84	0.86

Subsequently, we concatenate embeddings from DenseNet and CheXNet to train a 2-layer MLP classifier and observe that it gives an improvement in classification accuracy (91.57%). This implies that adding explicit information about various abnormalities present in Chest X-rays in the form of an embedding vector from CheXNet enhances the discriminatory power of CovidDiagnosis and improves the classification performance. Since, the network performance is already high in our case, there is very limited room for improvement on this small dataset. In order to show the effectiveness of CheXNet embeddings as an additional feature, we perform an experiment by training DenseNet on our dataset without using augmentation techniques during training. Here, we can see that CheXNet embeddings improved classification accuracy from 84.88% to 88.95%. We also present the confusion matrix, precision, recall and F1-score values of CovidDiagnosis for image sizes 448 × 448 to illustrate the class-wise performance in Table 2. We observe that CovidDiagnosis identifies COVID-19 positive samples with 0.98 for all the measures - precision, recall and F1-score.

The comparison of the performance of CovidDiagnosis against two baseline networks - Covid-Net and CovidAID is presented in Table 3. It is evident from the accuracy, AUC values and the confusion matrices that CovidDiagnosis outperforms both of the other methods for the 3-way classification problem. There is a boost of approx. 3% and 2% in classification accuracy of CovidDiagnosis when compared with Covid-Net and CovidAID respectively.

Table 3. Performance comparison with state-of-the-art networks for diagnosis of COVID-19 from Chest X-rays for 3-way classification

Confusion matrix		COVID	Healthy	Pneumonia	**AUC**	**Acc**
Covid-Net	COVID	**37**	0	9	0.9633	0.8934
	Healthy	3	**107**	0		
	Pneumonia	4	10	**74**		
CovidAID	COVID	**27**	1	18	0.9721	0.9061
	Healthy	0	**110**	0		
	Pneumonia	5	0	**83**		
Covid-Diagnosis	COVID	**46**	0	0	**0.9794**	**0.9221**
	Healthy	0	**107**	3		
	Pneumonia	2	14	**72**		

Figure 2 shows the reliability diagram of CovidDiagnosis for classifying Chest X-rays into 4 classes. The plot in Fig. 2(a) shows the confidence scores before calibration and we can see that the network is not well-calibrated and is overconfident in predicting outputs. But after using temperature scaling for network calibration, the reliability diagram is close to an identity plot as shown in Fig. 2(b) indicating that the network is not over-confident in its predictions. This builds up trust with medical practitioners to adopt our system for its practical use in hospitals, clinics, and public places like airports etc.

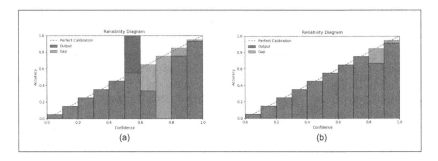

Fig. 2. Plots showing reliability diagrams (a) before and (b) after calibration of Covid-Diagnosis using temperature scaling [9].

We create activation maps for COVID-19 positive Chest X-rays using GRAD-Cam [23], as shown in Fig. 3. The activation maps indicate that the portions of the lungs that are actively examined by the model are in agreement with where abnormalities such as consolidations and opacities are present, showing that our network is indeed looking at the right locations for learning discriminating features for classification.

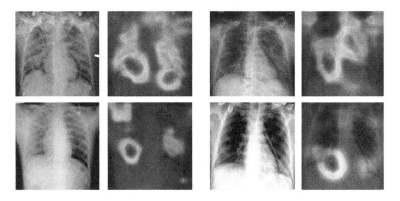

Fig. 3. Visualization maps of COVID-19 positive X-rays of patients using GRAD-Cam [23] highlighting regions of abnormalities.

6   Conclusion

We propose a system named CovidDiagnosis for segregating suspected COVID-19 positive patients having high confidence scores, thereby helping to reduce the spread of COVID-19 disease. We demonstrate that utilizing lung isolation and combining embeddings from CheXNet of visual disease symptoms in Chest X-rays enhances classification accuracy and enables the network to learn relevant discriminating features by focusing on correct lung regions. Thus, it produces improved classification performance compared to other existing COVID-19 X-ray classification approaches. The proposed method is well-calibrated via temperature scaling which can prove beneficial to radiologists as the predicted probabilities reflect the true correctness likelihood. We also aid radiologists by providing activation maps highlighting regions of disease symptoms for deeper investigation. Going forward, we wish to apply few-shot techniques such as meta-learning to train the network on limited available data and eventually, evaluate on larger and more diverse datasets.

References

1. Alom, M.Z., Yakopcic, C., Taha, T.M., Asari, V.K.: Nuclei segmentation with recurrent residual convolutional neural networks based u-net (r2u-net). In: NAE-CON 2018 - IEEE National Aerospace and Electronics Conference, pp. 228–233, July 2018. https://doi.org/10.1109/NAECON.2018.8556686
2. Asnaoui, K.E., Chawki, Y.: Using x-ray images and deep learning for automated detection of coronavirus disease. J. Biomolecular Structure Dyn. 1–12 (2020). https://doi.org/10.1080/07391102.2020.1767212
3. Basu, S., Mitra, S., Saha, N.: Deep learning for screening covid-19 using chest x-ray images. arXiv (2020), https://arxiv.org/abs/2004.10507
4. Bernheim, A., et al.: Chest ct findings in coronavirus disease-19 (covid-19): relationship to duration of infection. Radiology (2020). https://pubs.rsna.org/doi/10.1148/radiol.2020200463
5. Chen, S., Ma, K., Zheng, Y.: Med3d: Transfer learning for 3d medical image analysis. ArXiv abs/1904.00625 (2019)
6. Cohen, J.P., Morrison, P., Dao, L., Roth, K., Duong, T.Q., Ghassemi, M.: Covid-19 image data collection: Prospective predictions are the future. arXiv 2006.11988 (2020). https://github.com/ieee8023/covid-chestxray-dataset
7. Emery, S.L., et al.: Real-time reverse transcription-polymerase chain reaction assay for sars-associated coronavirus. Emerging Infectious Diseases (2004). https://www.ncbi.nlm.nih.gov/pmc/articles/PMC3322901/
8. Gozes, O., et al.: Rapid AI development cycle for the coronavirus (covid-19) pandemic: initial results for automated detection & patient monitoring using deep learning ct image analysis (2020)
9. Guo, C., Pleiss, G., Sun, Y., Weinberger, K.Q.: On calibration of modern neural networks. In: Proceedings of the 34th International Conference on Machine Learning, vol. 70. pp. 1321–1330. ICML 2017, JMLR.org (2017)
10. Huang, G., Liu, Z., Van Der Maaten, L., Weinberger, K.Q.: Densely connected convolutional networks. In: 2017 IEEE Conference on Computer Vision and Pattern Recognition (CVPR), pp. 2261–2269 (2017)
11. Irvin, J., et al.: Chexpert: a large chest radiograph dataset with uncertainty labels and expert comparison. CoRR abs/1901.07031 (2019). http://arxiv.org/abs/1901.07031
12. Jaeger, S., Candemir, S., Antani, S., Wáng, Y.X.J., Lu, P.X., Thoma, G.: Two public chest x-ray datasets for computer-aided screening of pulmonary diseases. Quantitative Imag. Med. Surgery 4(6), 475 (2014)
13. Kong, W., Agarwal, P.P.: Chest imaging appearance of covid-19 infection. Radiology (2020). https://pubs.rsna.org/doi/10.1148/ryct.2020200028

14. Kumar, P., Grewal, M., Srivastava, M.M.: Boosted cascaded convnets for multilabel classification of thoracic diseases in chest radiographs. In: Campilho, A., Karray, F., ter Haar Romeny, B. (eds.) Image Analysis and Recognition, pp. 546–552. Springer, Cham (2018)

15. Lan, L., Xu, D., Ye, G., Xia, C., Wang, S., Li, Y., Xu, H.: Positive RT-PCR test results in patients recovered from COVID-19. JAMA **323**(15), 1502–1503 (2020). https://doi.org/10.1001/jama.2020.2783

16. Lee, E.Y.P., Ng, M.Y., Khong, P.L.: COVID-19 pneumonia: what has CT taught us? The Lancet Infectious Diseases **20**(4), 384–385 (2020). http://www.sciencedirect.com/science/article/pii/S1473309920301341

17. Long, C., et al.: Diagnosis of the coronavirus disease (covid-19): RRT-PCR or CT? Euro. J. Radiol. **126**, 108961 (2020). http://www.sciencedirect.com/science/article/pii/S0720048X20301509

18. Mangal, A., Kalia, S., Rajgopal, H., Rangarajan, K., Namboodiri, V., Banerjee, S., Arora, C.: Covidaid: COVID-19 detection using chest x-ray (2020)

19. Oktay, O., et al.: Attention u-net: learning where to look for the pancreas. CoRR abs/1804.03999 (2018). http://arxiv.org/abs/1804.03999

20. Eng Pan, Ye, T., et al.: Time course of lung changes at chest ct during recovery from coronavirus disease 2019 (COVID-19). Radiology (2020). https://doi.org/10.1148/radiol.2020200370

21. Rajpurkar, P., et al.: Chexnet: Radiologist-level pneumonia detection on chest x-rays with deep learning. CoRR abs/1711.05225 (2017). http://arxiv.org/abs/1711.05225

22. Ren, S., He, K., Girshick, R., Sun, J.: Faster R-CNN: towards real-time object detection with region proposal networks. IEEE Trans. Pattern Anal. Mach. Intell. **39**(6), 1137–1149 (2017). https://doi.org/10.1109/TPAMI.2016.2577031

23. Selvaraju, R.R., Cogswell, M., Das, A., Vedantam, R., Parikh, D., Batra, D.: Gradcam: visual explanations from deep networks via gradient-based localization. In: 2017 IEEE International Conference on Computer Vision (ICCV), pp. 618–626 (2017)

24. Ozturk, T., et al.: Automated detection of COVID-19 cases using deep neural networks with x-ray images. Comput. Biol. Med. (2020). https://www.ncbi.nlm.nih.gov/pmc/articles/PMC7187882/

25. Tang, Y., Tang, Y., Xiao, J., Summers, R.M.: Xlsor: A robust and accurate lung segmentor on chest x-rays using criss-cross attention and customized radiorealistic abnormalities generation. In: MIDL (2019)

26. Toğaçar, M., Ergen, B., Cömert, Z.: Covid-19 detection using deep learning models to exploit social mimic optimization and structured chest x-ray images using fuzzy color and stacking approaches. Comput. Biol. Med. **121**, 103805 (2020). http://www.sciencedirect.com/science/article/pii/S0010482520301736

27. Wang, L., Wong, A.: Covid-net: A tailored deep convolutional neural network design for detection of covid-19 cases from chest x-ray images (2020)

28. Wang, X., Peng, Y., Lu, L., Lu, Z., Bagheri, M., Summers, R.M.: Chestx-ray8: hospital-scale chest x-ray database and benchmarks on weakly-supervised classification and localization of common thorax diseases. In: Proceedings of the IEEE Conference on Computer Vision and Pattern Recognition, pp. 2097–2106 (2017)

29. Xie, X., Zhong, Z., Zhao, W., Zheng, C., Wang, F., Liu, J.: Chest ct for typical 2019-ncov pneumonia: relationship to negative rt-pcr testing. Radiology (2020). https://pubs.rsna.org/doi/10.1148/radiol.2020200343

30. Yi, X., Walia, E., Babyn, P.: Generative adversarial network in medical imaging: a review. Med. Image Anal. **58**, 101552 (2019). http://www.sciencedirect.com/science/article/pii/S1361841518308430
31. Zu, Z.Y., Jiang, M.D., Xu, P.P., Chen, W., Ni, Q.Q., Lu, G.M., Zhang, L.J.: Coronavirus disease 2019 (covid-19): a perspective from china. Radiology (2020). https://pubs.rsna.org/doi/10.1148/radiol.2020200490

Can We Trust Deep Learning Based Diagnosis? The Impact of Domain Shift in Chest Radiograph Classification

Eduardo H. P. Pooch[1]([✉]), Pedro Ballester[2], and Rodrigo C. Barros[1]

[1] Machine Learning Theory and Applications Research Group (MALTA),
School of Technology, Pontifícia Universidade Católica do Rio Grande do Sul,
Rio Grande do Sul, Porto Alegre, Brazil
eduardo.pooch@edu.pucrs.br
[2] Neuroscience Graduate Program, McMaster University, Hamilton, Ontario, Canada

Abstract. While deep learning models become more widespread, their ability to handle unseen data and generalize for any scenario is yet to be challenged. In medical imaging, there is a high heterogeneity of distributions among images based on the equipment that generates them and their parametrization. This heterogeneity triggers a common issue in machine learning called domain shift, which represents the difference between the training data distribution and the distribution of where a model is employed. A high domain shift often results in a poor generalization performance from the models. In this work, we evaluate the extent of which domain shift damages model performance on four of the largest datasets of chest radiographs. We show how training and testing with different datasets (e.g., training in ChestX-ray14 and testing in CheXpert) drastically affects model performance, posing a big question over the reliability of deep learning models trained on public datasets. We also show that models trained on CheXpert and MIMIC-CXR generalized better to other datasets.

Keywords: Deep learning · Domain shift · Chest radiographs

1 Introduction

Radiography examinations are commonly used to diagnose chest conditions since they are a low-cost, fast, and widely available imaging modality. Abnormalities identified on radiographs are called radiological findings. Several chest radiological findings might indicate lung cancer, such as lesions, consolidation, and atelectasis. Lung cancer is the first cause of cancer death worldwide, and the lack of effective early-detection methods is one of the main reasons for its poor prognosis [8]. Lung cancer signs are mostly identified through imaging exams, but at the same time, 90% of the lung cancer misdiagnosis occurs in radiographs, often due to observer error [4].

© Springer Nature Switzerland AG 2020
J. Petersen et al. (Eds.): TIA 2020, LNCS 12502, pp. 74–83, 2020.
https://doi.org/10.1007/978-3-030-62469-9_7

Deep learning is a growing field for image analysis. It has recently been employed at several medical imaging tasks [14] and may help to overcome observer error. Considering chest radiographs, deep learning approaches are usually developed within a multi-label classification scenario, providing findings to assist physicians with the diagnosis process. Recent work in the field achieved near radiologist-level accuracy at identifying radiological findings by the use of convolutional neural networks [18], one of the most successful deep learning approaches.

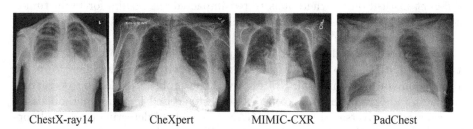

ChestX-ray14   CheXpert   MIMIC-CXR   PadChest

Fig. 1. Example of a chest radiograph positive for consolidation randomly sampled from each of the four analyzed datasets: ChestX-ray14, CheXpert, MIMIC-CXR, and PadChest.

One assumption underlying deep learning models is that training and test data are independent and identically distributed ($i.i.d$). This assumption often does not hold when data comes from different settings. This is a common case for medical imaging, a scenario in which image acquisition protocols and machines may vary among diagnostic centers, being defined by the quality of the machine, its parameters, and the acquisition protocol. Another aspect of medical imaging is the epidemiological variation among different populations, which may change the label distribution in different datasets. This difference in data distribution from the same task is called *domain shift*. The domain from where training data is sampled is the source domain, with distribution $p(X_s)$, and the one where the model is applied to is the target domain, with distribution $p(X_t)$. When $p(X_s) \sim p(X_t)$, it means the model most likely will handle test data the same way as it did in training. As $p(X_s)$ diverges from $p(X_t)$, trained models tend to yield poor results, failing to effectively handle the input data [19].

With deep learning becoming widespread, predictive models will inevitably become a big part of health care. We believe that before health care providers trust predictive models as a second opinion, we must understand the extent of their generalization capabilities and how well they perform outside the source domain. In this work, we propose to evaluate how well models trained on a hospital-scale database generalize to unseen data from other hospitals or diagnostic centers by analyzing the degree of domain shift among four large datasets of chest radiographs. We train a state-of-the-art convolutional neural network for multi-label classification on each of the four datasets and evaluate each model's performance in predicting labels on the other three datasets.

This paper is organized as follows: we first describe our methods, detailing our experiment design and datasets. Then, we summarize our results in Table 2 and discuss our findings.

2   Related Work

The impact of domain shift in medical imaging has been studied for brain tumors by AlBadawy et al. [1]. They showed how training models with data from a different institution to where it is tested impacted the results for brain tumor segmentation. They also found that using multiple institutions for training does not necessarily remove this limitation.

We also see methods focused on unsupervised domain adaptation, where the task is to mitigate the problems of domain shift with unlabeled data from the target domain. Madani et al. [15] observed the problem of domain overfitting on chest radiographs and developed a semi-supervised learning method based on generative adversarial networks (GANs) capable of detecting cardiac abnormality alongside the adversarial objective. Their method was able to overcome the domain shift between two datasets and increased the model performance when testing on a different domain. Chen et al. [3] developed a domain adaptation method based on CycleGANs. Their work resembles CyCADA [9], with the difference of also introducing a discriminator for the network output, creating what they called semantic-aware GANs. Javanmardi and Tasdizen [12] used a framework very similar to domain-adversarial neural networks [6] that employ a domain classification network with a gradient reversal layer to model a joint feature space.

Some works focus on domain adaptation for cross-modality segmentation. Dou et al. [5] designed an adversarial-based method that learns both domain-specific feature extraction layers and a joint high-level representation space that can segment data from both MRI or CT data.

Gholami et al. [7] propose a biophysics-based data augmentation method to produce synthetic tumor-bearing images to the training set. The authors argue that this augmentation procedure improves model generalization. Mahmood et al. [16] present a generative model that translates images from the simulated endoscopic images domain to a realistic-looking domain as data augmentation. The authors also introduce an L1-regularization loss between the translated and the original image to minimize distortions.

3   Materials and Methods

We wish to understand how trained models in each dataset behave when dealing with data from others.

3.1   Datasets

Three large datasets of chest radiographs are available to this date. ChestX-ray14 [20] from the National Institute of Health contains 112,120 frontal-view chest radiographs from 32,717 different patients labeled with 14 radiological findings. CheXpert [11] from the Stanford Hospital contains 224,316 frontal and lateral chest radiographs of 65,240 patients. MIMIC-CXR [13] from Massachusetts Institute of Technology presents 371,920 chest X-rays associated with 227,943 imaging studies from 65,079 patients. Both CheXpert and MIMIC-CXR are labeled with the same 13 findings. PadChest [2] contains 160,000 images obtained from 67,000 patients of San Juan Hospital in Spain. The radiographs are labeled with 174 different findings. Most labels from all four datasets are automatically extracted using natural language processing algorithms on the radiological reports.

We show the pixel intensity distribution of each dataset in Fig. 2. We see a spike at low intensities (especially 0) for most centers. However, the distribution for higher intensities is somewhat different for every center, which may imply in a decrease of the models' predictive performance, except for CheXpert and MIMIC-CXR, which show similar distributions. Figure 3 shows the average radiograph of each dataset (computed using 10,000 random samples), in which we can see small differences in pixel intensity and that a common artifact appears on the top left corner of PadChest radiographs. Another difference that might cause domain shift is that PadChest labels are extracted from reports in Spanish, while the other three are extracted from reports in English.

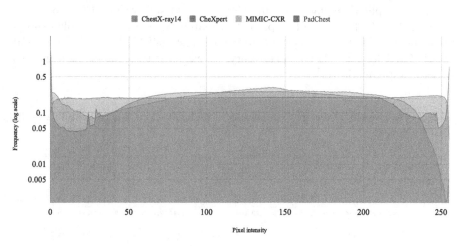

Fig. 2. Dataset pixel intensity probability density function.

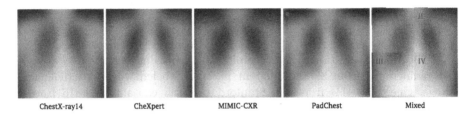

ChestX-ray14   CheXpert   MIMIC-CXR   PadChest   Mixed

Fig. 3. Average image of each of the four datasets. Last image cotains one quarter of each average image to better visualize pixel intensity differences (I - ChestX-ray14, II - CheXpert, III - MIMIC-CXR, IV - PadChest).

3.2 Experiment Design

We employ a multi-label classification approach reproducing CheXNet [18], which achieved state-of-the-art results in classification of multiple pathologies using a DenseNet121 convolutional neural network architecture [10]. The model is pre-trained on the ImageNet dataset, and the images are resized to 224×224 pixels and normalized using ImageNet mean and standard deviation. We train four models, one for each dataset, and subsequently evaluate our model at the other three. Each model is trained with the training set and evaluated on its own test set and the other three test sets. The four datasets have the same train, test, and validation sets across the experiments. For the ChestX-ray14 dataset, we use the original split, but since CheXpert and MIMIC-CXR test sets are not publicly available and PadChest does not have an original split, we randomly re-split their data, keeping ChestX-ray14 split ratio (70% train, 20% test, and 10% validation) and no patient overlap between the sets. Table 1 shows the frequency of the labels in each training and test split. As both CheXpert and MIMIC-CXR have labels for uncertainty, we assumed these labels as negatives (U-Zeros approach in [11]).

Table 1. Positive label frequency (in number of radiographs) in our train and test split for each dataset.

	Atelectasis		Cardiomegaly		Consolidation		Edema		Lesion		Pneumonia		Pneumothorax		No Finding	
	Train	Test	Train	Test	Train	Test	Train	Test	Train	Test	Train	Test	Train	Test	Train	Test
ChestX-ray14	7,996	2,420	1,950	582	3,263	957	1,690	413	7,758	2,280	978	242	3,705	1,089	42,405	11,928
CheXpert	20,630	6,132	15,885	5,044	9,063	2,713	34,066	10,501	4,976	1,411	3,274	935	12,583	3,476	12,010	3,293
MIMIC-CXR	34,653	10,071	34,097	9,879	8,097	2,430	20,499	5,954	5,025	1,341	12,736	3,711	8,243	2,231	58,135	16,670
PadChest	1,841	574	3,283	953	664	210	127	44	878	261	678	194	163	33	25,268	7,200

One limitation we encountered is that the datasets have a different set of labels between each other. We fix this by training each model with all labels available, but reporting the results only on the common labels for all four (Atelectasis, Cardiomegaly, Consolidation, Edema, Lesion, Pneumonia, Pneumothorax, and No Finding). We create a "Lesion" label on ChestX-ray14 by joining the samples annotated as "Nodule" or "Mass". For PadChest, we joined labels that can fit into the 8 common findings, (i.e. "Atelectasis Basal", "Total Atelectasis", "Lobar Atelectasis", and "Round Atelectasis" were merged into "Atelectasis"). Another limitation is that ChestX-ray14 has only frontal X-rays. Therefore, we only use the frontal samples from the other three datasets, which means 191,229 samples on CheXpert, 249,995 on MIMIC-CXR, and 111,176 on PadChest.

To evaluate domain shift, we use a standard performance metric in multi-label classification, the Area Under the Receiver Operating Characteristic curve (AUC), to report both individual radiological findings results and their average for an overall view of model performance. Both the true positive rate and the false positive rate are considered for computing the AUC. Higher AUC values indicate better performance.

4 Results

We train the same neural network architecture with the same hyperparameters on each of the four datasets individually. When training and testing on ChestX-ray14 achieve results similar to the ones reported by CheXnet [18], which exceeded radiologists' performance in detecting pneumonia. After training, we evaluate each of our models with images from the remaining three datasets.

Table 2. Resulting AUCs for the 8 radiological findings common to the four datasets. Best results for each test set are in bold.

Test set	Training set	Atelectasis	Cardiomegaly	Consolidation	Edema	Lesion	Pneumonia	Pneumothorax	No Finding	Mean
ChestX-ray14	ChestX-ray14	**0.8205**	**0.9104**	**0.8026**	**0.8935**	**0.7819**	0.7567	**0.8746**	**0.7842**	**0.8343**
	CheXpert	0.7850	0.8646	0.7771	0.8584	0.7291	0.7287	0.8464	0.7569	0.7933
	MIMIC-CXR	0.8024	0.8322	0.7898	0.8609	0.7457	**0.7656**	0.8429	0.7652	0.8006
	PadChest	0.7371	0.8124	0.7031	0.8213	0.6301	0.6487	0.7417	0.7384	0.7291
CheXpert	ChestX-ray14	0.6433	0.7596	0.6431	0.7145	0.6821	0.5967	0.7356	0.7717	0.6821
	CheXpert	**0.6930**	**0.8687**	**0.7323**	**0.8344**	**0.7882**	0.7619	**0.8709**	**0.8842**	**0.8042**
	MIMIC-CXR	0.6576	0.8197	0.7002	0.7946	0.7465	0.7219	0.8046	0.8564	0.7627
	PadChest	0.6127	0.7397	0.6352	0.6934	0.6978	0.6510	0.6209	0.7600	0.6764
MIMIC-CXR	ChestX-ray14	0.7616	0.7230	0.7567	0.8146	0.6880	0.6630	0.7773	0.8106	0.7406
	CheXpert	0.7587	0.7650	0.7936	0.8685	0.7527	0.6913	0.8142	0.8452	0.7861
	MIMIC-CXR	**0.8177**	**0.8126**	**0.8229**	**0.8922**	**0.7788**	0.7461	**0.8845**	**0.8718**	**0.8283**
	PadChest	0.7218	0.6899	0.7200	0.7828	0.6577	0.6454	0.6995	0.7976	0.7143
PadChest	ChestX-ray14	0.7938	0.8822	0.8300	0.8893	**0.7010**	0.7366	0.7176	0.8028	0.7929
	CheXpert	0.7566	0.8656	0.8511	**0.9390**	0.6833	0.7269	**0.8731**	0.8335	0.8161
	MIMIC-CXR	**0.7942**	0.8270	**0.8963**	0.9310	0.6761	**0.8060**	0.8308	0.8217	0.8229
	PadChest	0.7641	**0.9075**	0.8607	0.9107	0.6975	0.7990	0.8276	**0.8710**	**0.8298**

We summarize the results in Table 2. We can see that the best average result for each test set appears when the training set is from the same dataset. This shows that clinicians should expect a decrease in the reported performances of machine learning models when applying them in real-world scenarios. The decrease may vary according to the dataset distribution in which the model was trained. For instance, running a model trained on MIMIC-CXR on CheXpert's test set reduces the mean AUC in 0.04, while the model trained on ChestX-ray14 reduces it by 0.12. On MIMIC-CXR's test set, a model trained on CheXpert shows almost the same decrease in mean AUC (0.04), reducing the AUC in all of the findings. The model trained on ChestX-ray14 has the highest average AUC when testing on its own test set, but when testing in other datasets, it shows a significant performance drop, lowering CheXpert's mean AUC in 0.12, MIMIC-CXR's in 0.08 and PadChest in 0.04. Both the models trained on CheXpert and MIMIC-CXR mostly preserve the ChestX-ray14 baseline mean AUC, while the model trained on PadChest drops the average performance in 0.10. PadChest presented some variations on the best AUC for each disease, probably due to the smaller number of train instances. The models trained on CheXpert and MIMIC-CXR got very close results to PadChest's baseline.

Figure 4 shows the performance on the test set of the four trained models, represented as lines to better visualize AUC variations. The CheXpert and MIMIC-CXR models show smaller variations on the AUCs of the findings compared to their own test sets, presenting close lines, while PadChest and ChestX-ray14 shows the line of their own test set mostly on top and a drop in performance on the other test sets.

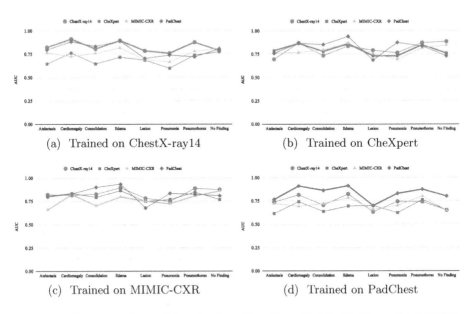

(a) Trained on ChestX-ray14   (b) Trained on CheXpert

(c) Trained on MIMIC-CXR   (d) Trained on PadChest

Fig. 4. Performance of a model trained on ChestX-ray14 (a), CheXpert (b), MIMIC-CXR (c), and PadChest (d) on each of the four test sets.

Clear evidence of the impact of domain shift over model performance is how frequently the best AUC for each radiological finding comes from the same dataset. In the ChestX-ray14 test set, the best AUC appears 7 out of 8 times when training with the same set. The same phenomenon happens on both CheXpert (8 out of 8) and MIMIC-CXR (8 out of 8). Furthermore, in all four test sets, the best average AUC comes from their respective training set. One possible cause of domain shift is the label extraction method. CheXpert and MIMIC-CXR used the same labeler, while ChestX-ray14 has its own.

ChestX-ray14 labeler has raised some questions concerning its reliability. A visual inspection study [17] states that its labels do not accurately reflect the content of the images. Estimated label accuracies are 10–30% lower than the values originally reported. It also might be that ChestX-ray14 and PadChest do not have representative training sets since models trained on CheXpert and MIMIC-CXR perform well on ChestX-ray14 and PadChest test sets, but the models trained on ChestX-ray14 and PadChest do not perform well on CheXpert and MIMIC-CXR's test sets.

5 Discussion and Conclusion

In this work, we show how a state-of-the-art deep learning model fails to generalize to unseen datasets when they follow a somewhat different distribution. Our experiments show that a model with reported radiologist-level performance had a huge drop in performance outside its source dataset, pointing the existence of domain shift in chest X-rays datasets. Despite recent efforts for the creation of large radiograph datasets in the hope of training generalizable models, it seems that the data acquisition methodology of some available datasets does not capture the required heterogeneity for this purpose.

Among the analyzed datasets, CheXpert and MIMIC-CXR seem to be most representative of the other datasets, as the models trained on them show a smaller performance drop when comparing to the baseline. Therefore, these two datasets should be preferred by researchers when developing models for chest radiograph analysis. The least representative seems to be ChestX-ray14, whose model did not perform as well outside its own test set, while the models trained on the other datasets performed well when testing on ChestX-ray14. Models trained on PadChest also show a significant performance drop in other test sets, but it might be because of the smaller amount of available data for each finding, as it has a way higher number of annotated findings than the other datasets.

Although deep learning advances allow for new application scenarios, more steps for model validation must be conducted with more emphasis on external validation. We argue that a case-by-case validation is ideal, where the model is validated on new data from each center. The reason is twofold. First, models must be able to handle data from a specific scenario properly. Second, the label distribution from each environment might change due to several external factors, which might not reflect prediction biases learned by the model. One alternative for these limitations is to create small datasets from specific machines where the model will be used, where we fine-tune them after pre-training on large available datasets.

References

1. AlBadawy, E.A., Saha, A., Mazurowski, M.A.: Deep learning for segmentation of brain tumors: impact of cross-institutional training and testing. Med. Phys. **45**(3), 50 (2018)
2. Bustos, A., Pertusa, A., Salinas, J.M., de la Iglesia-Vayá, M.: Padchest: a large chest x-ray image dataset with multi-label annotated reports (2019)
3. Chen, C., Dou, Q., Chen, H., Heng, P.A.: Semantic-aware generative adversarial nets for unsupervised domain adaptation in chest x-ray segmentation. In: Proceedings of the International Workshop on Machine Learning in Medical Imaging. Springer (2018)
4. del Ciello, A., Franchi, P., Contegiacomo, A., Cicchetti, G., Bonomo, L., Larici, A.R.: Missed lung cancer: when, where, and why? Diagnostic and Interventional Radiol. **23**(2), 118–126 (2017). https://doi.org/10.5152/dir.2016.16187
5. Dou, Q., Ouyang, C., Chen, C., Chen, H., Heng, P.A.: Unsupervised cross-modality domain adaptation of convnets for biomedical image segmentations with adversarial loss. In: Proceedings of the 27th International Joint Conference on Artificial Intelligence, pp. 691–697 (2018)
6. Ganin, Y., et al.: Domain-adversarial training of neural networks. J. Mach. Learn. Res. **17**(1), 4 (2016)
7. Gholami, A., et al.: A novel domain adaptation framework for medical image segmentation. In: Proceedings of the International Medical Image Computing and Computer Assisted Intervention Brainlesion Workshop, pp. 289–298. Springer, Cham (2018)
8. Hirsch, F.R., Franklin, W.A., Gazdar, A.F., Bunn, P.A.: Early detection of lung cancer: clinical perspectives of recent advances in biology and radiology. Clin. Cancer Res. **7**(1), 5–22 (2001)
9. Hoffman, J., et al.: Cycada: cycle consistent adversarial domain adaptation. In: Proceedings of the International Conference on Machine Learning, p. 15 (2018)
10. Huang, G., Liu, Z., Van Der Maaten, L., Weinberger, K.Q.: Densely connected convolutional networks. In: Proceedings of the IEEE Conference on Computer Vision and Pattern Recognition, pp. 4700–4708 (2017)
11. Irvin, J., et al.: Chexpert: a large chest radiograph dataset with uncertainty labels and expert comparison. arXiv preprint arXiv:1901.07031 (2019)
12. Javanmardi, M., Tasdizen, T.: Domain adaptation for biomedical image segmentation using adversarial training. In: Proceedings of the 15th International Symposium on Biomedical Imaging. IEEE (2018)
13. Johnson, A.E., et al.: Mimic-cxr: a large publicly available database of labeled chest radiographs. arXiv preprint arXiv:1901.07042 (2019)
14. Litjens, G., et al.: A survey on deep learning in medical image analysis. Med. Image Anal. **42**, 60–88 (2017)
15. Madani, A., Moradi, M., Karargyris, A., Syeda-Mahmood, T.: Semi-supervised learning with generative adversarial networks for chest X-ray classification with ability of data domain adaptation. In: IEEE 15th International Symposium on Biomedical Imaging (ISBI 2018). pp. 1038–1042. IEEE (2018). https://doi.org/10. 1109/ISBI.2018.8363749
16. Mahmood, F., Chen, R., Durr, N.J.: Unsupervised reverse domain adaptation for synthetic medical images via adversarial training. IEEE Trans. Med. Imag. **37**, 10 (2018)

17. Oakden-Rayner, L.: Exploring large scale public medical image datasets. Technical report, The University of Adelaide (2019). https://arxiv.org/pdf/1907.12720.pdf
18. Rajpurkar, P., et al.: Chexnet: Radiologist-level pneumonia detection on chest x-rays with deep learning. arXiv preprint arXiv:1711.05225 (2017)
19. Torralba, A., Efros, A.A., et al.: Unbiased look at dataset bias. In: Proceedings of the Conference on Computer Vision and Pattern Recognition. vol. 1, p. 7. Citeseer (2011)
20. Wang, X., Peng, Y., Lu, L., Lu, Z., Bagheri, M., Summers, R.M.: Chestx-ray8: Hospital-scale chest x-ray database and benchmarks on weakly-supervised classification and localization of common thorax diseases. CoRR abs/1705.02315 (2017)

A Weakly Supervised Deep Learning Framework for COVID-19 CT Detection and Analysis

Ophir Gozes[1(✉)], Maayan Frid-Adar[1], Nimrod Sagie[1,2], Asher Kabakovitch[1],
Dor Amran[1], Rula Amer[1], and Hayit Greenspan[1,2]

[1] Radlogics Inc., Boston, MA, USA
ophirgozes@mail.tau.ac.il
[2] Department of Biomedical Engineering, Tel-Aviv University,
Tel Aviv, Israel

Abstract. The outbreak of the COVID-19 global pandemic has affected millions and has a severe impact on our daily lives. To support radiologists in this overwhelming challenge, we developed a weakly supervised deep learning framework that can detect, localize, and quantify the severity of COVID-19 disease from chest CT scans using limited annotations. The framework is designed to rapidly provide a solution during the initial outbreak of a pandemic when datasets availability is limited. It is comprised of a pipeline of image processing algorithms which includes lung segmentation, 2D slice classification, and fine-grained localization. In addition, we present the Coronascore bio-marker which corresponds to the severity grade of the disease. Finally, we present an unsupervised feature space clustering which can assist in understanding the COVID-19 radiographic manifestations. We present our results on an external dataset comprised of 199 patients from Zhejiang province, China.

Keywords: Corona · Chest CT · Lung · COVID-19 · AI · Deep learning

1 Introduction

The Coronavirus disease 2019 (COVID-19) is an infectious disease caused by severe acute respiratory syndrome coronavirus 2 (SARS-CoV-2). First identified in 2019 in Wuhan, China, it has since become a global pandemic. Complementing the reverse-transcription polymerase chain reaction (RT-PCR) tests, non-contrast thoracic CT scans have been shown as a potential tool in the COVID-19 detection [1,2]. The disease can be characterized by the presence of lung ground-glass opacities in the early stages, followed by "crazy paving" and increasing consolidation. CT imaging studies of the suspected population can support decision making, providing for immediate isolation and appropriate patient treatment.

© Springer Nature Switzerland AG 2020
J. Petersen et al. (Eds.): TIA 2020, LNCS 12502, pp. 84–93, 2020.
https://doi.org/10.1007/978-3-030-62469-9_8

AI methods based on deep learning can contribute to faster CT diagnosis and analysis of the disease. Development of an algorithm in times of a pandemic is challenging and different than traditional algorithm development: In the early phase of a new disease, there is limited information regarding the disease characteristics, and the ability to collect data and perform exact annotation of the various radiological manifestations is limited.

Many studies have emerged in the last several months from the medical imaging community – swith many research groups as well as companies introducing deep learning based solutions to tackle the various tasks: mostly in detection of the disease (vs normal), and more recently also for staging disease severity. For a review of early works in this space we refer the reader to a recent review article [3] that covers the first papers published, up to and including March 2020 - in the entire pipeline of medical imaging and analysis techniques involved with COVID-19, including image acquisition, segmentation, diagnosis, and follow-up.

In the current work we focus on a weakly supervised deep learning framework, with limited data as input, for the tasks of COVID-19 detection and analysis. The system receives non-contrast chest CT scans and detects cases suspected of COVID-19. For cases classified as positive, the system outputs a 3D lung abnormality localization map and a "Corona-score" bio-marker which we show is related to the disease severity.

The solution is comprised of a sequence of 2D processing followed by a 3D fusion stage (Fig. 1). We employ data augmentation and ImageNet pre-training to address the challenge of training on smaller datasets [4].

The GradCam [7] method has become a common tool for providing visual explanations when using Deep Networks with Gradient-based localization. In addition to model interpretation, we show it can be used for the estimation of disease severity and for a 3D visualization of the case. In our method, a *fine-grained saliency map* is generated per each slice by performing a slice-based multi-scale application of the GradCam technique. As the deeper layers encode global context while shallower layers local concepts, a combination of the two allows a fine-grained map of the pathological areas to be obtained (Fig. 3).

To study representative disease manifestations, we explore the use of unsupervised k-means feature clustering. The feature space learned by COVID-19 classifier was selected for clustering since it encodes information specific to the disease. Our analysis shows prominent clusters of manifestations can be identified in an unsupervised manner corresponding to the study presented by Bernheim et al. [2]

The main contributions of this work are as follows:

- **Weakly supervision for training**: We present a method for COVID-19 case level detection and volumetric bio-marker extraction which is based on weakly annotated slice labels. Slices were annotated as COVID-19(+) or COVID-19(−).
- **Fine-grain localization**: We present an application of the GradCam technique for improving saliency map resolution and creation of a 3D overview and severity analysis.

- **Unsupervised exploration of disease manifestations**: We show the feature space learned by the detector can be utilized for unsupervised exploration of new disease imaging characteristics. Using gradient weighted k-means clustering, the method can produce meaningful insights on slice level disease manifestations.

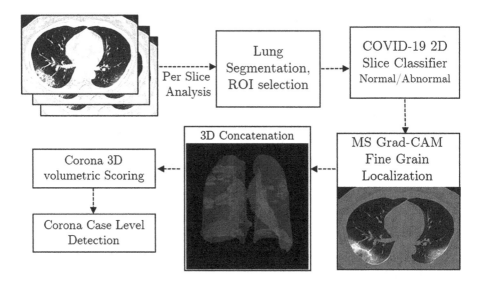

Fig. 1. Block diagram of the method

2 Methods

Figure 1 shows a block diagram of the proposed system, which is comprised of a series of 2D processing steps for each slice of the case; First, a lung segmentation step is performed to extract a 2D ROI of the lungs. Second, a 2D ROI classification is performed to classify each slice as Normal vs Abnormal. Lastly, a fine-grained localization map is generated by performing a multi-scale Grad-Cam. All slices localization maps are then concatenated to create a single 3D volume for a Corona 3D volumetric scoring and case-level detection decision. A detailed description of each component is given in the following subsections.

Several datasets are used throughout, for development and testing the system, as described in Table 1.

2.1 Lung Segmentation and Lung ROI Selection

The purpose of this stage is to provide 2D lung segmentation to support visualization and ROI selection as input for the classification stage. The model is

Table 1. Datasets used in this work

N°	Dataset	Description
1	Development Dataset, Chainz [12], Private Dataset	50 abnormal thoracic CT scans (slice thickness, {5–10} mm) of patients that were diagnosed by a radiologist as suspicious for COVID-19 (from Jan-Feb 2020). The cases were extracted by querying a cloud PACS system for cases that were referred for laboratory testing following the scan. Cases were annotated at the slice level by a trained specialist as COVID-19(−) (n = 1036), COVID-19(+) (n = 829)
2	Testing Dataset, Wenzhou Medical University, China, Private Dataset	109 patients with a confirmed diagnosis of COVID-19 infection by RT-PCR, 90 patients with fever symptoms and upper respiratory tract symptoms diagnosed by a radiologist as negative for COVID-19
3	Lung Segmentation Development, El-Camino Hospital (CA), Private Dataset	In-house pre-pandemic dataset containing CT scans of cases with lung opacities and their corresponding lung masks
4	Lung Segmentation Development, University Hospitals of Geneva (HUG), Public Dataset	ILD database - A multimedia collection of cases with interstitial lung diseases (ILDs) built at the University Hospitals of Geneva (HUG) [13]

based on a U-net architecture [9] in which the encoder is pre-trained with ImageNet [11]. Since the algorithm is required to support cases of abnormal lung appearance, we train it on a collection of slices belonging to datasets containing interstitial lung disease cases and opacities. We use 6,150 CT slices of cases with lung abnormalities and their corresponding lung masks which were taken from Datasets-3,4. Input slices were clipped and normalized to [0,1] using a window of [−1000, 0] HU. A diagram of the architecture is displayed in Fig. 2. In order to perform lung ROI selection, for each slice, we predict a segmentation mask and compute a bounding box. The lung ROI is then defined as the 2D union of all bounding boxes. In the next stage, we crop each slice using the ROI to allow the classifier to focus the learning process on lung related areas.

2.2 COVID-19 Classifier

The second step focuses on classifying the lung ROIs as normal vs abnormal for COVID-19. We use ResNet-50 which is a 2D deep convolutional neural network architecture [5] pre-trained on ImageNet [6]. The ROI obtained by the segmentation phase is resized to fit the network's input size, 224×224. To train

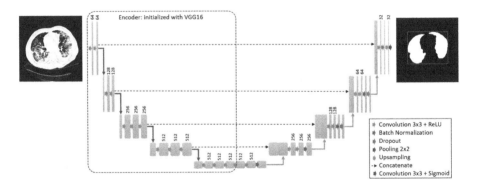

Fig. 2. The proposed U-Net architecture with a VGG-16 based encoder.

the network, we used 1275 slices belonging to 50 patients that were suspected as COVID-19(+) following a radiologist review (Table 1: Dataset-1). The slices were labeled as COVID-19(+) if there were any subregions that are COVID-19(+). From a total of 1865 slices collected, 1036 slices were COVID-19(−) and 829 were COVID-19(+). We randomly split the dataset to training (n = 1275), validation (n = 320), and testing (n = 270) slices with no patient overlap between the test set and the development sets. To further enrich our training set, we employed data augmentation techniques which included image rotations, horizontal flips, and cropping. Binary cross-entropy loss function was used and optimized by the Adam Optimizer (lr = 1E-4).

2.3   Model Interpretation and Multi-scale GradCam for Localization

To verify that the learning process focused on pathological areas, we employed the GradCam technique in two image resolutions. GradCam is performed on the activation layers corresponding to a resolution of 14×14 and 28×28 following normalization to the range $[0,1]$. The two maps are resized to the input shape(224×224) followed by multiplication to achieve a fine-grained localization map. The selection of the specific layers was chosen to match the observed scale of the infected regions. In Fig. 3 we display the activation maps corresponding to the two scales and the resulting heatmap obtained by fusion. In the heatmap view, a high activation can be observed in a COVID-19 region manifested by a groundglass opacity.

2.4   Case-Wise COVID-19 Volumetric Scoring for Severity Estimation

To provide a complete review of a case, we combine the fine-grained maps to create 3D localization maps. The resulting volume corresponds to the extent of the disease spread throughout the lungs and can provide valuable insight to the radiologist (Fig. 1). In order to extract a quantitative bio-marker, we propose the

Corona score (Eq. 1). The score is computed by summation over the activation maps ($Cmap_z$) of positive detected slices, considering only the activation above a certain pre-defined threshold $T_{activation}$. The threshold used in our experiments was determined to be 0.6 by means of visual evaluation by expert.

$$CoronaScore = \sum_{z=1}\sum_{ij} Cmap_{zij} \cdot \mathbb{1}(cmap_{zij} > T_{activation}) \cdot voxel\_volume \quad (1)$$

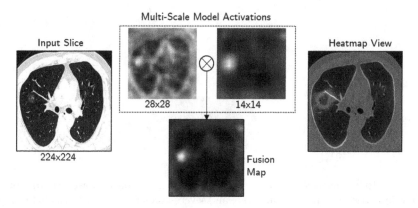

Fig. 3. Creation of fine-grained localization maps. The resulting heatmap view is a fusion of activation maps of two scales

3 Experiments and Results

3.1 Slice Classification Results and Experiments

We start with an evaluation of the ability to detect slice-level COVID-19. The performance of this step is crucial for obtaining overall case wise detection. For testing, we used 270 of the slices from the development dataset (Table 1: Dataset-1). The split was patient wise and there is no overlap with the slices used for training. A total of 270 slices were analyzed: 150 normal slices and 120 COVID-19 suspected slices. We achieved an Area Under Curve (AUC) result of 0.994 with 94% sensitivity and 98% specificity (at threshold 0.5).

3.2 Corona Score for Disease Detection

To evaluate the case level detection performance, a collection containing confirmed COVID-19 patients (n = 109) and negative COVID-19 patients (n = 90) was used (Table 1: Dataset-2). Using the Corona score as a predictive variable, an ROC analysis was performed. The results are shown in Fig. 4a. An AUC score of 0.948 (95% CI: 0.912-0.985) was attained. We cannot compare directly to other works, as each work trained and tested on different datasets. For example, in the method presented by Mei et al. [8]: based on Inception-ResNet-v2 and ResNet-18 2D ImageNet pre-trained networks, the reported AUC was 0.86 (95%CI: 0.82-0.90). Their private test set contained 279 cases; 134 COVID-19(+) cases and 145 COVID-19(−).

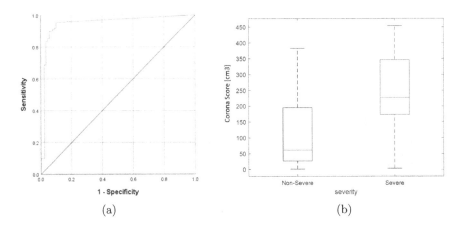

(a)   (b)

Fig. 4. (a) ROC analysis for case level COVID-19 detection (Dataset-2) (b) Corona Score volumetric measure for non-severe and severe-grade COVID-19 patients (a subset of 49 patients of Dataset-2)

3.3 Corona Score Agreement with Specialist Annotation

For analyzing the correlation between the corona score and manual delineation of infected lung regions, 28 cases belonging to Dataset-2 were annotated by a trained specialist at the pixel level to normal areas vs areas of consolidation or ground-glass opacities. Regression analysis showed a pearson correlation coefficient of 0.8 between the corona score and the volume of abnormal areas labeled by the specialist.

3.4 Corona Score as a Bio-Marker for Disease Severity

The corona score is a volumetric score related to the extent of the disease in a patient's lungs. In order to examine the correspondence between our bio-marker and the radiologist severity grading, we performed the following experiment: A subset of CT scans of 49 patients from Dataset 2 were graded by a radiologist to severe (n = 13) vs non-severe (n = 36). For the analysis, we create a box-plot diagram comparing the score distributions of severe and non-severe patients. Results are shown in Fig. 4b: The p-value of a two-sided Wilcoxon rank-sum test for equality of distributions was p = 0.0064. The median corona score for the non-severe cases was 61.5 cm3 while for the severe cases the median corona score was 227.5 cm3.

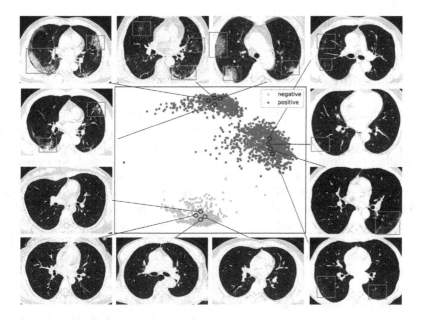

Fig. 5. Gradient weighted Feature Space and representative key slices

3.5 Study of the Disease Manifestations

In an initial study to explore and identify prominent manifestations of the COVID-19 disease we use unsupervised k-means feature clustering. The feature space created by the COVID-19 2D classifier was selected as it encodes information relevant to the pathology and is more specific than ImageNet pre-trained feature extractors. To further focus on disease-related features, we weight each feature vector by the gradient of this layer, computed using GradCam. For each input slice, we extract the features by flattening the output of the last convolutional layer to a $d = 2048$ feature vector, followed by element-wise multiplication with the corresponding gradients vector and pre-clustering normalization. K-means clustering was performed using the euclidean metric. The optimal number of clusters ($k = 3$) was found using the elbow method [14]. Prior to clustering, we perform normalization to zero mean and unit standard deviation.

Our analysis was conducted on predicted positive key slices from 109 patients ($n = 1592$) and predicted negative slices from 81 patients ($n = 701$) belonging to the test set [Dataset 2]. We constructed a high-dimensional feature space to cluster the samples, and for visualization purposes only, a dimensionality reduction was performed by using Principal Components Analysis (PCA) from $d = 2048$ to $d = 2$.

The resulting feature space is visualized in Fig. 5: each sample point (Fig. 5, center) represents a slice in the feature space. For each cluster center, we present 4 key slices chosen by minimal L2 distance to the corresponding cluster's center (Fig. 5, exterior). It is noticeable that the positive data points can be divided into two distinguishable groups: slices with subtle focal lesions and slices with diffuse severe patterns.

4   Discussion

In this work, designed to address the outbreak of a new pandemic, we present results for COVID-19 detection, quantification, and feature space clustering using weakly-supervised deep-learning techniques on chest CT.

Utilizing the deep-learning image analysis system developed, we achieved a high detection AUC of 0.948 (95%CI: 0.912-0.985) on a dataset comprised of negative and positive COVID-19 patients (Dataset 2). We show a fine-grained localization method that is able to provide radiologists insight into the "black-box" model prediction as well as provide a 3D visualization of the disease. Using the fine-grained activation masks, we propose a Coronascore bio-marker. This score was shown to have a high correlation with the volume of infection as annotated by the specialist. In addition, we show it corresponds to the severity grade of the disease; paving the way for it to be used as a means for patient monitoring and management.

An advantage of the proposed approach for estimating the disease severity grade, lies in the fact that it is a data-driven approach to localize disease manifestations. It requires weak slice-based COVID-19 labeling which reduces the need for collecting pixel-level annotation. This in turn means that we do not focus in the current work on pixel-level accurate segmentation maps; if such maps are desired, additional high-resolution annotation and development is needed; we leave this for future work.

In the outbreak of a new disease, medical research is focused on mapping and understanding the disease radiographic manifestations [2]. In order to support this endeavor, we present a method for unsupervised clustering of the feature space that can identify prominent imaging manifestations. The initial exploratory analysis identified main feature space clusters, which correspond to different COVID-19 manifestations. In the future, such computational tools may assist the radiologists in the early phases of disease study and exploration.

References

1. Ai, T., et al.: Correlation of chest CT and RT-PCR testing in coronavirus disease (COVID-19) in China: a report of 1014 cases. Radiology **2020**, 200642 (2019)
2. Bernheim, A., et al.: Chest CT findings in coronavirus disease-19 (COVID-19): relationship to duration of infection. Radiology **295**(3), 200463 (2020)
3. Shi, F., et al.: Review of artificial intelligence techniques in imaging data acquisition, segmentation and diagnosis for COVID-19. IEEE Rev. Biomed. Eng. (2020)
4. Gozes, O., Greenspan, H.: Deep feature learning from a Hospital-scale chest X-ray dataset with application to TB detection on a small-scale dataset. In: 2019 41st Annual International Conference of the IEEE Engineering in Medicine and Biology Society (EMBC), IEEE (2019)

5. Kaiming, H., et al. Deep residual learning for image recognition. In: Proceedings of the IEEE Conference on Computer Vision and Pattern Recognition (2016)
6. Deng, J., et al.: Imagenet: a large-scale hierarchical image database. In: IEEE Conference on Computer Vision and Pattern Recognition, CVPR 2009, pp. 248–255. IEEE (2009)
7. Selvaraju, R.R., et al. Grad-cam: visual explanations from deep networks via gradient-based localization. In: Proceedings of the IEEE international conference on computer vision (2017)
8. Xueyan, M., et al. Artificial intelligence-enabled rapid diagnosis of patients with COVID-19. Nature Med. 1–5 (2020)
9. Ronneberger, O., Fischer, P., Brox, T.: U-Net: convolutional networks for biomedical image segmentation. In: Navab, N., Hornegger, J., Wells, W.M., Frangi, A.F. (eds.) MICCAI 2015. LNCS, vol. 9351, pp. 234–241. Springer, Cham (2015). https://doi.org/10.1007/978-3-319-24574-4_28
10. Simonyan, K. and Zisserman, A.: Very deep convolutional networks for large-scale image recognition (2014). arXiv preprint arXiv:1409.1556
11. Frid-Adar, M., Ben-Cohen, A., Amer, R., Greenspan, H.: Improving the segmentation of anatomical structures in chest radiographs using U-Net with an ImageNet Ppe-trained encoder. In: Stoyanov, D. (ed.) RAMBO/BIA/TIA -2018. LNCS, vol. 11040, pp. 159–168. Springer, Cham (2018). https://doi.org/10.1007/978-3-030-00946-5_17
12. ChainZ (www.ChainZ.cn)
13. Depeursinge, A., et al.: Building a reference multimedia database for interstitial lung diseases. Comput. Med. Imaging Graphics 36(3), 227–238 (2012)
14. Dhendra, M., Handaka, S.H., Wijaya, E.: The determination of cluster number at k-mean using elbow method and purity evaluation on headline news. In: 2018 International Seminar on Application for Technology of Information and Communication, IEEE (2018)

Deep Reinforcement Learning for Localization of the Aortic Annulus in Patients with Aortic Dissection

Marina Codari[1]([✉]) [ID], Antonio Pepe[2] [ID], Gabriel Mistelbauer[3] [ID],
Domenico Mastrodicasa[1] [ID], Shannon Walters[1], Martin J. Willemink[1] [ID],
and Dominik Fleischmann[1] [ID]

[1] Department of Radiology,
Stanford University School of Medicine, Stanford, CA, USA
mcodari@stanford.edu
[2] Institute of Computer Graphics and Vision,
Graz University of Technology, Graz, Austria
[3] Department of Simulation and Graphics,
Otto-von-Guericke University, Magdeburg, Germany

Abstract. Accurate localization of the aortic annulus is key to several imaging tasks, like cross-sectional aortic valve plane estimation, aortic root segmentation, and annulus diameter measurements. In this project, we propose an end-to-end trainable deep reinforcement learning (DRL) algorithm aimed at identification of the aortic annulus in patients with aortic dissection. We trained 5 different agents on a dataset of 75 CT scans from 66 patients following a sequential model-upgrading strategy. We evaluated the effect of performing different image preprocessing steps, adding batch normalization and regularization layers, and changing terminal state definition. At each step of this sequential process, the model performance has been evaluated on a validation sample composed of 24 CTA scans from 24 independent patients. Localization accuracy was defined as the Euclidean distance between estimated and target aortic annulus locations. Best model results show a median localization error equal to 2.98 mm with an interquartile range equal to $[2.25, 3.81]$ mm, and a failure rate (i.e., percentage of samples with localization error > 10 mm) of 0% in validation data. We proved the feasibility of DRL application for aortic annulus localization in CTA images of patients with aortic dissection, which are characterized by a large variability in aortic morphology and image quality. Nevertheless, further improvements are needed to reach expert-human level performance.

Keywords: Deep reinforcement learning · Landmark localization · Aortic annulus

1 Introduction

The aortic annulus is an important landmark in the cardiovascular system, denoting the virtual boundary between the left ventricular outflow tract and

© Springer Nature Switzerland AG 2020
J. Petersen et al. (Eds.): TIA 2020, LNCS 12502, pp. 94–105, 2020.
https://doi.org/10.1007/978-3-030-62469-9_9

the aortic root [16]. Accurate localization of the aortic annulus is key to several imaging tasks, such as cross-sectional aortic valve plane estimation, aortic root segmentation, and annulus diameter measurements, which are critical for device sizing in the setting of transcatheter aortic valve replacement (TAVR). The aortic annulus also serves as the starting point of the centerline and hence the first of a series of landmarks along the entire thoracoabdominal aorta in the setting of aortic surveillance, where aortic dimensions are followed over months or years in patients with aortic aneurysms or dissections.

Several attempts have been made to automatically identify and measure the aortic annulus, predominantly in the setting of TAVR planning, using ECG-gated submillimeter CT angiographic datasets [3–5,12]. However, most of the current approaches require aortic root segmentation [4,5] and/or a-priori knowledge of the aortic root morphology [5,12] to detect the desired landmarks. Vascular segmentation remains a considerable challenge when dealing with diseased vessels, where model-based approaches may fail [10]. The high variability in aortic morphology and hemodynamics in patients with aortic dissection and the presence of metallic prostheses (e.g. mechanical aortic valves and endovascular stent grafts) strongly affect the overall anatomical appearance and CT angiography (CTA) image quality. To overcome this issue, deep learning approaches were explored, since they allow to capture the patient-specific anatomy while generalizing to unseen data with excellent performance [1,3,15]. The identification of the aortic annulus in CT datasets obtained in patients with aortic dissection poses additional challenges [11]. ECG gating is not always used in patients presenting with acute aortic dissection, resulting in more motion artifacts. The slice thickness and in-plane resolution are coarser. Other than TAVR candidates, patients with aortic dissection may have undergone prior surgical aortic valve and root replacement with a mechanical aortic valve, which adds to the wider variability of the aortic annulus appearance on CT.

In this project, we propose an end-to-end trainable deep reinforcement learning (DRL) network to overcome these limitations, and developed and validated a set of agents aimed at localizing the aortic annulus in patients with aortic dissection. In DRL, an artificial agent interacts with the image environment to learn the optimal trajectory towards a target landmark position, thus learning the patient anatomy appearance and the optimal search strategy at the same time [2,6]. This characteristic allows DRL models to efficiently search the object of interest in a large 3D image without scanning it exhaustively, which would be computationally expensive in large image volumes such as aortic CTA [6].

Starting from a publicly available model [2] we evaluated the effect of: performing different image preprocessing steps; adding batch normalization and regularization layers in the fully connected part of the used CNN; changing terminal state definition.

This is the first step and prerequisite towards automation of these otherwise time-consuming measurements required for aortic surveillance in patients with aortic dissection.

2   Background

Reinforcement learning (RL) is a sub-field of machine learning. In a RL problem, an agent learns by interacting with the environment, how to map situations (states) to actions in order to maximize a quantitative reward signal [14]. At each time step t, the agent chooses an action among $a_t \in \mathcal{A}$, where $\mathcal{A}$ defines a set of actions, based on its current state $s_t \in \mathcal{S}$, with $\mathcal{S}$ being a finite space of states. By performing this action, the agent receives from the environment a quantitative reward r and a new state s'. The agent learns the optimal probability distribution that maps an action $a \in \mathcal{A}$ to a state $s_t \in \mathcal{S}$, that maximizes the accumulated reward signal [17].

Landmark detection can be formulated as a RL problem, where an agent interacts with the image environment to learn the optimal trajectory from any starting position towards a target landmark position. This decision-making process can be formulated as a Markov decision process, in which s_t and a_t are conditionally independent from previous states and actions, thus holding the Markov property. At each state s of the sequential decision-making process, the agent selects the optimal action a that maximizes the state-action value function $Q(s, a)$, which quantifies the quality of choosing a_t given s_t. The state-action function is defined as the expected discounted future rewards accumulated during the agent lifetime and can be estimated iteratively using the Bellman equation:

$$Q_{t+1}(s, a) = E[r + \gamma \max_{a'} Q_t(s', a')], \tag{1}$$

where $\gamma \in [0, 1]$ is the discount factor, r is the quantitative reward, and s' and a' are the future state and action [2].

In DRL, deep convolutional neural networks (CNNs) are used as nonlinear approximators of $Q(s, a) \approx Q(s, a, \theta)$, where θ indicates the CNN parameters [18]. These networks, called deep Q-networks (DQN), enrich the cognitive modeling through reinforcement learning with the representational power of CNNs, thus allowing them to learn the anatomy appearance and the optimal search strategy at the same time [2,6]. In this formulation of the RL problem, the approximation of the optimal parameters θ^* can be learned end-to-end using stochastic gradient descent of the partial derivative of the loss function $\mathcal{L}$ over θ, whit $\mathcal{L}$ defined as:

$$\mathcal{L}_{DQN}(\theta) = E_{s,r,a,s' \sim D}[(r + \gamma \max_{a'} Q(s', a'; \theta^-) - Q(s, a; \theta))^2], \tag{2}$$

where θ^- are the fixed network parameters of a target network that is updated periodically and D is an experience replay memory used to store transactions between $[s, a, r, s']$ and randomly sampling mini-batches for training. To prevent large Q values, the rewards r are clipped between $[-1, 1]$ [2].

DQNs were successfully applied to segmentation, registration and detection, localization and tracing tasks [17]. Notably, DQNs were applied to CT images to trace the aortic centerline [18] and detect aortic arch bifurcation landmarks [6], achieving promising results with limited prior knowledge.

3   Method

Inspired by the promising results achieved in anatomical landmark detection [2,6], we implemented a DRL agent to automatically localize the aortic annulus. We built on top of the model proposed by Alansary et al. [2][1]. The DQN agent interacts with the image environment $\mathbf{I} : \mathbb{Z}^3 \to \mathbb{R}$ by taking an action among six valid actions starting from a location $\mathbf{p_0} = [x_0, y_0, z_0]$ and a current state s_0, which is defined as a 3D region of interest (ROI) cropped around $\mathbf{p_0}$. Valid actions represent translations along x, y and z axes $(\pm \Delta x, \pm \Delta y, \pm \Delta z)$. The DQN model calculates the Q value for all valid actions and selects the one that maximizes the expected discounted future reward. Afterwards, the current state is updated to a new position $\mathbf{p_1} = [x_1, y_1, z_1]$.

The scalar reward was defined as suggested by both Ghesu et al. [6] and Alansary et al. [2]:

$$r = ||\mathbf{p_{t-1}} - \mathbf{p_T}|| - ||\mathbf{p_t} - \mathbf{p_T}||, \tag{3}$$

where $\mathbf{p_{t-1}}$ represents the last landmark position and $\mathbf{p_t}$ is the current landmark position and $\mathbf{p_T}$ is the target landmark position. So defined, the reward is therefore higher when the agent gets closer to the target position when compared to the previous state.

The agent navigates through the 3D volume using a multi-scale strategy, which proved to increase both accuracy and speed in noisy images with large field of views, such as CTA images. The search ends once the terminal state or the maximum number of steps have been reached. During training, the landmark search successfully ends when the Euclidean distance between the current and target landmark d_{Err} is less than 1 mm. During validation, the search ends when the agent reaches the maximum number of steps allowed per game, or when it oscillates among multiple sub-optimal locations [2]. In the second case, defining the terminal state is not trivial. According to Alansary et al. [2], the terminal state is defined as the location that corresponds to the lowest Q value. In our implementation, we defined it as the barycenter of the last four locations stored in the frame history buffer. Intuitively, we assumed that if the agent oscillates among a finite set sub-optimal solutions, it might be because it is orbiting around the optimal final location.

Network Architecture. The original DQN model proposed by Alansary et al. was composed by four convolutional and three dense layers followed by an output layer representing the six possible actions along x, y, and z axes. The first two convolutional layers had 32 filters with a kernel size of $5 \times 5 \times 5$, the third layer had 64 filters with size $4 \times 4 \times 4$ and the last convolutional layer had 64 filters with size $3 \times 3 \times 3$. All convolutional layers had a stride value equal to 1 and were followed by a max-pooling layer. The number of hidden units in the dense layers was 512, 216, and 128, respectively. PReLU was set as the activation function for convolutional layers, while leakyReLU was set for dense layers. Adam was used as optimizer [2]. We modified the DQN model (see Fig. 1) by adding a

---

[1] Publicly available at https://github.com/amiralansary/rl-medical.

batch normalization layer after each dense layer to reduce the internal covariate shift issue and speed-up the training process [7]. Moreover, to reduce possible overfitting, we also added a dropout layer after each batch normalization layer.

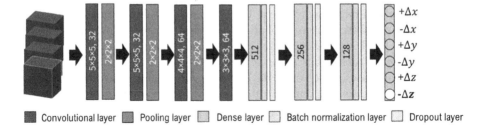

Convolutional layer ▢ Pooling layer ▢ Dense layer ▢ Batch normalization layer ▢ Dropout layer

Fig. 1. Architecture of the proposed CNN model used by the DRL agent for aortic annulus detection. Green and yellow have been used to highlight layers added to the model proposed by Alansary et al. [2] (Color figure online)

Training Strategy. As suggested by Alansary et al. [2], we trained our agent in an episodic manner. Each episode represents an attempt at finding the target landmark position. During training, the agent follows an ϵ-greedy strategy in which the agent randomly selects an action among valid actions with a probability $(\epsilon) \in [0, 1]$ and follows the greedy policy with probability $1 - \epsilon$. To encourage exploration during early training steps, ϵ was initialized to 1.0 and then decreased over epochs [9].

Agent Comparison. In this work, we evaluated the model performance according to different terminal states definitions, dropout rate values, and image preprocessing steps. In particular, we evaluated the effect of different dropout rate values on model performance in both training and validation data. Moreover, we estimated the effect of histogram-based intensity range clipping prior to image intensity min-max normalization. We started using the initial 12-bit intensity range and then we clipped Hounsfield units (HU) values accordingly to different clinically used intensity ranges. Further details are reported in the following section. All agents were trained and validated using the same data.

Since medical imaging data is usually acquired around the region of interest, we initialize the landmark search for unseen data at the dataset center position. The accuracy of the localization process was estimated as the Euclidean distance between estimated and the target aortic annulus locations:

$$d_{Err} = ||\mathbf{p}_E - \mathbf{p}_T||, \tag{4}$$

where $\mathbf{p}_E$ and $\mathbf{p}_T$ represent the 3D position of the estimated and target location of the annulus landmark, respectively.

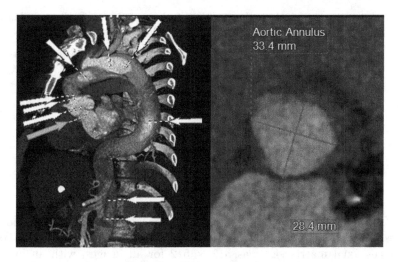

Fig. 2. Example of the sequence aortic landmarks annotated as part of the aortic surveillance program at our institution. The left panel shows a 3D reconstruction of a dissected aorta. The orange arrow indicates the aortic annulus. The right panel shows the manually drawn major- and minor-axis cross-sectional diameter at the level of the aortic annulus landmark. (Color figure online)

4 Experiment

4.1 Dataset

We estimated the aortic annulus landmark location in a database of 99 CTA scans from 90 patients who underwent CTA as part of the aortic surveillance program at our institution. All images were retrospectively collected. We obtained approval from the institutional ethical research board (IRB-47939). Patient informed consent was waived due to the retrospective design of the study. Our aortic surveillance protocol requires to assess the major- and minor-axis cross-sectional diameter in the imaging plane perpendicular to the blood-flow axis and originating in the aortic annulus landmark. We defined the ground truth aortic annulus landmark location as the midpoint of the aortic annulus major axis, manually traced by experienced radiology technologists as part of their clinical routine. Figure 2 shows an example of manually traced major and minor aortic annulus diameters in a CTA volume of a patient with aortic dissection.

To ensure annotation quality, 12 scans were annotated twice by three experienced radiology technologists. Accuracy was estimated as the Euclidean distance between each operator's landmark location estimation and the mean of all landmarks for each patient. Jones' analysis [8] showed a high reproducibility among operators, bias was 0 mm and the 95% limits of agreement with the mean were ± 0.44 mm. Table 1 provides the descriptive statistics of the inter-observer variability of Euclidean distances (d_{Err}) between operators.

Table 1. Inter-observer analysis. Descriptive statistic of Euclidean distance between manually placed landmark d_{Err}. $Op1$: Operator 1; $Op2$: Operator 2; $Op3$: Operator 3; q_1: first quartile; q_2: second quartile; q_3: third quartile.

	Op_1 vs. Op_2	Op_2 vs. Op_3	Op_1 vs. Op_3
$min(d_{Err})$ [mm]	0.38	0.50	0.17
$q_1(d_{Err})$ [mm]	0.78	0.86	0.50
$q_2(d_{Err})$ [mm]	1.12	1.04	0.64
$q_3(d_{Err})$ [mm]	1.62	1.67	1.27
$max(d_{Err})$ [mm]	2.42	3.15	2.48

We split our dataset (75:25) to train and validate the developed models. The resulting training set was composed of 75 scans from 66 patients. Training images axial matrix size was 512×512 for all images, with an in-plane isotropic resolution ranging between $[0.55, 0.98]$ mm. Slice number ranged within $[568, 2091]$, with slice thickness ranging within $[0.30, 1.25]$ mm. The validation set was composed of 24 scans from 24 independent patients. Axial matrix size was 512×512 for all images, with an in-plane isotropic resolution ranging within $[0.53, 0.71]$ mm. Slice number ranged in $[781, 1579]$, while slice thickness ranged within $[0.40, 0.70]$ mm.

Conversely to other published methods dealing with CT data of the aorta, we did not resample images to a fixed isotropic resolution. Existing literature resamples to a resolution within the range $[1, 2]$ mm [2,6,18]. We kept the original sub-millimeter 3D resolution to preserve all fine details related to small anatomical structures, like the aortic valve leaflets that are essential to accurately localize the aortic annulus landmark. We initially preserved the entire 12-bit intensity range $([-1024, 3071]$ HU).

4.2   Implementation

The size of the ROI cropped around the landmark location was set to $45 \times 45 \times 45$ voxels [2]. During the training phase, the starting location was randomly selected in ROI equal to 80% of the original image volume [2]. While evaluating unseen data, the starting landmark location was set as the image center. We limited the maximum number of steps per framework to 1500 and the maximum number of epochs to 1000. Moreover, during model development we trained our agents using an early stop strategy, which monitors success rate improvement over epochs with a patience value set to 3 epochs. We set our batch size to 32, while other hyper-parameters were set as proposed by Alansary et al. [2]. The trained agent was implemented using Python v3.6, TensorFlow GPU v1.14.0, and Tensorpack v.0.9.5. The training was performed using two GPUs NVidia GeForce RTX 2080Ti 11 GB, on a Linux workstation equipped with a CPU AMD Threadripper 3960X and 128 GB RAM.

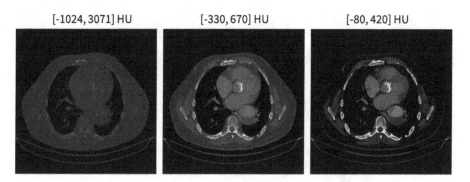

Fig. 3. Examples of the different windowing functions applied in this study.

5 Results and Discussion

We trained 5 different agents following a sequential model upgrading strategy. At each step of this sequential process, the model performance has been evaluated in both training and validation datasets. The characteristics of the developed agents were:

Agent 1: In the first experiment, we preserved the original 12-bit voxel intensity range prior to intensity normalization between [0, 1], see Fig. 3 (left). The CNN architecture and the terminal state definition were set as proposed by Alansary et al. [2].

Agent 2: In the second experiment, we improved the CNN architecture adding batch normalization and dropout layers. The initial dropout rate was set to 0.25. Moreover, we changed the terminal state definition as proposed in the Method section. Image preprocessing was equivalent to the one performed in the first experiment.

Agent 3: In this experiment, we changed the dropout rate to 0.40 to evaluate the effect of a stronger regularization on DQN-model accuracy and generalizability.

Agent 4: Given the results obtained by the previous agents, we evaluated the effects of different preprocessing steps on the outcome of Agent 2. We trained from scratches a new DQN agent defined like Agent 2 but clipping the intensity range to [−330, 670] HU prior to intensity normalization. This range corresponds to a symmetric histogram window centered in a 170 HU and with a width of 1000 HU. These parameters reflect the ones used by Rubin et al. [13]. An example of obtained image contrast is displayed in Fig. 3 (center).

Agent 5: Finally, we repeated the same experiment with a narrower HU range. We halved the window width, thus clipping the intensity range to [−80, 420] HU prior to intensity normalization. An example of the obtained image contrast is presented in Fig. 3 (right). Figure 4 shows the success rate over epochs during training for all agents. Success is defined as percentage of games ending with a final $d_{Err} < 1$ mm. Distributions of d_{Err} values obtained evaluating each agent on training and validation data are summarized in Fig. 5. In Fig. 5 the d_{Err} axis maximum value was set to 10 mm for visualization purposes. Detailed results of

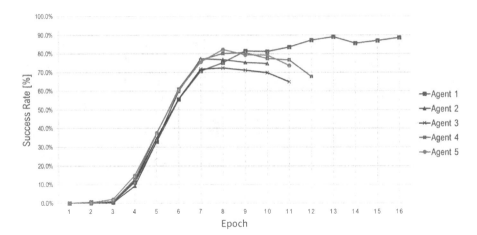

Fig. 4. DQN model success rate trend over epochs. Different lines correspond to different agents.

trained agents, including the percentage of cases exceeding the 10 mm threshold (i.e., localization failure) are reported in Table 2.

In this work, we evaluated the feasibility of performing aortic annulus landmark localization using DRL. The comparison of different agents showed the positive effect of including batch normalization and regularization layers to the DQN model.

The huge variability in aortic anatomy and the relatively limited sample size (≈100 scans) could be a major cause for overfitting. Indeed, Fig. 5 shows a remarkable difference in terms of model performance between training and validation data for *Agent 1*. Our results showed how the introduction of dropout

Table 2. Agent validation performance. Descriptive statistic of Euclidean distance between manually and automatically placed landmarks d_{Eff}. Op1: Operator 1; Op2: Operator 2; Op3: Operator 3. q_1: first quartile; q_2: second quartile; q_3: third quartile.

	Agent 1	Agent 2	Agent 3	Agent 4	Agent 5
Training epochs	16	10	11	12	11
Max success rate [%]	89.0	77.2	72.3	80.6	82.3
$min(d_{Err})$ [mm]	0.69	1.38	0.70	0.98	0.00
$q_1(d_{Err})$ [mm]	2.53	2.79	2.02	2.24	2.15
$q_2(d_{Err})$ [mm]	3.53	3.51	2.97	3.06	2.98
$q_3(d_{Err})$ [mm]	4.66	4.46	5.03	4.05	3.81
$max(d_{Err})$ [mm]	127.55	49.69	33.74	124.30	9.74
$d_{Err} > 5$ mm [%]	16.7	20.8	25.0	20.8	16.7
$d_{Err} > 10$ mm [%]	8.3	8.3	4.2	8.3	0

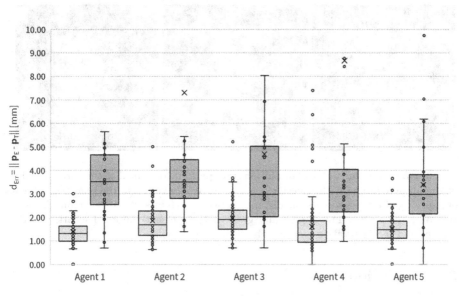

Fig. 5. Distributions of d_{Err} values obtained on validation data with all trained agents. Gray boxes represent training set samples while blue boxes represent validation set samples. The cross identifies the mean d_{Err} value, which is sensitive to the presence of outliers. (Color figure online)

layers allows to reduce the uncertainty in aortic annulus localization by reducing the magnitude and the number of outlines. *Agent 2* showed a good trade-off between model generalization and accuracy, while *Agent 3* seemed to improve median model performances at the cost of a higher localization uncertainty.

Not surprisingly, histogram windowing helped reducing the intensity variability, thus improving model accuracy in both *Agent 4* and *Agent 5*. The best results were obtained with the narrowest intensity range. This was more evident in the presence of hyperdense structures near the aortic valve, such as mechanical valves or calcifications. The reduced contrast between different hyper-dense structures (e.g., contrast-enhanced blood and the metal components of the mechanical valve) might improve model performance by masking unnecessary intensity variability, thus allowing the extraction of more meaningful imaging features, see Fig. 6. Even though the performances of *Agent 5* look promising, it does not yet reach the performance of expert radiology technologists.

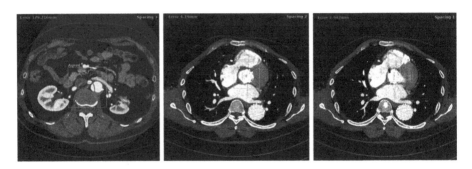

Fig. 6. Example of hierarchical resolution steps performed to localize the aortic annulus landmark in a patient with a mechanic aortic valve. The radius of the semi-transparent orange circle (left) represents the distance between current and target landmarks position over the z axis. The orange and green dots represent the axial location of the current and target position respectively. (Color figure online)

6   Conclusion

In this project we evaluated the performance of several DRL agents in aortic annulus localization in CTA data. Our results showed promising performance on a dataset of CTA images of patients with aortic dissection, which are usually characterized by a large variability in term of aortic morphology and image quality. Obtained results were achieved without any a priori knowledge on patient anatomy or image segmentation, thus confirming DRL as a versatile approach able to generalize to unseen data with good performance, even in pathological subjects. Further improvement will include the enlargement of the selected ROI around the current landmark location. In case of an enlarged aorta, the ROI may completely fall within the aortic lumen. In such cases, the limited variability of ROI voxel intensities hinders the extraction of meaningful features, causing the model to converge to a sub-optimal location. Moreover, future investigations will be focused on improving the performance of the best performing agent, which will be trained longer, relaxing early stopping criteria, on an enlarged database.

Acknowledgements. A. Pepe was supported by the TU Graz LEAD project *Mechanics, Modeling and Simulation of Aortic Dissection*. M.J. Willemink was supported by a Postdoctoral Fellowship Grant from the American Heart Association (18POST34030192). D. Mastrodicasa was supported in part by a grant from National Institute of Biomedical Imaging and Bioengineering (5T32EB009035).

References

1. Al, W.A., Yun, I.D.: Partial policy-based reinforcement learning for anatomical landmark localization in 3D medical images. IEEE Trans. Med. Imaging **39**(4), 1245–1255 (2019)
2. Alansary, A., et al.: Evaluating reinforcement learning agents for anatomical landmark detection. Med. Image Anal. **53**, 156–164 (2019)

3. Astudillo, P., et al.: Automatic detection of the aortic annular plane and coronary ostia from multidetector computed tomography. J. Intervent. Cardiol. **2020**, 1–9 (2020)

4. Elattar, M., et al.: Automatic aortic root landmark detection in CTA images for preprocedural planning of transcatheter aortic valve implantation. Int. J. Cardiovasc. Imaging **32**(3), 501–511 (2016). https://doi.org/10.1007/s10554-015-0793-9

5. Gao, X., et al.: Quantification of aortic annulus in computed tomography angiography: validation of a fully automatic methodology. Eur. J. Radiol. **93**, 1–8 (2017)

6. Ghesu, F.C., et al.: Multi-scale deep reinforcement learning for real-time 3D-landmark detection in CT scans. IEEE Trans. Pattern Anal. Mach. Intell. **41**(1), 176–189 (2017)

7. Ioffe, S., Szegedy, C.: Batch normalization: accelerating deep network training by reducing internal covariate shift. arXiv preprint arXiv:1502.03167 (2015)

8. Jones, M., Dobson, A., O'Brian, S.: A graphical method for assessing agreement with the mean between multiple observers using continuous measures. Int. J. Epidemiol. **40**(5), 1308–1313 (2011)

9. Mnih, V., et al.: Human-level control through deep reinforcement learning. Nature **518**(7540), 529–533 (2015)

10. Moccia, S., De Momi, E., El Hadji, S., Mattos, L.S.: Blood vessel segmentation algorithms-review of methods, datasets and evaluation metrics. Comput. Methods Programs Biomed. **158**, 71–91 (2018)

11. Pepe, A., Li, J., Rolf-Pissarczyk, M., et al.: Detection, segmentation, simulation and visualization of aortic dissections: a review. Med. Image Anal. **65**, 101773 (2020)

12. Queirós, S., et al.: Automatic 3D aortic annulus sizing by computed tomography in the planning of transcatheter aortic valve implantation. J. Cardiovasc. Comput. Tomogr. **11**(1), 25–32 (2017)

13. Rubin, G.D., Shiau, M.C., Leung, A.N., Kee, S.T., Logan, L.J., Sofilos, M.C.: Aorta and iliac arteries: single versus multiple detector-row helical CT angiography. Radiology **215**(3), 670–676 (2000)

14. Sutton, R.S., Barto, A.G.: Reinforcement Learning: An Introduction. MIT Press, Cambridge (2018)

15. Theriault-Lauzier, P., et al.: Recursive multiresolution convolutional neural networks for 3D aortic valve annulus planimetry. Int. J. Comput. Assist. Radiol. Surg. **15**, 577–588 (2020). https://doi.org/10.1007/s11548-020-02131-0

16. Tops, L.F., et al.: Noninvasive evaluation of the aortic root with multislice computed tomography: implications for transcatheter aortic valve replacement. JACC: Cardiovasc. Imaging **1**(3), 321–330 (2008)

17. Yu, C., Liu, J., Nemati, S.: Reinforcement learning in healthcare: a survey. arXiv preprint arXiv:1908.08796 (2019)

18. Zhang, P., Wang, F., Zheng, Y.: Deep reinforcement learning for vessel centerline tracing in multi-modality 3D volumes. In: Frangi, A., Schnabel, J., Davatzikos, C., Alberola-López, C., Fichtinger, G. (eds.) MICCAI 2018. LNCS, vol. 11073, pp. 755–763 (2018). Springer, Cham. https://doi.org/10.1007/978-3-030-00937-3_86

Image Translation and Inpainting

Functional-Consistent CycleGAN for CT to Iodine Perfusion Map Translation

Pietro Nardelli[(✉)] [ID], Rubén San José Estépar, Farbod N. Rahaghi [ID], and Raúl San José Estépar [ID]

Applied Chest Imaging Laboratory, Brigham and Women's Hospital, Harvard Medical School, Boston, MA, USA
{pnardelli,rsanjose}@bwh.harvard.edu

Abstract. Image-to-image translation from a source to a target domain by means of generative adversarial neural network (GAN) has gained a lot of attention in the medical imaging field due to their capability to learn the mapping characteristics between different modalities. Cycle-GAN has been proposed for image-to-image translation with unpaired images by means of a cycle-consistency loss function, which is optimized to reduce the difference between the image reconstructed from the synthetically-generated domain and the original input. However, CycleGAN inherently implies that the mapping between both domains is invertible, i.e., given a mapping G (forward cycle) from domain A to B, there is a mapping F (backward cycle) that is the inverse of G. This is assumption is not always true. For example, when we want to learn functional activity from structural modalities. Although it is well-recognized the relation between structure and function in different physiological processes, the problem is not invertible as the original modality cannot be recovered from a given functional response.

In this paper, we propose a functional-consistent CycleGAN that leverages the usage of a proxy structural image in a third domain, shared between source and target, to help the network learn fundamental characteristics while being cycle consistent. To demonstrate the strength of the proposed strategy, we present the application of our method to estimate iodine perfusion maps from contrast CT scans, and we compare performance of this technique to a traditional CycleGAN framework.

Keywords: CycleGAN · Cycle-consistency · Image translation · Iodine perfusion map

1 Introduction

Due to their demonstrated problem-solving capabilities, generative adversarial neural networks (GANs) [6] have become very popular in the computer vision

This work has been partially funded by the National Institutes of Health NHLBI awards R01HL116473, R01HL149877, and by the Brigham Health BWH Radiology Department Pilot Grant Award. We gratefully acknowledge the support of NVIDIA Corporation with the donation of the GPU used for this research.

© Springer Nature Switzerland AG 2020
J. Petersen et al. (Eds.): TIA 2020, LNCS 12502, pp. 109–117, 2020.
https://doi.org/10.1007/978-3-030-62469-9_10

community. In its original setup, two neural networks, a generator G and a discriminator D, are trained alternately and fight with each other in a minimax game that helps convert input noise to the desired output. Since the GAN approach was first introduced, several variations and improvements have been proposed in the literature. As an example, auxiliary information can be presented to the generator G to condition the network to output images with specific characteristics [10]. In the computer vision field, a typical approach is to use an image as conditional input to force the network to learn the characteristics of an image in different domains and solve image-to-image translation problems [7].

More recently, a new method for image-to-image translation, called Cycle-GAN, has been proposed to relax the requirement of aligned training pairs and learn essential characteristics between sets of unpaired samples [13]. Two generators, G (from domain A to domain B) and F (from domain B to domain A), are combined and trained simultaneously along with two discriminators, while a cycle-consistency loss is introduced to force G and F to be consistent with each other and reconstruct the original input from synthetically-generated outputs.

While CycleGAN was originally proposed to overcome the constraint of aligned training pairs [13], in cases in which paired data is available, the same underlying concept can be used and extended by including a new loss function term that compares synthesized images and original outputs [2].

The primary underlying assumption of the CycleGAN is that a transformation G: $A \rightarrow B$ is invertible so that there always exist a second transformation F: $B \rightarrow A$ that can be used to retrieve the original input in the source domain A from the synthesized image in the target domain B. In some kinds of image translations problems, this assumption is often violated, and the search for a joint distribution between the two domains represents an ill-posed problem.

Our hypothesis is that for ill-posed problems a proxy image may be generated in a third functional domain, C, by a pair of corresponding inputs in the two domains to obtain a well-posed problem on which a CycleGAN can be applied. To this end, the requirement of cycle-consistency on the original input in domain A - difficult to retrieve from domain B - is relaxed, and a functional-consistency between domains B and C is introduced.

To demonstrate the strength of the presented strategy, we applied the proposed framework to synthesize chest iodine perfusion map images from contrast pulmonary chest CT images using the distance map of the vascular tree as proxy image. The estimation of perfusion from contrast chest CT scans can be relevant to examine perfusion defects related to pathologies that preclude a normal gas exchange. CT is the core imaging modality for the evaluation of pulmonary disorders. However, a new dual energy CT (DECT) technique has been recently proposed to allow the estimation of relative parenchymal iodine concentration in different parts of the lung [8]. This shows the distribution of pulmonary perfusion and can be used, for example, as a marker to detect perfusion defects in pulmonary thromboembolic disease [5,9].

Results are first compared with the original CycleGAN, as proposed in [13], through mean squared error (MSE), the structural similarity (SSIM) index, and

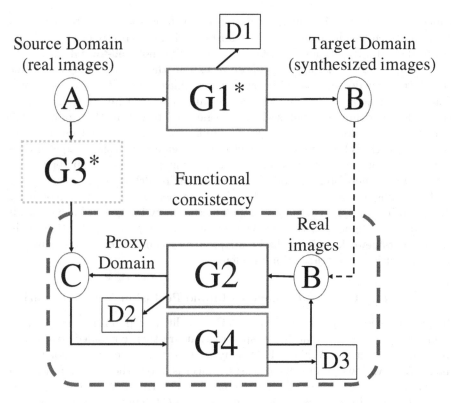

Fig. 1. Scheme of functional-consistent CycleGAN. A functional domain is shared between source and target to help the network improve accuracy and relax the cycle-consistency requirement. Non-invertible transformations are indicated with *. G indicate generation functions, while D are the corresponding discriminators. (Color figure online)

local correlations on patches of 15×15 pixels. Finally, we show the practical use of the method to quantify the perfusion defects in pulmonary embolism (PE).

2   Materials and Methods

Figure 1 shows the flow diagram of the proposed functional-consistent CycleGAN that automatically generates synthesized images in the target domain, B, from the source domain, A. The framework consists of three GAN networks, including three generators (G1, G2, and G4) and corresponding adversarial discriminators (D1, D2, and D3), and one generator, G3, which might consist in another neural network (e.g, U-Net [11]) or a traditional generative algorithm (e.g, segmentation technique).

In the medical imaging field, very often the original input image cannot be easily reconstructed from a synthetically-generated output, as some essential information has been lost in the transformation from the source to the target domain. When this happens, the G1 transformation (green box in Fig. 1) is not invertible and a traditional CycleGAN framework is not well-formulated.

To overcome this issue, we propose to extend the CycleGAN network and introduce a new domain, called *proxy domain*, which represents a common space that can be generated from both the source and the target inputs. While a non-invertible algorithm (G3, yellow box) can be used to obtain the shared image from the source domain, two generative functions, G2 and G4 (red and blue boxes, respectively), are used in a CycleGAN scheme to translate target images to the proxy outputs, and viceversa, in a functional consistent manner (purple dashed box). Therefore, G2 and G4 are invertible by definition.

Depending on the specific task that the neural network model has to perform, the generators and discriminators as well as the proxy image can be specifically selected and designed. In the following section, we show the application of the proposed framework as it might be adapted to a contrast chest CT image to iodine perfusion map translation problem.

2.1   Contrast Chest CT Image to Iodine Perfusion Map Translation

To generate a iodine perfusion map, two CTs at different potentials are acquired in order to obtain different X-ray spectra that are then combined together to form the final image. While DECT may represent an important tool for the diagnosis of various pulmonary diseases, concerns about the radiation dose the patient is exposed to have limited its use [8]. For this reason, having a tool that automatically synthesizes iodine map from a CT image might be crucial to improve diagnosis of lung disorders.

Iodine perfusion maps are generated based on the difference in attenuation at different energies normalized by the mean density in the pulmonary artery [8]. While a neural network, G1, can be found to translate a CT to iodine map, structural information about major vessels, airways and other organs is not present on the target image, making the reconstruction of the original CT from the synthesized map an ill-posed problem. Therefore, the generative function G1 is not invertible and the cycle-consistency requirement of a traditional CycleGAN approach is not respected.

In the framework we propose in this work, we acknowledge that there is a connection between vascular structures and functional perfusion [12]. Therefore, we can define a proxy image form the source CT scan where a cycle consistent connection with the functional domain can be established. In our case, we utilize as proxy image a vessel distance map obtained from a vessel segmentation [*], followed by signed Daniellson distance map [4] (G3 transformation). This proxy vessel distance map can also be generated from a iodine map with an invertible transformation (G4 in Fig. 1) using a CycleGAN approach, as proposed in [13]. This way, cycle-consistency is transferred to a more well-posed problem, while functional consistency is required to the whole network.

The goal of this work is to compare the proposed functional-consistent GAN to a traditional CycleGAN and demonstrate that the introduction of a new common domain helps improve the network accuracy. For this reason, all generative (G1, G2, and G4) and discriminative models (D1, D2, and D3), as well as optimizer and main parameters are the same as introduced in [13]. In particular, a mean absolute error is used to optimize G1, while a cycle-consistency loss, as defined in [13], is utilized for the G2-G4 optimization. For all 3 discriminators, a mean squared error is used as loss function. The difference with [13] is that in this work both the proposed network and the CycleGAN take input images of 512×512 pixels and predict images of the same size.

Training was performed on 6,000 2D axial slices randomly extracted from 40 clinical cases - for which both contrast CT images and iodine perfusion maps (extracted with a dual-source Siemens CT scanner) were available - using a NVIDIA Titan X GPU machine and the deep learning framework Keras [3] on top of TensorFlow [1]. Since we had access to corresponding inputs in the two domains, a paired images approach was taken.

3 Experimental Setup

To evaluate accuracy of the proposed approach in comparison to CycleGAN, agreement between real and synthesized iodine map images extracted from 30 clinical cases (not used for training) were compared using MSE, SSIM index and local correlations on randomly selected patches (500 per case) of 15×15 pixels. To this end, the three indices were computed independently on rind (defined as the area at a distance $\leq 10\,\mathrm{mm}$ from the rind) and core (area at distance $> 10\,\mathrm{mm}$) of the lung region to evaluate where the network attention is focused. Difference between methods were assessed using t-test or Wilcoxon test.

Finally, we performed an indirect validation by assessing perfusion defect differences between the clot-affected lung side and the normally perfused lung side in 20 subject with PE from the CAD-PE challenge (www.cad-pe.org). An expert reviewed those cases to define the lung region affected by a clot. 7 cases had clots in the right lung and 1 case in the left lung. In 8 cases the clot affected both lungs and 4 cases were excluded due to additional parenchymal injury. In total, 8 subjects with unilateral clotting were used in this study.

4 Results

To justify the usage of the proposed approach in our experiments, an example of a CT slice reconstructed using CycleGAN is shown in Fig. 2(a). As expected, the reconstructed image does not efficiently recover some important structures, such as airways and small vessels, and lung rind as well as texture are deformed. On the other hand, the reconstruction of a vessel distance map from iodine map is much more feasible, as shown in Fig. 2(b).

Two examples of iodine perfusion map as synthesized by CycleGAN and the proposed method in comparison to real maps are presented in Fig. 3.

The MSE and mean SSIM obtained on the testing set using the traditional CycleGAN and the proposed method are presented in Table 1 along with the

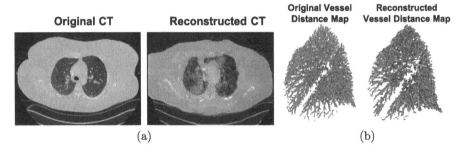

(a)   (b)

Fig. 2. Example of reconstructed contrast CT images (a) and vessel distance map (b) from iodine perfusion map. While reconstructing a CT is complicated, a reconstructed vessel distance map is more feasible to obtain

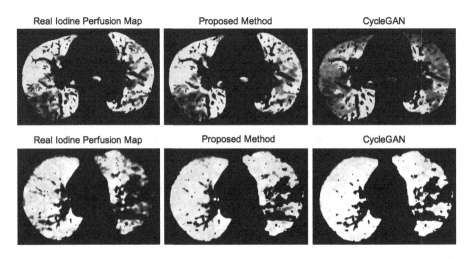

Fig. 3. Two examples of iodine perfusion maps in comparison to real maps (left) as obtained using the proposed method (center) and traditional cycleGAN (right).

local Spearman's correlation coefficient obtained on patches of 15×15 pixels randomly extracted from the test dataset.

Finally, results for the PE study are shown in Fig. 4. As expected, lung regions with clot showed a clear tendency to have lower mean perfusion than regions without the clot when using our method. However, the difference was not noticeable when using the CycleGAN. In both cases, the difference was not statistically significant due to the limited number of cases used in this study.

Table 1. Performance comparison between CycleGAN and our method in terms of mean squared error (MSE), mean structural similarity (SSIM) index, and local Spearman's correlation coefficient obtained on local patches of 15 × 15 pixels. Evaluation has been computed independently on rind and core of the lung region. Best results are presented in bold.

	Core			Rind		
	CycleGAN	Our Method	pval	CycleGAN	Our Method	pval
MSE	0.046 ± 0.006	**0.035 ± 0.005**	0.229	0.059 ± 0.013	**0.045 ± 0.009**	0.167
SSIM	0.689 ± 0.014	**0.712 ± 0.014**	0.473	0.578 ± 0.014	**0.617 ± 0.017**	0.244
ρ_{local}	0.494 ± 0.375	**0.524 ± 0.354**	<0.0001	0.641 ± 0.331	**0.668 ± 0.307**	<0.0001

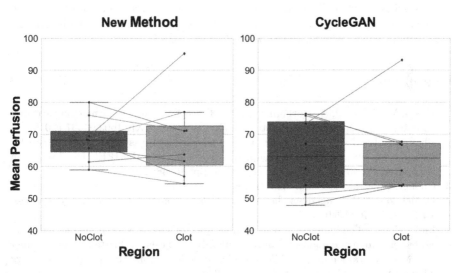

Fig. 4. Difference in mean perfusion between clot and non-clot regions in cases with PE

5   Discussion and Conclusion

In this paper, we presented a novel approach to image-to-image translation for medical images that employs a proxy image to impose functional consistency on the network. This may be particularly helpful in cases in which the forward translation is not invertible, making cycle-consistency challenging to respect.

To demonstrate the validity of our approach, we proposed an example of translation from contrast CT to iodine perfusion map for which corresponding images in the two domains were available. Comparison to traditional CycleGAN, as proposed in [13], was performed. The presented preliminary results show that the inclusion of a proxy domain shared between source and target helps improve network performance. We want to point out that the final goal of this experiment was not to obtain an optimal image-to-image translation, but to demonstrate that if the proposed approach is utilized, results improve compared to the usage of a traditional CycleGAN.

Interestingly enough, MSE and SSIM values were better on the core of the iodine maps, while local correlations were higher results on the lung rind. This effect should be explored in future analysis.

From a thorough analysis of results, we also noticed that both networks have a strong tendency to overfitting. Therefore, data augmentation, as well as modification of the network generators and parameters optimization should be considered in the future. Also, 3D information might further help the network correctly identify perfusion regions and should be investigated.

In conclusion, we believe that the proposed method represents an innovative approach to a CycleGAN scheme that may particularly help in the medical image analysis field in which a backward cycle is not feasible.

References

1. Abadi, M., Agarwal, A., Barham, P., et al.: Tensorflow: large-scale machine learning on heterogeneous distributed systems. arXiv preprint arXiv:1603.04467 (2016)
2. Chang, H., Lu, J., Yu, F., Finkelstein, A.: Pairedcyclegan: asymmetric style transfer for applying and removing makeup. In: Proceedings of the IEEE Conference on Computer Vision and Pattern Recognition, pp. 40–48 (2018)
3. Chollet, F., et al.: Keras. https://keras.io (2015)
4. Danielsson, P.E.: Euclidean distance mapping. Comput. Graph. Image Process. **14**(3), 227–248 (1980)
5. Fink, C., et al.: Dual-energy CT angiography of the lung in patients with suspected pulmonary embolism: initial results. In: RöFo-Fortschritte auf dem Gebiet der Röntgenstrahlen und der bildgebenden Verfahren, vol. 180, pp. 879–883. Georg Thieme Verlag KG Stuttgart New York (2008)
6. Goodfellow, I., et al.: Generative adversarial nets. In: Advances in Neural Information Processing Systems, pp. 2672–2680 (2014)
7. Isola, P., Zhu, J.Y., Zhou, T., Efros, A.A.: Image-to-image translation with conditional adversarial networks. In: Proceedings of the IEEE Conference on Computer Vision and Pattern Recognition, pp. 1125–1134 (2017)
8. Kang, M.J., Park, C.M., Lee, C.H., Goo, J.M., Lee, H.J.: Dual-energy CT: clinical applications in various pulmonary diseases. Radiographics **30**(3), 685–698 (2010)
9. Kang, M.J., Park, C.M., Lee, C.H., Goo, J.M., Lee, H.J.: Focal iodine defects on color-coded iodine perfusion maps of dual-energy pulmonary CT angiography images: a potential diagnostic pitfall. Am. J. Roentgenol. **195**(5), W325–W330 (2010)
10. Mirza, M., Osindero, S.: Conditional generative adversarial nets. arXiv preprint arXiv:1411.1784 (2014)
11. Ronneberger, O., Fischer, P., Brox, T.: U-net: convolutional networks for biomedical image segmentation. In: Navab, N., Hornegger, J., Wells, W.M., Frangi, A.F. (eds.) MICCAI 2015. LNCS, vol. 9351, pp. 234–241. Springer, Cham (2015). https://doi.org/10.1007/978-3-319-24574-4_28

12. Weibel, E.R.: It takes more than cells to make a good lung. Am. J. Respir. Crit. Care Med. **187**(4), 342–346 (2013)
13. Zhu, J.Y., Park, T., Isola, P., Efros, A.A.: Unpaired image-to-image translation using cycle-consistent adversarial networks. In: Proceedings of the IEEE International Conference on Computer Vision, pp. 2223–2232 (2017)

MRI to CTA Translation for Pulmonary Artery Evaluation Using CycleGANs Trained with Unpaired Data

Maialen Stephens[1(✉)], Raúl San José Estepar[2], Jesús Ruiz-Cabello[3],
Ignacio Arganda-Carreras[4], Iván Macía[1,5], and Karen López-Linares[1,5]

[1] Vicomtech Foundation, San Sebastián, Spain
mstephens@vicomtech.org
[2] Applied Chest Imaging Laboratory, Brigham and Women's Hospital,
Harvard Medical School, Boston, USA
[3] CIC biomaGUNE, Basque Research and Technology Alliance (BRTA), CIBERES,
Ikerbasque, Basque Foundation for Science, Departamento de Química en Ciencias
Farmacéuticas, Universidad Complutense de Madrid, Madrid, Spain
[4] Department of Computer Science and Artificial Intelligence, Ikerbasque, Basque
Foundation for Science, University of the Basque Country (UPV/EHU),
Donostia International Physics Center (DIPC), San Sebastián, Spain
[5] Biodonostia Health Research Institute, San Sebastián, Spain

Abstract. Pulmonary Hypertension (PH) is a cardiovascular disease
where the pulmonary arterial pressure and resistance increases, causing
functional and morphological changes in structures like the Pulmonary
Artery (PA). Magnetic Resonance (MR) is a noninvasive image modality
whose importance is raising as it allows a complete functional evaluation
of the affected structures, as well as complex blood flow pattern analysis. However, anatomical information is more accurately estimated from
Computed Tomography (CT), where structures are better defined. Thus,
both image modalities are required for a complete PH evaluation and generating CT images from MR seems to be a good alternative to reduce
patient radiation, time and expense for a complete characterization of
PH only from MR images. Previous approaches have shown CycleGANs
to successfully complete image-to-image translation tasks with different
medical image modalities, yet, lung MR-CT translation for PA characterization has barely been exploited using CycleGANs. Hence, in this
work we propose generating synthetic CT Angiography (CTA) images
from pulmonary MR images training a CycleGAN with unpaired data,
to further evaluate the ability of the synthetic CT images to provide
structural PA information. We demonstrate to generate synthetic CTA
images that correctly resemble real CTA images by automatically segmenting the PA with a 2D CNN trained with real CTA scans. We also
prove to preserve PA structural information comparing the ground truth

Electronic supplementary material The online version of this chapter (https://
doi.org/10.1007/978-3-030-62469-9_11) contains supplementary material, which is
available to authorized users.

PA annotations of the real CTA images and the predicted PA segmentations of the reconstructed CTA scans.

Keywords: CycleGAN · CT synthesis · Pulmonary hypertension · Segmentation · Convolutional neural network

1 Introduction

Magnetic Resonance (MR) is a noninvasive imaging modality whose role is increasing during the diagnosis and follow up of Pulmonary Hypertension (PH). PH is a cardiovascular disease defined as the rise of pulmonary arterial pressure and resistance, responsible for right heart failure and functional decline. In patients with PH, MR images allow evaluating changes in the functionality of structures like the Pulmonary Artery (PA) or the Right Ventricle (RV). Furthermore, advanced techniques like 4D flow MR provide complex blood flow pattern visualization and retrospective quantification of flow parameters [1]. The assessment of the PA morphology is also essential in PH management, as the disease produces a widening of the central PA area. However, this structural analysis is more accurately performed using Computed Tomography (CT) images as they provide more detailed anatomical information. Thus, both imaging modalities are required for a precise PH characterization and management, yet, the acquisition of both volumes is time-consuming, expensive, and it exposes patients to stress and radiation. Hence, the generation of CT images from MR may be a good alternative to acquire both imaging studies, enabling a complete functional and structural characterization of PH.

In recent years, CycleGAN networks [2] have emerged as a powerful tool for image-to-image translation tasks when having unpaired image datasets. These networks remove the burden of traditional Generative Adversarial Networks (GANs) needing a paired dataset to generate a model able to translate images from one domain to another, which is especially a disadvantage when working with medical images. Different image modalities are rarely acquired for the same subject, leading to a lack of paired images to train GANs. CycleGANs have shown positive results in the synthesis of medical images with unpaired data for several body areas, such as brain [3,4], pelvis [5], fundus [6] or abdominal aorta [7].

The purpose of this study is to evaluate the use of CycleGANs to obtain PA structural biomarkers from MR images, which in itself provide functional information, by generating synthetic pulmonary CT scans from unpaired pulmonary MR images, for a correct PH evaluation. Particularly, we generate CT Angiography (CTA) images where the PA is highly contrasted from T1 weighted MR images, training a CycleGAN with human CTA images and pig MR images. To ensure the validity of our approach and to confirm that the synthetically generated images resemble real CTA scans, we train a 2D convolutional neural network (CNN) [8] to automatically segment the PA from real CTA scans and test it using the synthetically generated scans.

2 State-of-the-Art

Image-to-image translation has been for years a challenge in computer vision, image processing and computer graphics, where researchers have proposed many different formulations to find an optimal solution to this problem. With the advances in deep learning techniques, CNNs have been widely applied for many different computer vision tasks, including image-to-image translation, surpassing state of the art results. For medical imaging, CNNs have shown to provide promising results when generating CT images from MR images [9,10], yet misalignment in the ground truth causes inaccuracies that lead to wrong synthetic CT predictions.

Recently, GAN models [11] have demonstrated to generate more realistic images by introducing an extra CNN that aims at predicting whether the output images are real or fake. Several studies have used GANs to accurately translate MR images to CT images [12–14]. However, the aforementioned approaches require paired and perfectly aligned CT-MR datasets, which in the medical domain is difficult to obtain.

To overcome this issue, CycleGANs were first introduced in [2], allowing to train an image translation model without the need of a paired dataset. Compared to traditional GANs, they make use of an extra cycle consistency loss that forces the reconstructed image to match the original image, using the difference between these two as a regularization term during the training process. Moreover, this method avoids different original images from one domain to converge to the same synthetic image and generates unique synthetic images that resemble original images correctly. CycleGANs have successfully been employed in medical image synthesis for different body parts like brain, pelvis, fundus or abdominal aortic images [3–7]. Nevertheless, lung MR-CT translation for PA characterization has rarely been exploited using CycleGANs. In this study, we take advantage of the CycleGANs to demonstrate that a complete PH evaluation could be carried out by a functional study of the MR images and a structural analysis of the PA by generating corresponding CTA images from MR images.

3 Methods

As both CT and MR images are necessary for a complete subject PH evaluation, but CT exposes patients to radiation and acquiring different image modalities is expensive and time-consuming, we aim at generating CT angiography (CTA) images from MRI for an accurate structural analysis of the PA. For this purpose, we first train an adaptation of the CycleGAN model, proposed by [3], with unpaired data to generate CTA images from MRI. Then, employing the architecture presented in [8], we train a 2D CNN to automatically segment the PA from CTA images to evaluate the performance of the CycleGAN to produce realistic CTA images, where the PA is clearly visible, aiding the extraction of relevant biomarkers that characterize the PH.

3.1 Datasets

T1 weighted PA cine MR images have been provided by CICBiomaGUNE obtained from 6 pigs (25–35 kg Sus scrofa domesticus) used for a study related to PH secondary to acute lung injury. For each subject, images were acquired in several conditions: normal condition, after inducing acute respiratory distress syndrome and up to three different positive end-expiratory pressure conditions. This leads to a total of 24 cine MR studies that we have further divided according to the trigger time, resulting in 403 volumes of $158 \times 158 \times 50$ voxels in size.

Moreover, we have worked with 51 CTA volumes of different patients obtained from the Brigham and Women's Hospital: 39 patients with pulmonary embolism, 8 control with PH and 4 subjects with hypertension. As we have a higher number of MR images, we have applied 6 translations per each original CTA image, summing a total of 357 volumes of $158 \times 158 \times 50$ voxels in size. Ground truth PA annotations from these CTA images to train the automatic PA segmentation network have been obtained semi-automatically.

Finally, we have resized CTA images to match the size of MR volumes and rescaled the intensities of images from both domains to 0–1.

3.2 CycleGAN Training

Synthesis of CTA images from MR images is carried out using the CycleGAN approach [2], described in Fig. 1. The training process consists in optimizing 4 different networks: two generators and two discriminators that are trained in an adversarial way, where the generators aim at learning the mapping between two domains and the discriminators try to classify real and synthetic images. Discriminators are trained to predict whether an image is real (1) or fake (0), so the CTA discriminator will minimize the function shown in Eq. 1 while the MR discriminator will minimize the function in Eq. 2.

$$L_{CTA} = (1 - D_{CTA}(Real_{CTA}))^2 + D_{CTA}(G_{CTA}(Real_{MR}))^2 \qquad (1)$$

$$L_{MR} = (1 - D_{MR}(Real_{MR}))^2 + D_{MR}(G_{MR}(Real_{CTA}))^2 \qquad (2)$$

where D_{CTA} is the CTA discriminator, D_{MR} is the MR discriminator and $Real_{CTA}$ and $Real_{MR}$ are the real CTA and MR images, respectively.

On the contrary, both generators are trained in an adversarial way to maximize the previous losses, ensuring synthetic images to correctly resemble real images from the other domain. As we have unpaired data, this model allows us to exploit supervised training with an extra cycle consistency loss L_{Cyc} (Eq. 3) that also updates generator weights to enforce forward-backward consistency, avoiding generators to provide images that are unrelated to the inputs, making the reconstructed image match the real input image. The original generator loss proposed in [2], built as the sum of the adversarial and cycle consistency loss, uses a single parameter λ to control the impact of L_{Cyc} with respect to the adversarial losses in the backward propagation of both generators. Comparing to

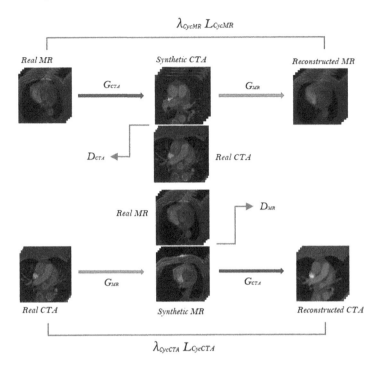

Fig. 1. Representation of the used CycleGAN architecture. G_{CTA} is trained to generate CTA from MR images, while G_{MR} generates MR images from CTA scans. D_{CTA} and D_{MR} aim at discriminating between real and synthetic CTA and MR images, respectively. L_{CycCTA} compares the original and the reconstructed CTA scans weighted by $\lambda_{Cyc_{CTA}}$ for the L_{Cyc} and L_{CycMR} compares the original and the reconstructed MR images weighted by $\lambda_{Cyc_{MR}}$. Both generator and discriminator architectures are detailed in the supplementary file.

the original one, we use 4 different λ parameters to better weight the influence of each component of the loss function that updates the generators: $\lambda_{Cyc_{MR}}$, $\lambda_{Cyc_{CTA}}$, $\lambda_{Adv_{MR}}$ and $\lambda_{Adv_{CTA}}$.

$$L_{Cyc} = \lambda_{Cyc_{MR}} \| G_{MR}(G_{CTA}(Real_{MR})) - Real_{MR} \|_1 + \\ + \lambda_{Cyc_{CTA}} \| G_{CTA}(G_{MR}(Real_{CTA})) - Real_{CTA} \|_1 \qquad (3)$$

where G_{MR} generates MR images from CTA scans, G_{CTA} generates CTA images from MR and $\lambda_{Cyc_{MR}}$ and $\lambda_{Cyc_{CTA}}$ control the impact of the MR and CTA cycle consistency loss in the total loss independently.

Both generators G_{CTA} and G_{MR} have the network architectures similar to the ones proposed by [2]: 2D fully convolutional networks with stride 2 convolutional layers, nine residual blocks and two fractionally-strided convolutional layers with stride $\frac{1}{2}$, which remove checkerboard artifacts. We use instance normalization, which normalizes each batch independently, i.e, across spatial locations. To build the discriminators D_{CT} and D_{MRI} we use 70×70 PatchGANs that classify whether 70×70 overlapping patches are real or fake.

Hyperparameters are experimentally defined, selecting the ones providing highest quality synthetic and reconstructed images for both domains. We set $\lambda_{Cyc_{MR}}$, $\lambda_{Cyc_{CTA}}$, $\lambda_{Adv_{MR}}$ and $\lambda_{Adv_{CTA}}$ initial values to 14, 12, 4, and 1, respectively and adjusted during training according to the loss value, as explained in Sect. 4.1. We use Adam optimizer with a batch size of 4 and a constant learning rate of 2e−04 for all models in the network.

3.3 2D CNN for Pulmonary Artery Segmentation in CTA

To validate the effectiveness of the CycleGAN to produce reliable CTA images from MR, we proceed to train the CNN proposed in [8] with real CTA images. However, as this network is used to predict the PA in 2D images generated by G_{CTA}, we have modified the network to output 2D segmentations of the PA, preserving the same network architecture. The main difference is the use of a weighted Dice loss function, assigning a weight of 0.9 to the foreground and 0.1 to the background Dice score, instead of the cross-entropy loss as it provided more accurate results. We train the network with an initial learning rate of 1e−3, batch size 16 and Adam optimizer. All networks are trained on a TITAN X Pascal (NVIDIA) GPU card.

4 Results

After training both networks, our objective is to test the possibility of extracting relevant structural biomarkers that CT images offer, only having MR images and a network that computes the translation from MR to CTA. An important parameter clinicians assess is the PA diameter that enlarges in patients with PH. Hence, having a well defined PA in synthetic CTA images is critical for a real application of our approach, which would allow a precise PA measurement that could not have been done in a MR image due to its low anatomical resolution.

4.1 Synthetic Image Generation Using CycleGANs

For a correct CycleGAN training, we change the λ values according to the loss curves during the training process. If initially weighting adversarial losses with very low λ, generators are mainly updated by L_{Cyc}, producing nearly perfect reconstructed images but hardly leaning to generate correct synthetic images that resemble images in the other domain. We find a balance between correct synthetic image generation and reconstruction by initially defining $\lambda_{Cyc_{MR}}$, $\lambda_{Cyc_{CTA}}$, $\lambda_{Adv_{MR}}$ and $\lambda_{Adv_{CTA}}$ as 14, 12, 4, and 1, respectively. Maintaining these weights constant, our models learn to generate accurate synthetic images in both domains in early epochs, but later all start to converge to a same image, without changing according to the input image. Consequently, all the reconstructed images also converge to a same image, increasing the cycle consistency loss abruptly due to the mismatch between the reconstruction and the original image. Thus, when identifying an excessive increase in the L_{cyc}, the λ values are updated increasing $\lambda_{Cyc_{MR}}$ and $\lambda_{Cyc_{CTA}}$ to ensure a correct reconstruction, which also leads to a different synthetic image per each input image. In Fig. 2 we can observe that the proposed procedure allows cycle loss training curves to decrease or oscillate around a same value. The training process is stopped once the curves are stable around a certain value without improving.

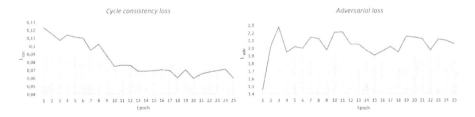

Fig. 2. Training cycle consistency loss (left) and adversarial loss (right) curves updating the λ values when L_{cyc} increases.

Figure 3 shows an example of a real MR image, a synthetic CTA image and a reconstructed MR image. It can be seen that anatomical structures are better defined in CTA, and structures in synthetic images have different sizes and shapes depending on the input MR image, meaning that structures are generated in a consistent way. In fact, although there are errors with respect to the original image, the shape of the main structures is conserved in the reconstructed images, which implies that the synthesized CTA image is unique for the corresponding input image.

Furthermore, we can assume a correct translation to CTA images because when we have reconstructed a 3D image from synthetic 2D slices corresponding to the same MR volume, we notice that the synthetic image is spatially consistent, where anatomical structures can be detected and quantified (Fig. 4). Despite 3D reconstruction being slightly discontinuous, for PH evaluation the PA diameter is the most relevant biomarker and is extracted locating the PA bifurcation and estimating the diameter in a oblique slice to the PA centerline. Thus, we believe that a misaligned 3D image would not affect PH patient diagnosis and follow-up, as shape and size remains consistent. Nevertheless, this would have to be evaluated in more detail.

However, MR-CTA-MR cycle offers poor information about the PA shape and size conservation, as this structure is not clearly visible in MR images. Therefore, reconstructing a CTA image from a synthetic MR using G_{CTA} seems to allow us to evaluate how good the PA is conserved compared to the original CTA. We can observe in Fig. 3 that our model is able to generate reliable MR images and correctly reconstruct the original CTA scans. In this case, we can sense a slight blur in the reconstructed images, which is logical as CTA images are harder to reconstruct as they contain more detailed structural information.

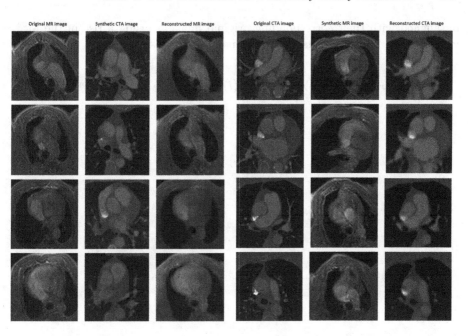

Fig. 3. Examples of generated synthetic and reconstructed images.

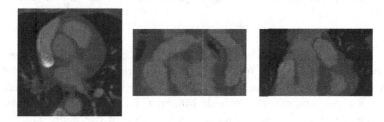

Fig. 4. Three views of a synthetic CTA image: axial, sagital, coronal.

Nevertheless, the PA apparently preserves its shape and size in the reconstructed image compared to the corresponding original one, meaning that the model is translating PA structural information in a correct way, confirming that our approach seems to be useful for further PH evaluation.

In order to quantitatively evaluate the overall consistency among real and reconstructed images, we have computed the Mean-Squared-Error (MSE) defined in Eq. 4 (for CTA) and represented in Fig. 5 for both image modalities. The MSE for CTA images yields a mean value of 0.007 ± 0.006 while for MR this value increases to 0.01 ± 0.007. As we can appreciate in Fig. 3, the original MR images are not registered before training and have a slight difference in the subject orientation. Thus, the generators might have learnt to generate synthetic images in a specific orientation that causes some reconstructed MR images to be misaligned with their corresponding original image, causing a rise in the MSE value for MR images as images are compared pixel-wise.

$$MSE_{CTA} = \frac{1}{N} \sum_{i=1}^{N} (Real_{CTA}(i) - G_{CTA}(G_{MR}(Real_{CTA}))^2 \qquad (4)$$

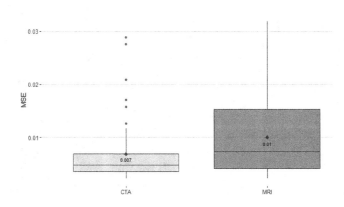

Fig. 5. Plots representing the MSE in both directions: CTA-MR-CTA (left) and MR-CTA-MR (right). The mean MSE is also displayed for each case in red. (Color figure online)

It is important to note that unlike other MR to CT translation studies, apart from translating from one image modality to another, our models are also learning to translate anatomical differences between pigs and human, the reason why the shape of the synthetic human CTA images do not match the original pig MR image. Yet, the shape preservation of the main structures in the reconstructed images demonstrates that synthetic images are appropriately generated.

4.2   Pulmonary Artery Segmentation from Synthetic CTAs

In order to further validate the quality of the generated synthetic CTA images, we test the ability of a CNN trained with real CTA scans to automatically segment the PA in the generated CTA images. As displayed in Fig. 6, the PA is segmented unsuccessfully in MR images with the 2D CNN trained on CTA data, while this structure is more precisely segmented in the synthetic CTA images. Although 3D segmentation reconstructions lacking of continuity due to slice misalignment in the synthetic CTA images, the segmentations may allow extracting the PA centerline to locate the PA bifurcation and directly calculate its diameter for the PH evaluation.

Additionally, we segment the reconstructed CTA images to corroborate PA shape and diameter are correctly preserved when changing from one domain

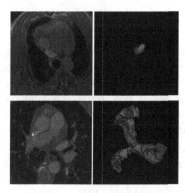

Fig. 6. In red, the output of the segmentation model in an original MR image (top) and its corresponding synthetic CTA image (bottom). In blue, the real PA in the MR. (Color figure online)

to another, by comparing those segmentations to the ground truth annotations of the original CTA images. Figure 7 demonstrates that, even if small artery branches are lost, our models are capable of accurately recovering the main PA in the reconstructed images. We also calculate the difference between the ground truth and the corresponding reconstructed main PA size of 50 different CTA scans, which results in a mean value of 1.06 ± 1.09 mm, having original PA sizes vary from 17 mm to 39 mm. Results suggest that synthetic CTA images may be used for PH assessment as the PA size varies depending on the input MR image apparently in a coherent manner.

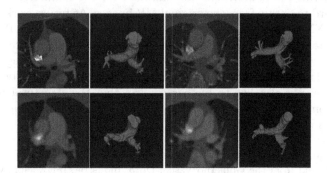

Fig. 7. First row shows two original CTA images with the ground truth segmentations and the second row images are the corresponding CTA reconstructions together with the predicted PA. We can visually confirm PA diameter remains the same from the original image to the reconstructed CTA.

5   Conclusions

Hereby, we have proposed a MR to CTA translation approach based on Cycle-GANs as a tool for a complete PH assessment. MR imaging allows clinicians a precise functional evaluation of structures that are altered due to the PH. In addition, MR provides blood flow pattern visualization and quantification, which are essential for the analysis of cardiovascular diseases. Still, MR grants poor anatomical information of relevant structures that are affected by PH, for example, the PA. Therefore, CT scans are crucial for the estimation of structural biomarkers, where experts can easily distinguish between the different structures within the image. In order to avoid acquiring both image modalities and exposing patients to radiation with CT imaging, MR to CT image translation is a helpful tool that permits only acquiring MR images for a exhaustive PH evaluation.

We have demonstrated to successfully generate CTA images from MR, allowing simpler PA diameter size evaluation. For this purpose, we have weighted each component of the generator loss using different initial λ values, which are changed during the training process if the cycle consistency loss increases abruptly, avoiding all generated images converging to an identical synthetic image. We have also quantitatively compared the quality of the reconstructed CTA and MR images, by calculating the MSE between the original and reconstructed images. We notice that the mean MR reconstruction error is higher than the CTA reconstruction error, which could be caused by the misalignment of the original MR images. Thus, a part from increasing $\lambda_{Cyc_{MR}}$, we aim at registering the input MR images to train our network and obtain lower MSE errors.

Moreover, we have validated our approach by automatically segmenting the PA in the synthetic CTA images using a 2D CNN, showing that the output allows extracting relevant structural biomarkers for PH characterization, which would be hard to obtain from the original MR images. As future work, we aim at training a CNN directly on MR data and calculating the error of the PA diameter estimation from the predicted PA. Then, we would compare the results to the PA diameter estimation from the corresponding synthetic CTA images to verify our proposed methodology improves PH biomarker extraction only using MR images. We would also like to further confirm that the structural biomarkers extracted from synthetic CTA images are sufficient to differentiate a healthy PA from a PA of a patient with PH.

Acknowledgement. This work was supported by grants from MEIC (SAF2017-84494-C2-R), and from the Gobierno Vasco, Dpto. Industria, Innovación, Comercio y Turismo under the ELKARTEK Program (Grant No. KK-2019/bmG19). JR-C received an Ayuda from the Fundación contra la Hipertensión Pulmonar (2018).

References

1. Stankovic, Z., Allen, B.D., Garcia, J., Jarvis, K.B., Markl, M.: 4D flow imaging with MRI. Cardiovasc. Diagn. Ther. 4(2), 173 (2014)

2. Zhu, J.-Y., Park, T., Isola, P., Efros, A.A.: Unpaired image-to-image translation using cycle-consistent adversarial networks. In: Proceedings of the IEEE International Conference on Computer Vision, pp. 2223–2232 (2017)

3. Wolterink, J.M., Dinkla, A.M., Savenije, M.H.F., Seevinck, P.R., van den Berg, C.A.T., Išgum, I.: Deep MR to CT synthesis using unpaired data. In: Tsaftaris, S.A., Gooya, A., Frangi, A.F., Prince, J.L. (eds.) SASHIMI 2017. LNCS, vol. 10557, pp. 14–23. Springer, Cham (2017). https://doi.org/10.1007/978-3-319-68127-6_2

4. Armanious, K., Jiang, C., Abdulatif, S., Küstner, T., Gatidis, S., Yang, B.: Unsupervised medical image translation using Cycle-MedGAN. In: 2019 27th European Signal Processing Conference (EUSIPCO), pp. 1–5 (2019)

5. Lei, Y., et al.: MRI-only based synthetic CT generation using dense cycle consistent generative adversarial networks. Med. Phys. 46(8), 3565–3581 (2019)

6. Schiffers, F., Yu, Z., Arguin, S., Maier, A., Ren, Q.: Synthetic fundus fluorescein angiography using deep neural networks. Bildverarbeitung für die Medizin 2018. I, pp. 234–238. Springer, Heidelberg (2018). https://doi.org/10.1007/978-3-662-56537-7_64

7. Wang, C., Macnaught, G., Papanastasiou, G., MacGillivray, T., Newby, D.: Unsupervised learning for cross-domain medical image synthesis using deformation invariant cycle consistency networks. In: Gooya, A., Goksel, O., Oguz, I., Burgos, N. (eds.) SASHIMI 2018. LNCS, vol. 11037, pp. 52–60. Springer, Cham (2018). https://doi.org/10.1007/978-3-030-00536-8_6

8. López-Linares Román, K., et al.: 3D pulmonary artery segmentation from CTA scans using deep learning with realistic data augmentation. In: Stoyanov, D., et al. (eds.) RAMBO/BIA/TIA - 2018. LNCS, vol. 11040, pp. 225–237. Springer, Cham (2018). https://doi.org/10.1007/978-3-030-00946-5_23

9. Nie, D., Cao, X., Gao, Y., Wang, L., Shen, D.: Estimating CT image from MRI data using 3D fully convolutional Networks. In: Carneiro, G., et al. (eds.) LABELS/DLMIA - 2016. LNCS, vol. 10008, pp. 170–178. Springer, Cham (2016). https://doi.org/10.1007/978-3-319-46976-8_18

10. Han, X.: MR-based synthetic CT generation using a deep convolutional neural network method. Med. Phys. 44(4), 1408–1419 (2017)

11. Goodfellow, I., et al.: Generative adversarial nets. In: Advances in Neural Information Processing Systems, pp. 2672–2680 (2014)

12. Nie, D., et al.: Medical image synthesis with context-aware generative adversarial networks. In: Descoteaux, M., Maier-Hein, L., Franz, A., Jannin, P., Collins, D.L., Duchesne, S. (eds.) MICCAI 2017. LNCS, vol. 10435, pp. 417–425. Springer, Cham (2017). https://doi.org/10.1007/978-3-319-66179-7_48

13. Nie, D., et al.: Medical image synthesis with deep convolutional adversarial networks. IEEE Trans. Biomed. Eng. 65(12), 2720–2730 (2018)

14. Emami, H., Dong, M., Nejad-Davarani, S.P., Glide-Hurst, C.K.: Generating synthetic CTs from magnetic resonance images using generative adversarial networks. Med. Phys. 45(8), 3627–3636 (2018)

Semi-supervised Virtual Regression of Aortic Dissections Using 3D Generative Inpainting

Antonio Pepe[1,2,3](✉)(iD), Gabriel Mistelbauer[2,4](iD), Christina Gsaxner[1,3,5](iD), Jianning Li[1,3](iD), Dominik Fleischmann[2](iD), Dieter Schmalstieg[1](iD), and Jan Egger[1,3,5](✉)(iD)

[1] Institute of Computer Graphics and Vision, Graz University of Technology, Graz, Austria
{antonio.pepe,egger}@tugraz.at
[2] School of Medicine, Department of Radiology, Stanford University, Stanford, CA, USA
apepe@stanford.edu
[3] Computer Algorithms in Medicine Laboratory, Graz, Austria
[4] Department of Simulation and Graphics, University of Magdeburg, Magdeburg, Germany
[5] Department of Oral and Maxillofacial Surgery, Medical University of Graz, Graz, Austria

Abstract. Aortic dissection (AD) is a condition of the main artery of the human body, resulting in the formation of a new flow channel, or false lumen (FL). The disease is usually diagnosed with a computed tomography angiography (CTA) scan during the acute phase. A better understanding of the causes of AD requires knowledge of aortic geometry prior to the event, which is available only in very rare circumstances. In this work, we propose an approach to reconstruct the aorta before the formation of a dissection by performing 3D inpainting with a two-stage generative adversarial network (GAN). In the first stage of our two-stage GAN, a network is trained on the 3D edge information of the healthy aorta to reconstruct the aortic wall. The second stage infers the image information of the aorta to reconstruct the entire dataset. We train our two-stage GAN with 3D patches from 55 non-dissected aortic datasets and evaluate it on 20 more non-dissected datasets, demonstrating that our proposed 3D architecture outperforms its 2D counterpart. To obtain pre-dissection aortae, we mask the entire FL in AD datasets. Finally, we provide qualitative feedback from a renown expert on the obtained pre-dissection cases.

Keywords: Inpainting · Aortic dissection · Deep learning · Edge reconstruction · Generative adversarial networks

© Springer Nature Switzerland AG 2020
J. Petersen et al. (Eds.): TIA 2020, LNCS 12502, pp. 130–140, 2020.
https://doi.org/10.1007/978-3-030-62469-9_12

1   Introduction

The aortic dissection (AD) is an uncommon, but life-threatening condition of the aorta (Fig. 1), caused by a diseased medial layer inside the aortic wall [9]. Characteristic is the sudden development of a so-called *primary entry tear*, a defect on the luminal side of the aorta [11]. This allows blood to enter the teared aortic wall, further dissect it, and form a new 'false' blood flow channel inside the aortic wall. As the dissected aortic wall is thinner and of lower mechanical strength, it may rupture, leading to a typically lethal event [19]. When the newly formed blood channel reconnects with the original 'true' blood flow channel of the aorta, two separate flow channels are generated, referred to as true lumen (TL) and false lumen (FL), as the interior of a blood vessel is called *lumen* [11].

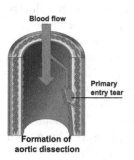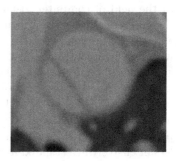

Fig. 1. Illustration of an AD. Left, in color: The formation of a FL with a primary entry tear. It is clearly visible that the FL grows within the medial layer of the dissected aortic wall, i.e. the central layer in yellow. In gray: actual CTA images of AD showing a rendered sagittal view (center) and a cropped axial view (right). (Color figure online)

Diagnosing ADs is typically done by acquiring CTA that provides detailed anatomic information of therapeutically relevant features, such as the anatomy of TL and FL [5]. A more in-depth discussion is provided in two recent reviews on the biomechanics of the aortic wall [22] and on the adopted techniques in medical imaging [19]. Once AD has been diagnosed, patients undergo life-long surveillance, comprising CTA scans after three months, six months and annually thereafter to monitor the progression of the aortic growth [7,15]. Investigating the onset of the disease remains rather unexplored, since acquiring data before the diagnosis of AD is highly unlikely [19]. Such data would only exist from an earlier examination that required a thorax CTA. Having such data would help simulate and understand the causes of ADs as well as visually convey the progression over time [15]. The aortic diameter is currently used for risk assessment, as this increases with the growth of the FL [15,19].

In this work, we address this shortage using image processing via generative adversarial networks (GANs) [6], which have found applications in different research areas, such as image artifact reduction [24]. By using a free-form

3D inpainting approach we are able to generate plausible pre-dissection CTA datasets. We consider the FL of an AD as an image 'artifact' to be masked for removal.

1.1   Background

A large body of recent research in image processing employs GAN, including free-form inpainting problems [17,26]. A GAN consists of two distinguished deep networks, a generator and a discriminator [6]. The two networks are trained in a zero-sum game, where the generator learns to generate realistic fake data, the discriminator, to distinguish it from real data.

Due to the availability of large databases like ImageNet [1], GAN inpainting has been widely and intensively tested on 2D images with rectangular masks. In the field of computer vision, Liu et al. [12] claim to be the first to address the problem of free-form inpainting with deep learning, using partial convolution and a U-Net as generator. Yu et al. [26] use GAN with gated convolution to deal with free-form masks. They also introduce the idea of adding manual sketches as guidelines to reinforce particular shapes in the inpainted images. Nazeri et al. [17] automate the creation of these guidelines using adversarial edge learning. They suggest a two-stage GAN with 2D inputs, which initially hallucinates the edges inside the masked area, successively it uses this information as a guideline and performs the actual inpainting task. Free-form inpainting approaches have been less intensively investigated in the medical imaging community. Mirsky et al. [14] qualitatively evaluated the effectiveness of CT inpainting using 3D GANs. The authors used a rectangular ROI to add or remove a tumor in thoracic CT images. In their evaluation, they show how the method can *fool* expert radiologists in different cases. Armanious et al. [2] evaluated the role of perceptual losses, as considered also by Nazeri et al. [17], in CT and MRI inpainting.

1.2   Contribution

Using a semi-supervised approach, we apply a free-form mask to exclude the region occupied by the FL and train a two-stage 3D GAN to first hallucinate the edges of the masked volume and then, secondly, perform an edge-guided inpainting. Our contributions are:

- a two-stage, semi-supervised 3D GAN network for the reconstruction of corrupted or missing content in CTA images,
- the virtual regression of AD via prediction of the pre-dissection aortic shape,
- the evaluation of the generated data by a clinical expert.

2   Data Acquisition and Preprocessing

Since before-AD/with-AD image pairs are unavailable, we use public datasets of healthy aortae for training. A total of 75 CTA datasets were acquired, 40 from the CAD-PE challenge (www.cad-pe.org) and 35 from Masoudi et al. [13]. Both data sources contain images of pulmonary embolism, which usually does not affect the original shape of the aorta. For a qualitative evaluation of the virtual AD regression, we use 52 non-public datasets with Type-B AD. Type-B indicates that the dissection only involves the descending aorta, after the arch [4].

To contain the computational cost, the datasets were manually cropped to a variable size of approximate $100 \times 100 \times D$ voxels, with the number of slices, D, depending on the length of the aorta. The extent of the smallest cropped volume is $100 \times 100 \times 133$, whereas the extent of the largest is $104 \times 104 \times 473$. All images contain the descending aorta and its immediate surroundings.

3   Method

Aortic dissection (AD) can extend along the whole aorta. For this reason, inpainting techniques can easily fail when considering single-view, 2D approches. Extending the idea from Nazeri et al. [17], we define a 3D inpainting method based on a two-stage GAN. Each stage consists of a 3D-GAN with spectral normalization [16]. Each layer is initialized using the Xavier method [23]. A scheme of the overall architecture is shown in Fig. 2. The network input is obtained from a 3D slab, $\mathbf{V}$, of size $I = 100 \times 100 \times 12$; this can be interpreted as a 3D sliding window, $\mathbf{V}$, which slides along the descending aorta. The sliding window with overlap allows the information to be transmitted to the following slabs.

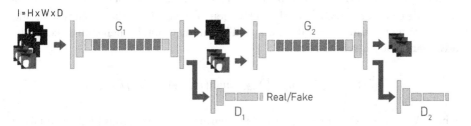

Fig. 2. Architecture of the two-stage 3D network. Each input volume has size I. In yellow, the convolution and deconvolution layers. In red, the residual blocks. The layers of the discriminators follow the Patch-GAN architecture [17]: each layer consists of a 3D convolution (Kernel size: 3, stride: 2, channels, in order: {64, 128, 256, 512, 1}), spectral normalization and LeakyRELU activation with threshold 0.2. For the generators, the encoding layers consist of 3d convolution (cubic kernel size, in order: {7, 4, 4}, stride: {1, 2, 2}, channels: {64, 128, 256}), spectral normalization, instance normalization and ReLU activations. The residual blocks are similar to the encoding layers with 256 channels and dilation factor 2. The decoding layers mirror the encoding layers. (Color figure online)

Given the 3D slab $\mathbf{V}$, its edges $\mathbf{C} = edge(\mathbf{V})$ and a mask $\mathbf{M}$; we define the following inputs and output for the first generator G_1:

$$\mathbf{C}_M = \mathbf{C} \odot (1 - \mathbf{M}), \tag{1}$$

$$\mathbf{V}_M = \mathbf{V} \odot (1 - \mathbf{M}), \tag{2}$$

$$\mathbf{C}_G = G_1(\mathbf{V}_M, \mathbf{C}_M, \mathbf{M}), \tag{3}$$

where $\odot$ is the Hadamard product; $\mathbf{C}_M$, the masked edge volume; $\mathbf{V}_M$, the masked original volume, and $\mathbf{C}_G$, the output of the first generator, which contains the reconstructed edges. We provide both the edge volume and the original volume as we empirically found that this reduces the training time. The output volume $\mathbf{C}_G$ is then used to evaluate the adversarial loss, $\mathcal{L}_{adv1}$, and the feature matching loss, $\mathcal{L}_{FM}$, used in the objective function. In particular, having defined with $\mathbb{E}$ the expectation operator,

$$\mathcal{L}_{adv1} = \mathbb{E}_{(\mathbf{C}, \mathbf{V})} \left[\log D_1(\mathbf{C}, \mathbf{V}) \right] + \mathbb{E}_{(\mathbf{V})} \log \left[1 - D_1(\mathbf{C}_G, \mathbf{V}) \right] \tag{4}$$

defines a metric of the average distance between the two distributions $(\mathbf{C}_G, \mathbf{V})$ and $(\mathbf{C}, \mathbf{V})$.

$$\mathcal{L}_{FM} = \mathbb{E} \left[\sum_{i=1}^{L} \frac{1}{N_i} \left\| D_1^{(i)}(\mathbf{C}) - D_1^{(i)}(\mathbf{C}_G) \right\|_1 \right] \tag{5}$$

defines a metric in the feature space; where L is the number of convolution layers in the discriminators, $D_1^{(i)}$ is the activation of layer i. Similar volumes should therefore have similar activation maps. This information is then combined in the adversarial objective function:

$$\min_{G_1} \max_{D_1} \mathcal{L}_{G_1} = \min_{G_1} \left[\lambda_{adv1} \max_{D_1} (\mathcal{L}_{adv1}) + \lambda_{FM} \mathcal{L}_{FM} \right], \tag{6}$$

where λ_{adv1} and λ_{FM} are regularization parameters. We extend this evaluation also to the second generator, G_2:

$$\mathbf{C}_I = \mathbf{C}_M + \mathbf{C}_G \odot \mathbf{M}, \tag{7}$$

$$\mathbf{V}_G = G_2(\mathbf{V}_M, \mathbf{C}_I), \tag{8}$$

$$\mathbf{V}_I = \mathbf{V}_M + \mathbf{V}_G \odot \mathbf{M}, \tag{9}$$

where $\mathbf{C}_I$ represents the inpainting of $\mathbf{C}_M$; $\mathbf{V}_G$, the output of the second generator, and $\mathbf{V}_I$, the final inpainting of $\mathbf{V}_M$.

Ad-hoc loss functions have been defined for 2D image outputs. These include the style loss and the perceptual loss [10], which provide a metric based on the activation maps of a pre-trained VGG-19 network. Practical experiments revealed that the distances in the feature space are not significantly affected by the dataset used to train the network. Nonetheless, VGG-19 is trained on 2D images; therefore we introduced an averaged perceptual loss and style loss,

$$\mathcal{L}_{perc,av} = \mathbb{E}\left[\sum_{i,j} \frac{1}{N_i} \|\phi_i(\mathbf{I}_j) - \phi_i(\mathbf{I}_{G_j})\|_1\right], \tag{10}$$

$$\mathcal{L}_{style,av} = \mathbb{E}_{k,j}\left[\|G_k^\phi(\mathbf{I}_j) - G_k^\phi(\mathbf{I}_{G_j})\|_1\right], \tag{11}$$

where we compute the loss values on a per-slice level j and average them over the volume. This considers the fact that medical experts evaluate the volume by analyzing single 2D axial views. Each ϕ_i is the activation map of the layer i in the VGG-19 network; G_k^ϕ is a Gram matrix derived from the activation map ϕ_k [10]. Thus, we define a composite objective function:

$$\min_{G_2}\max_{D_2}\mathcal{L}_{G_2} = \min_{G_2}\max_{D_2}\left[\lambda_{adv2}\mathcal{L}_{adv2} + \lambda_{l_1}\mathcal{L}_{l_1} + \lambda_p\mathcal{L}_{perc,av} + \lambda_s\mathcal{L}_{style,av}\right] \tag{12}$$

where λ_{adv2}, λ_{l_1}, λ_p, and λ_s are regularization parameters; $\mathcal{L}_{adv2}$ is the adversarial loss (Eq. 4), and $\mathcal{L}_{l_1}$ is the L1 loss.

Previously, 2D networks were trained with the masks provided by Liu et al. [12] or with rectangular masks [12,17]. In this work, we generate random 3D masks by filling each of the 12 slices with a mask from Liu et al., a random super-ellipse (SE), or a segmentation mask. During training, the masks and the patch volumes are selected randomly. During testing, the patch volumes are consecutively extracted with a sliding window, together with the relative masks, with a pace of four slices.

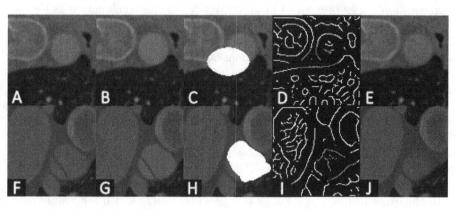

Fig. 3. Example of two inpainted slices. A) A healthy aorta, F) A dissected aorta, B) G) Segmentation of true lumen (green) and false lumen (red), C) H) masked image, D) I) hallucinated edges (green), E) J) inpainting result on the aorta and surroundings. (Color figure online)

Table 1. Quantitative results of the inpainting, compared to the previous 2D version [17]. Precision (Prec.) and Accuracy (Acc.) refer to the edge reconstruction.

Input	Mask	Prec	Acc	$\mathcal{L}_{l_1}$	$\mathcal{L}_{perc,av}$	$\mathcal{L}_{style,av}$	HDD	PSNR	MAE
2D	SE	32.26	28.64	0.349	0.048	0.065	0.610	30.465	0.017
2D	SE/FF	10.32	10.34	0.192	0.099	0.102	1.248	17.049	0.186
3D	**SE**	**58.89**	**55.44**	**0.261**	**0.045**	**0.020**	**0.082**	**45.898**	**0.003**
3D	**SE/FF**	**88.67**	**86.53**	**0.201**	**0.049**	**0.027**	**0.168**	**41.81**	**0.005**

4 Experiments and Results

To evaluate our approach, we train the network on cropped regions of interest (ROI) from 55 non-dissected aortae, which we augment through reflections, as the aorta can be situated on both sides of the spine. We evaluate its performance over a separate pool of 20 images of non-dissected aortae, to be able to quantify the results. Moreover, we test our approach with after-AD images and ask medical experts to evaluate the results.

The training was performed using PyTorch v1.2 on a desktop computer (CPU: Intel i7-8700, 64 GB RAM, GPU: NVIDIA Titan RTX 24 GB) and with a batch size of 16. The learning rate was set to 10^{-4}, λ_{adv1} and λ_{adv2} to 0.1, λ_{FM} to 10, λ_s to 250, λ_{l_1} to 1 and λ_p to 0.1.

Initially, we only train the first stage, where the volume edges are reconstructed. First, we train with stacks of random SE to provide the training with more degrees of freedom than the usual rectangles. We continue training by mixing the SE slices with the free-form masks from Liu et al. [12] and further segmentation masks of medical images. We refer to this combination as FF.

Table 1 summarizes the measured precision and accuracy for this stage. The 3D information enhances the performances considerably, especially, for FF. Probably due to size and shape variety of masks, the 3D approach outperformed the 2D approach. Convolution in 3D can use information from adjacent slices, resulting in a network capable of inpainting in larger planar areas.

We repeat the same experiments for the second stage. Here, precision and recall may not be reliable measures, as small differences are acceptable. Therefore, we evaluate the performance of the inpainting stage using the loss metrics, together with the peak signal-to-noise ratio (PSNR), the mean absolute error (MAE) and the Hausdorff distance (HDD).

The measures in Table 1 show a trend comparable with the first stage. In both the experiments, the 3D approach provides results which are visibly more accurate. Nonetheless, a detailed comparison between the two trends shows that there is still space for improvements in the second stage. Figure 3 provides a visual overview of the results.

From a qualitative point of view, we further saw that the edge reconstruction step guarantees more natural edges for the aorta reconstruction, compared to the second-stage network trained without the edge information. The images of

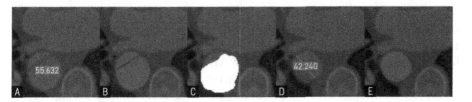

Fig. 4. Example of size change during AD regression. Values in millimeter. A) Original image. The aorta presents a higher diameter due to the presence of the FL, B) Segmentation of TL (green) and FL (red), C) Masked image, D) Reconstructed pre-dissection state. The diameter is now lower. E) Segmentation of the pre-dissection aorta. (Color figure online)

the resulting pre-dissection case were reviewed by a cardiovascular radiologist with more than 20 years of experience in the interpretation of CT angiograms of patients with aortic diseases. The expert was asked to evaluate if the virtual pre-dissection aorta reasonably resembled the expected appearance of non-diseased aorta. Specifically, the expert was asked to assess if the following key features of a dissection were suppressed in the virtual pre-dissection dataset: (a) Presence of a dissection flap, (b) difference in contrast enhancement between TL and FL, (c) shape of the outer contour of the aorta, and (d) introduced artifacts or unexpected findings.

(a) The dissection flap – the diagnostic hallmark of aortic dissection in CT imaging – was successfully eliminated in almost all images.
(b) The contrast opacification of the simulated pre-dissection aorta appeared homogeneous, with elimination of the typical attenuation difference between TL versus FL blood. There is a contrast heterogeneity without an abrupt transition caused by a dissection flap. The contrast heterogeneity exhibits commonly observed mixing artifacts.
(c) The shape of the virtual pre-dissection aorta was considered remarkably similar to the expected appearance of a normal aorta, with circular or slightly oval cross section on transverse CT images, with coronal and sagittal reformats. This is in contradiction to the typically more eccentric shape of a dissected aorta, where the outer wall of the FL stretches and dilates due to thinning and loss of elastic tissue.
(d) Even though, subjectively, the appearance of the virtual regression was remarkably similar to a non-dissected aorta, the interface between the inserted aorta and its surrounding, typically a few millimeters outside of the aortic contour, was noticeable (see Fig. 4). However, these artifacts did not distract from the evaluation of the important features of the aorta.

5   Conclusion

We have evaluated the potential of 3D image inpainting for visually regressing images of aortic dissection. In particular, we define a two-stage 3D-GAN for medical image inpainting and train it with patch volumes containing healthy aortae and free-form masks obtained with different approaches. We mask only the dissected traits of the aorta and use the GAN to reconstruct their original healthy state, before the development of AD. We obtain quantitative results by inpainting a separate image pool of healthy aortae, and compare them with a 2D approach. Moreover, we perform a qualitative evaluation of the inpainting operation on AD cases under the guidance of a senior radiologist specialized in cardiovascular diseases. To the best of our knowledge, this is a unique application of GAN and the first evaluation of AD regression leveraging the strengths of neural networks. The results show how the suggested 3D inpainting approach performs considerably better than the state-of-the-art 2D counterpart. Although expected, this underlines the necessity to process the aorta as a whole or, at least, as a union of overlapping segments. Furthermore, the network is trained with randomly located masks, and provides enough generalization to reconstruct also other objects near the aorta, such as the spine. The 2D version has been currently integrated in the online open-science platform www.studierfenster.at [25] and a video tutorial is available on YouTube[1] [21]. Future work sees the extension to the whole aorta as well as the segmentation of these pairs [20] and their use in biomechanical simulations [3]. Additionally, we will evaluate long-short term memory approaches to remove the need for an overlap between slabs [8].

Acknowledgement. This work received fundings from the TU Graz LEAD Project *Mechanics, Modeling and Simulation of Aortic Dissection* (https://www.tugraz.at/projekte/biomechaorta/*BioMechAorta*), the Austrian Science Fund (FWF) KLI 678-B31 *enFaced* and the COMET K-Project 871132 *CAMed* of the Austrian Research Promotion Agency (FFG). Antonio Pepe was also supported by an Austrian Marshall Plan Foundation Scholarship (Scholarship n. 942121022222019) [18]. Additionally, the authors would like to thank Professor Dr. Gerhard A. Holzapfel (Graz University of Technology) for his advice.

References

1. ImageNet. www.image-net.org. Accessed 10 July 2020 07:10:23
2. Armanious, K., Mecky, Y., Gatidis, S., Yang, B.: Adversarial inpainting of medical imaging modalities. In: Proceedings of International Conference on Acoustics, Speech and Signal Processing (2019). https://doi.org/10.1109/ICASSP.2019.8682677
3. Bäumler, K., Vedula, V., Sailer, A.M., et al.: Fluid-structure interaction simulations of patient-specific aortic dissection. Biomech. Model. Mechanobiol. (2020). https://doi.org/10.1007/s10237-020-01294-8
4. Daily, P.O., Trueblood, H.W., Stinson, E.B., et al.: Management of acute aortic dissections. Ann. Thoracic Surg. **10**(3), 237–247 (1970). https://doi.org/10.1016/S0003-4975(10)65594-4

---

[1] Deep Learning Inpainting of Aortic Dissections with Studierfenster: https://www.youtube.com/watch?v=c85qV-CDOX4.

5. Egger, J., Gunacker, S., Pepe, A., et al.: A comprehensive workflow and framework for immersive virtual endoscopy of dissected aortae from CTA data. In: SPIE Medical Imaging 1131531 (2020). https://doi.org/10.1117/12.2559239
6. Goodfellow, I., Pouget-Abadie, J., Mirza, M., et al.: Generative adversarial nets. In: Proceedings of Advances in Neural Information Processing Systems, vol. 27, pp. 2672–2680 (2014). https://doi.org/10.5555/2969033.2969125
7. Hahn, L.D., Mistelbauer, G., Higashigaito, K., et al.: Ct-based true- and false-lumen segmentation in type b aortic dissection using machine learning. Radiol. Cardiothor. Imaging **2**(3), 1–10 (2020)
8. Hochreiter, S., Schmidhuber, J.: Long short-term memory. Neural Comput. **9**(8), 1735–1780 (1997). https://doi.org/10.1162/neco.1997.9.8.1735
9. Howard, D.P., Banerjee, A., Fairhead, J.F., et al.: Population-based study of incidence and outcome of acute aortic dissection and premorbid risk factor control: 10-year results from the oxford vascular study. Circulation **127**(20), 2031–2037 (2013). https://doi.org/10.1161/circulationaha.112.000483
10. Johnson, J., Alahi, A., Fei-Fei, L.: Perceptual losses for real-time style transfer and super-resolution. In: Leibe, B., Matas, J., Sebe, N., Welling, M. (eds.) ECCV 2016. LNCS, vol. 9906, pp. 694–711. Springer, Cham (2016). https://doi.org/10.1007/978-3-319-46475-6_43
11. LeMaire, S.A., Russell, L.: Epidemiology of thoracic aortic dissection. Nat. Rev. Cardiol. Nat. Publ. Group **8**(2), 103–113 (2011). https://doi.org/10.1038/nrcardio.2010.187
12. Liu, G., Reda, F.A., Shih, K.J., Wang, T.-C., Tao, A., Catanzaro, B.: Image inpainting for irregular holes using partial convolutions. In: Ferrari, V., Hebert, M., Sminchisescu, C., Weiss, Y. (eds.) ECCV 2018. LNCS, vol. 11215, pp. 89–105. Springer, Cham (2018). https://doi.org/10.1007/978-3-030-01252-6_6
13. Masoudi, M., Pourreza, H.R., Saadatmand-Tarzjan, M., et al.: A new dataset of computed-tomography angiography images for computer-aided detection of pulmonary embolism. Sci. Data **5**, 180180 (2018). https://doi.org/10.1038/sdata.2018.180
14. Mirsky, Y., Mahler, T., Shelef, I., Elovici, Y.: CT-GAN: Malicious tampering of 3D medical imagery using deep learning. In: Proceedings of the 28th USENIX Security Symposium (2019). https://doi.org/10.5555/3361338.3361371
15. Mistelbauer, G., Schmidt, J., Sailer, A.M., et al.: Aortic dissection maps: comprehensive visualization of aortic dissections for risk assessment. In: Proceedings of Eurographics Workshop on Visual Computing for Biology and Medicine, pp. 143–152 (2016). https://doi.org/10.2312/vcbm.20161282
16. Miyato, T., Kataoka, T., Koyama, M., et al.: Spectral normalization for generative adversarial networks. In: Proceedings of International Conference on Learning Representations (2018)
17. Nazeri, K., Ng, E., Joseph, T., et al.: Edgeconnect: generative image inpainting with adversarial edge learning. In: Proceedings of International Conference on Computer Vision Workshops (2019)
18. Pepe, A., Fleischmann, D., Schmalstieg, D., Egger, J.: Visual computing of dissected aortae. In: Technical Report for the Austrian Marshall Plan Foundation, pp. 1–32 (2020, to appear)
19. Pepe, A., Li, J., Rolf-Pissarczyk, M., et al.: Detection, segmentation, simulation and visualization of aortic dissections: a review. Med. Image Anal. (2020). https://doi.org/10.1016/j.media.2020.101773

20. Pepe, A., Schussnig, R., Li, J., et al.: Iris: interactive real-time feedback image segmentation with deep learning. In: Medical Imaging 2020: Biomedical Applications in Molecular, Structural, and Functional Imaging, vol. 11317 (2020). https://doi.org/10.1117/12.2551354

21. Prutsch, A., Pepe, A., Egger, J.: Design and development of a web-based tool for inpainting of dissected aortae in angiography images. In: Proceedings of Central European Seminar on Computer Graphics, pp. 1–8 (2020)

22. Sherifova, S., Holzapfel, G.A.: Biomechanics of aortic wall failure with a focus on dissection and aneurysm: a review. Acta Biomaterialia **99**, 1–17 (2019). https://doi.org/10.1016/j.actbio.2019.08.017

23. Sun, W., Su, F., Wang, L.: Improving deep neural networks with multi-layer maxout networks and a novel initialization method. Neurocomputing **278**, 34–40 (2018). https://doi.org/10.1016/j.neucom.2017.05.103

24. Wang, J., Zhao, Y., Noble, J.H., Dawant, B.M.: Conditional generative adversarial networks for metal artifact reduction in CT Images of the Ear. In: Frangi, A.F., Schnabel, J.A., Davatzikos, C., Alberola-López, C., Fichtinger, G. (eds.) MICCAI 2018. LNCS, vol. 11070, pp. 3–11. Springer, Cham (2018). https://doi.org/10.1007/978-3-030-00928-1_1

25. Wild, D., Weber, M., Egger, J.: Client/server based online environment for manual segmentation of medical images. In: 41st Annual International Conference of the IEEE Engineering in Medicine and Biology Society (EMBC), pp. 3463–3467. IEEE (2019). https://doi.org/10.1109/EMBC.2019.8856481

26. Yu, J., Lin, Z., Yang, J., et al.: Free-form image inpainting with gated convolution. In: Proceedings of International Conference on Computer Vision (2019). https://doi.org/10.1109/ICCV.2019.00457

Image Registration

Registration-Invariant Biomechanical Features for Disease Staging of COPD in SPIROMICS

Muhammad F. A. Chaudhary[1](✉), Yue Pan[2], Di Wang[2], Sandeep Bodduluri[3],
Surya P. Bhatt[3], Alejandro P. Comellas[5], Eric A. Hoffman[1,4],
Gary E. Christensen[2,4], and Joseph M. Reinhardt[1,4](✉)

[1] Roy J. Carver Department of Biomedical Engineering, The University of Iowa,
Iowa City, IA 52242, USA
{faizyab-chaudhary,joe-reinhardt}@uiowa.edu

[2] Department of Electrical and Computer Engineering, The University of Iowa,
Iowa City, IA 52242, USA

[3] UAB Lung Imaging Core, University of Alabama at Birmingham, Birmingham, AL
35294, USA

[4] Department of Radiology, College of Medicine, The University of Iowa, Iowa City,
IA 52242, USA

[5] Division of Pulmonary, Critical Care, and Occupational Medicine, The University
of Iowa, Iowa City, IA 52242, USA

Abstract. Chronic Obstructive Pulmonary Disease (COPD) manifests
itself as a heterogeneous mixture of airways disease and parenchymal
tissue damage. Computed tomography (CT) imaging has been used to
detect, assess, and characterize COPD. One approach for using CT imaging to assess COPD relies on image registration to match inspiratory and
expiratory images to extract biomarkers reflective of local tissue biomechanics. Despite the initial success of such biomarkers, their diagnostic
performance and stability across registration methods is yet to be studied. In this study, we evaluated the ability of pulmonary biomechanical features to explain several clinical parameters across four state-of-
the-art image registration algorithms. We extracted features from three
registration-based measures of lung mechanics: the Jacobian determinant, the anisotropic deformation index, and the slab-rod index. Four
state-of-the-art registration methods were used to derive these measures and consequently four different biomechanical feature sets were
constructed. We analyzed and compared the stability of these features
for predicting airflow obstruction, COPD severity, and different spirometric measures. Biomechanical features were consistent across all four
registration methods and were independently able to explain most of
the variance in the spirometric measures. These variables predicted airflow obstruction and COPD stage with an average area under receiver
operating characteristic curve of 0.86 and 0.80, respectively.

Keywords: Image registration · Lung biomechanics · Machine
learning · COPD

© Springer Nature Switzerland AG 2020
J. Petersen et al. (Eds.): TIA 2020, LNCS 12502, pp. 143–154, 2020.
https://doi.org/10.1007/978-3-030-62469-9_13

1   Introduction

Chronic Obstructive Pulmonary Disease (COPD) is characterized by a heterogeneous distribution of abnormalities in both the airways and lung parenchyma. The spectrum includes chronic bronchitis, functional small airways disease (fSA D), and emphysema [9,15]. With few curative options, COPD is one of the leading causes of morbidity and mortality worldwide [16]. Currently, spirometry is used as the principal tool for diagnosing and staging COPD. Based on spirometry, the Global Initiative for Chronic Obstructive Lung Disease (GOLD) has devised a four-stage system to measure COPD severity [31]. However, spirometry alone fails to provide detailed information about the underlying pathogenesis.

Due to the need to gain better insights into genetic and epigenetic causes of COPD, major multi-center initiatives, such as the Genetic Epidemiology of COPD (COPDGene) [25] and the SubPopulations and Intermediate Outcome Measures in COPD Study (SPIROMICS) [11], are underway. Such studies have successfully led to the development of CT-based markers of COPD progression [5,6,15]. One class of approaches relies on image registration to align an expiratory image with an inspiratory image, thus providing insight into lung function. For example, Galbán et al. [15] used registered inspiratory-expiratory image pairs to define the parametric response mapping (PRM) for quantifying emphysema and fSAD. Bodduluri et al. [6] extracted biomechanical indices from registered inspiratory-expiratory images and demonstrated the effectiveness of these features for predicting airflow obstruction (AFO), COPD GOLD stage and lung function measures, such as forced expiratory volume in one second (FEV_1). In another study, Bodduluri et al. [5] showed the mean Jacobian of the image registration transformation from the expiratory image to inspiratory image (a measure of local volume change) to be significantly associated with COPD-related clinical measures such as FEV_1, emphysema, six-minute walk distance, and exercise capacity (BODE) index.

The success of registration-based methods, however, can be influenced by the choice of the underlying registration method. Recently, a study [22,23] examined the impact of registration algorithm on three lung biomechanical parameters: the Jacobian determinant (J), the anisotropic deformation index (ADI), and the slab-rod index (SRI) [2]. Ideally, biomarkers used for clinical assessment should be robust to registration algorithm. In this study, we analyzed the robustness of biomechanical features extracted from J, ADI, and SRI to the underlying registration algorithm. Following [22,23], we computed these measures using four different state-of-the-art registration methods, namely, the sum-of-squared-tissue-volume-difference (SSTVD) [8], the geodesic density regression (GDR), the greedy symmetric normalization (GSyN) [29] and the pulmonary vessel and lobe surface varifold (PVSV) [10]. We extracted feature sets using each of these registration algorithms and compared their performance for predicting clinical measures of COPD. Further, the measures from each algorithm were also compared with density-based features popular for characterizing COPD.

2   Methods

This section describes the image processing and analysis pipeline developed to assess and compare the performance of biomechanical markers from four different registration algorithms.

2.1   Notation

We denote images as I and different feature sets used for analysis as curved capitals B. A subscript is used to identify the underlying image used for constructing the feature set. For instance, B_{SSTVD} denotes the set of biomechanical features generated using SSTVD as the registration method.

2.2   Image Datasets

We conducted this analysis using 250 subjects randomly selected from the larger SPIROMICS cohort [11]. SPIROMICS is an on-going cohort study aimed at identifying biomarkers that could identify novel, clinically relevant sub-types of COPD [11]. In this study, nearly 3000 subjects were scanned using CT and staged longitudinally at different follow-up visits. Following the GOLD criteria [31], spirometry was used to stage subjects into one of four categories of COPD severity ranging from GOLD 1 (mild) through GOLD 4 (severe). In this work, we use GOLD 0 to represent asymptomatic smokers. CT images were acquired for all subjects at total lung capacity (TLC) and residual volume (RV).

To develop a model for predicting AFO and GOLD stage, the baseline scans from 250 subjects with a varying degree of disease severity were used. Images for these subjects were acquired at 12 different clinical sites and were randomly sampled from each GOLD Stage. Initially, there were 50 subjects from each group, but 12 cases had at least one failed registration, leaving 238 subjects for analysis – 48 subjects from GOLD 0, 49 subjects from GOLD 1, 46 subjects from GOLD 2, 48 subjects from GOLD 3, and 47 subjects from GOLD 4. Multivariable regression models were used to investigate the associations between the biomechanical measures and clinical parameters such as FEV_1, forced vital capacity (FVC), forced expiratory flow between 25% and 75% of FVC ($FEF_{25-75\%}$) and FEV_1/FVC. Four subjects had missing values for $FEF_{25-75\%}$, so these subjects were excluded from models with $FEF_{25-75\%}$ as an outcome variable.

As a preprocessing step, the TLC and RV scans were resampled isotropically to a resolution of 1mm $\times$ 1mm $\times$ 1mm. The entire lung regions were segmented using a multi-resolution convolutional neural network [17].

2.3   Image Registration Algorithms

Four state-of-the-art image registration methods were used to align the TLC (moving) and RV (target) scans [22,23]. These methods are SSTVD [8], GDR [28], GSyN [29], and PVSV [10,13,24]. Full details on the image registration process and algorithm parameters are given in [22,23].

The SSTVD approach assumes the tissue density is constant from TLC to RV [8]. The cost function of SSTVD algorithm consists of the SSTVD metric, sum of squared vesselness measure difference (SSVMD), and a Laplacian regularization term [8]. The displacement field is parametrized by cubic BSpline.

The GDR algorithm, which is short for geodesic density regression, was originally designed for matching 4DCT [28]. In addition to the SSTVD metric, the images are aligned using the large deformation model (LDDMM) [3].

The GSyN, or greedy symmetric normalization [29], method estimates two transformations: one from the fixed image domain and the other from the moving image domain to the mid point of the two, respectively. The final transformation from moving image to fixed image is computed by composing the two. The transformation model of GSyN is also LDDMM, and the similarity metric is normalized cross correlation.

The PVSV, or pulmonary blood vessel and lobe surface varifold, algorithm registers the shapes, including pulmonary vessel trees and lung surfaces, using a varifolds representation [10]. This method does not use any intensity information for matching the shapes [24], and employs a sparse representation of the LDDMM [13].

Using the four registration methods, we independently computed three lung deformation indices – J, SRI, and ADI. Jacobian determinant J is a measure of local lung expansion and contraction; ADI quantifies the amount of deformation of each voxel and is complemented by SRI, which explains the nature of deformation of each voxel [2]. These measures provide three-dimensional insights into lung tissue mechanics and their statistics were evaluated over different registration methods.

2.4   Feature Extraction

A total of eight different feature sets were computed for this study: four biomechanical feature sets (one from each of the image registration algorithms SSTVD, GDR, GSyN, and PVSV), texture feature sets from each of the TLC and RV images, a densitometric feature set computed from the TLC and RV images, and a PRM feature set computed from the registered TLC and RV images.

Biomechanical Feature Sets: Each registration algorithm was used to register the TLC to RV scans. After registration, the J, ADI, and SRI were computed from the registration deformation field. To extract biomechanical features spanning multiple scales and sizes, we processed each of the J, ADI, and SRI images using a filter bank containing Laplacian of Gaussian (LoG) filters and wavelet filters (see Fig. 1). Each biomechanical parameter image was filtered using four LoG filters with standard deviations 3.0 mm, 3.5 mm, 4.0 mm, 4.5 mm, producing four intermediate output images. Similarly, base level wavelet decomposition was used to produce eight intermediate output images at multiple resolutions. Coiflets [4] were used as the basis for wavelet decomposition. These $4 + 8 = 12$ intermediate filtered images were combined with the original biomechanical parameter image, and these 13 images are summarized by computing

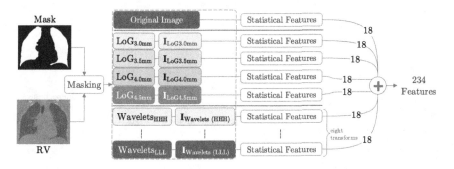

Fig. 1. Feature extraction pipeline used to extract multi-resolution statistical features from an example RV scan (it could be TLC, J, ADI, or SRI). The input image is transformed by a small bank of 12 filters – four LoG and eight Wavelets. Each filter produces a transformed image denoted as $\mathbf{I}_{filter}$. On top, an identity filter is present to indicate feature extraction from the original image. A total of 18 statistical features are extracted from the original and 12 filtered images, to form a set of 234 features ($18 + 12 \times 18 = 234$).

18 statistical features over the lung region in each image. The 18 statistical features used are the mean, median, 10th percentile, 90th percentile, maximum, minimum, energy, total energy, entropy, kurtosis, skewness, range, interquartile range, variance, root mean squared, mean absolute deviation, robust mean absolute deviation, and uniformity. As illustrated in Fig. 2, the result of this process produces $13 \times 18 = 234$ features for each biomechanical parameter image, resulting in a total of 702 features. This process was repeated for each registration algorithm producing four separate sets of 702 biomechanical features denoted $\mathcal{B}_{SSTVD}$, $\mathcal{B}_{GDR}$, $\mathcal{B}_{GSyN}$, and $\mathcal{B}_{PVSV}$. We used PyRadiomics [30], an open source python package, for feature extraction.

TLC and RV Texture Feature Sets: CT texture features are extracted from the TLC and RV scans using the same multi-scale strategy as that employed for the biomechanical parameter images. Each TLC and RV image is filtered using four LoG filters with standard deviations 3.0 mm, 3.5 mm, 4.0 mm, 4.5 mm, producing four intermediate output images. Similarly, wavelet decomposition is used to produce eight intermediate output images. These 12 intermediate filtered images are combined with the original TLC or RV image, and these 13 images are summarized using the same 18 statistical features used to create the biomechanical feature sets. Thus, each CT texture feature sets contains $13 \times 18 = 234$ features, and there is one feature set for each of the TLC and RV images. We denote these feature sets as $\mathcal{T}_{TLC}$ and $\mathcal{T}_{RV}$.

Densitometry Features: The densitometry feature set was computed by thresholding the TLC and RV scans. Percent emphysema was defined as the number of lung voxels with CT attenuation below -950 Hounsfield units (HU)

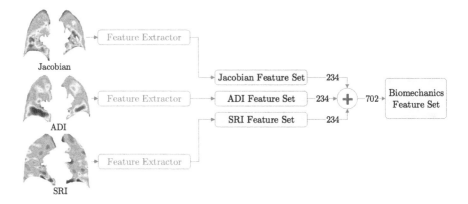

Fig. 2. Biomechanical feature set development. For each registration method, J, SRI, and ADI were used to extract 234 features. These smaller feature sets were then combined to construct the large biomechanical signature set. The feature extractor box highlighted in Fig. 1.

divided by the total number of lung voxels in the TLC scan [20]. Similarly, air-trapping was quantified as the fraction of lung voxels in RV scan having CT attenuation below -856 HU [7,21]. These two features together form the densitometry feature set $\mathcal{S}_{\text{Density}}$.

PRM Features: Parametric response mapping was proposed as a CT biomarker to quantify the extent of emphysema and fSAD – two components of COPD [15]. To compare the performance of biomechanical features with PRM, we compute two PRM features, the percent fSAD and the percent emphysema. These two features comprise the PRM feature set $\mathcal{S}_{\text{PRM}}$. In this work, the PRM was computed using the SSTVD algorithm for image registration.

2.5 Problem-Specific Feature Selection

We devised two feature selection pipelines optimized independently for classification (AFO and GOLD stage prediction) and regression (FEV$_1$, FVC, FEV$_1$/ FVC, and FEF$_{25-75\%}$ prediction) tasks.

Classification: The subjects with AFO were defined to have FEV$_1$/ FVC less than 0.7 [14]. For classification tasks, we selected the optimal features in two steps. First, the Mann Whitney U test [26] was used as a univariate filter to select significant features for predicting AFO. Similarly, for GOLD stage classification, we used the Kruskal Wallis H test [32] to eliminate insignificant features. To avoid the multiple comparisons problem, we performed Bonferroni correction [1] to both of these tests with a type-I error rate of 0.05. After adjusting the p-values, an even more conservative threshold ($p < 0.001$) was used to filter insignificant features. Next, we used random forest [18] classifier to recursively eliminate irrelevant features from the model. Using recursive feature elimination (RFE), we selected a smaller, more optimal feature set.

Multivariable Regression: We developed multivariable models for explaining four clinical outcomes, FEV_1, FVC, $FEV_1/$ FVC, and $FEF_{25-75\%}$. To minimize multicollinearity, Pearson's correlation was first used to remove redundant features from the model at a threshold of 0.85. Next, we used Akaike's Information Criterion (AIC) [27] to select an optimal variable set. This was done using a bi-directional, stepwise regression [33] method that minimizes AIC to arrive at a smaller number of relevant features. Lastly, we used variance inflation factor (VIF) [12] to eliminate remaining multicollinearity, wherein, the features with VIF >10 were excluded from the final model.

2.6 Statistical Learning Experiments

The selected feature subsets were then used for classification and regression experiments. For AFO and GOLD stage classification, random forest classifier with 50 estimators was used. The dataset was randomly divided into train and test sets, where bootstrapping with a large number of repeats ($n = 1000$) was used to evaluate the model. We used area under the receiver operating characteristic curve (AUC) to quantify the performance of our model. AUCs computed at each bootstrap were averaged to report the final performance of our model. We used a one-vs-rest approach for GOLD stage classification.

After feature subset selection, multiple regression was used to assess the amount of variance explained by each feature set. We evaluated the performance of our features by using the penalized adjusted r-squared values (adjusted r^2) [19]. In our experiments, we also investigated the collective performance of different feature set combinations, to ultimately identify some synergistically optimal feature set unions.

Table 1. SSTVD Results. Adjusted r^2 values (top 4 rows) and AUCs (last 2 rows) for $\mathcal{B}_{SSTVD}$ vs. $\mathcal{S}_{Density}$, $\mathcal{S}_{PRM}$, $\mathcal{T}_{RV}$, and $\mathcal{T}_{TLC}$. The columns $\{\mathcal{T}_{RV}, \mathcal{B}_{SSTVD}\}$ and $\{\mathcal{T}_{TLC}, \mathcal{B}_{SSTVD}\}$ indicate the performance of specified feature sets combined.

Response	$\mathcal{B}_{SSTVD}$	$\mathcal{S}_{Density}$	$\mathcal{T}_{RV}$	$\mathcal{T}_{TLC}$	$\mathcal{S}_{PRM}$	$\{\mathcal{T}_{RV}, \mathcal{B}_{SSTVD}\}$	$\{\mathcal{T}_{TLC}, \mathcal{B}_{SSTVD}\}$	All
FEV_1	0.74	0.67	0.72	0.61	0.67	0.85	0.83	0.88
$FEV_1/$ FVC	0.71	0.70	0.76	0.69	0.70	0.82	0.81	0.85
FVC	0.64	0.34	0.43	0.38	0.33	0.68	0.69	0.70
$FEF_{25-75\%}$	0.48	0.47	0.59	0.47	0.47	0.64	0.58	0.66
AFO	0.84	0.88	0.89	0.88	0.89	0.90	0.89	0.90
GOLD Stage	0.79	0.78	0.80	0.77	0.78	0.83	0.83	0.84

3   Results

3.1   Classifying AFO and GOLD Stage

The optimal features obtained after feature selection were used to predict AFO and GOLD stage. RFE empirically identified a subset of 50 features for both tasks and the results from classification experiment conducted over 1000 bootstraps are reported in Tables 1, 2, 3 and 4. Each table shows results from one registration method, compared with texture, density, and PRM feature sets. The final column of each table reports the performance with all feature sets combined. The biomechanical set $\mathcal{B}_{\mathrm{SSTVD}}$ predicted AFO and GOLD Stage with AUCs of 0.84 and 0.79, respectively (Table 1). Similarly, the set $\mathcal{B}_{\mathrm{GDR}}$ achieved a higher AUC of 0.86 (AFO) and 0.82 (GOLD stage) for both the tasks (Table 2). A small increase was further observed when we moved to the biomechanics set $\mathcal{B}_{\mathrm{GSyN}}$, where AUC for AFO was 0.87. In this case, the AUC for GOLD stage prediction was comparable to GDR, 0.81. (Table 3). PVSV predicted AFO and GOLD stage with almost similar AUCs of 0.87 and 0.79 (Table 4).

Table 2. GDR Results. Adjusted r^2 values (top 4 rows) and AUCs (last 2 rows) for $\mathcal{B}_{\mathrm{GDR}}$ vs. $\mathcal{S}_{\mathrm{Density}}$, $\mathcal{S}_{\mathrm{PRM}}$, $\mathcal{T}_{\mathrm{RV}}$, and $\mathcal{T}_{\mathrm{TLC}}$. The columns $\{\mathcal{T}_{\mathrm{RV}}, \mathcal{B}_{\mathrm{GDR}}\}$ and $\{\mathcal{T}_{\mathrm{TLC}}, \mathcal{B}_{\mathrm{GDR}}\}$ indicate the performance of specified feature sets combined.

Response	$\mathcal{B}_{\mathrm{GDR}}$	$\mathcal{S}_{\mathrm{Density}}$	$\mathcal{T}_{\mathrm{RV}}$	$\mathcal{T}_{\mathrm{TLC}}$	$\mathcal{S}_{\mathrm{PRM}}$	$\{\mathcal{T}_{\mathrm{RV}}, \mathcal{B}_{\mathrm{GDR}}\}$	$\{\mathcal{T}_{\mathrm{TLC}}, \mathcal{B}_{\mathrm{GDR}}\}$	All
FEV_1	0.72	0.67	0.72	0.61	0.67	0.81	0.80	0.84
$FEV_1/$ FVC	0.65	0.70	0.76	0.69	0.70	0.79	0.78	0.82
FVC	0.58	0.34	0.43	0.38	0.33	0.60	0.61	0.64
$FEF_{25-75\%}$	0.52	0.47	0.59	0.47	0.47	0.64	0.64	0.70
AFO	0.86	0.88	0.89	0.88	0.89	0.90	0.90	0.89
GOLD Stage	0.82	0.78	0.80	0.77	0.78	0.85	0.85	0.85

Table 3. GSyN Results. Adjusted r^2 values (top 4 rows) and AUCs (last 2 rows) for $\mathcal{B}_{\mathrm{GSyN}}$ vs. $\mathcal{S}_{\mathrm{Density}}$, $\mathcal{S}_{\mathrm{PRM}}$, $\mathcal{T}_{\mathrm{RV}}$, and $\mathcal{T}_{\mathrm{TLC}}$. The columns $\{\mathcal{T}_{\mathrm{RV}}, \mathcal{B}_{\mathrm{GSyN}}\}$ and $\{\mathcal{T}_{\mathrm{TLC}}, \mathcal{B}_{\mathrm{GSyN}}\}$ indicate the performance of specified feature sets combined.

Response	$\mathcal{B}_{\mathrm{GSyN}}$	$\mathcal{S}_{\mathrm{Density}}$	$\mathcal{T}_{\mathrm{RV}}$	$\mathcal{T}_{\mathrm{TLC}}$	$\mathcal{S}_{\mathrm{PRM}}$	$\{\mathcal{T}_{\mathrm{RV}}, \mathcal{B}_{\mathrm{GSyN}}\}$	$\{\mathcal{T}_{\mathrm{TLC}}, \mathcal{B}_{\mathrm{GSyN}}\}$	All
FEV_1	0.73	0.67	0.72	0.61	0.67	0.79	0.79	0.84
$FEV_1/$ FVC	0.63	0.70	0.76	0.69	0.70	0.80	0.78	0.82
FVC	0.55	0.34	0.43	0.38	0.33	0.58	0.59	0.64
$FEF_{25-75\%}$	0.55	0.47	0.59	0.47	0.47	0.67	0.65	0.70
AFO	0.87	0.88	0.89	0.88	0.89	0.90	0.90	0.91
GOLD Stage	0.81	0.78	0.80	0.77	0.78	0.83	0.84	0.84

3.2   Predicting FEV_1, FVC, FEV_1/FVC and $FEF_{25-75\%}$

Biomechanical feature sets, were evaluated in terms of their ability to explain the variance in four clinical variables associated with lung function – FEV_1, FVC, FEV_1/FVC, and $FEF_{25-75\%}$. We used adjusted r^2 instead of multiple r^2 values. This ensured robustness to an increase in number of model parameters. For SSTVD, the variable selection process yielded an average of 45 independent features after final stage of feature reduction – VIF-based filtering. Similarly, the mean number of selected features for GDR, GSyN, PVSV, RV, and TLC were, 24, 38, 20, 16, and 15, respectively. Using these feature subsets, multivariable regression models were developed (adjusted r^2 values reported in Tables 1, 2, 3 and 4).

4   Discussion

We investigated the predictive stability of biomechanical features extracted from three measures of lung deformation (J, ADI, and SRI). These indices were computed using four state-of-the-art lung registration methods. All four methods employed different schemes for matching the TLC and RV scans, which allowed us to fairly evaluate the performance of these features across different registration algorithms. Feature sets from all methods performed consistently well for classification as well as regression tasks. For instance, the feature sets $\mathcal{B}_{SSTVD}$, $\mathcal{B}_{GDR}$, $\mathcal{B}_{GSyN}$, $\mathcal{B}_{PVSV}$ were each independently able to explain much of the variance in FEV_1, FVC, FEV_1/FVC, and $FEF_{25-75\%}$ (column 1 of Tables 1, 2, 3 and 4). This helped us arrive at registration-invariant features, that were robustly able to explain various measures of lung function.

Furthermore, we analyzed the performance of biomechanical features across a number of spirometric measures. For instance, we incorporated the less-explored measures like FVC and $FEF_{25-75\%}$ in our analysis, which helped us assess the stability of biomechanics across a variety of clinical parameters. The feature sets performed well across all of these measures. This enabled us to highlight the two-way stability of biomechanical features – across registration methods and across different clinical parameters. All biomechanical feature sets performed well when compared to density, RV, TLC, and PRM-based features. The r^2-values were a slightly higher for density, PRM, and TLC in case of FEV_1 and FEV_1/FVC. But when extended to FVC and $FEF_{25-75\%}$, the biomechanical features were stable, whereas the performance of density, TLC, and PRM features dropped. RV feature set also performed consistently well with all registration methods.

A similar trend can be observed for predicting AFO and GOLD stage (see Tables 1, 2, 3 and 4), where all biomechanical features performed well across different registration methods. When compared to other feature sets, the AUCs of biomechanical sets were comparable to density, texture, and PRM sets for AFO prediction. However, in case of GOLD stage, the biomechanical measures were better able to classify SPIROMICS subjects into different GOLD stages, as compared to density, texture, or PRM markers.

We also investigated the performance of various feature set combinations. It was observed that the combination of texture with biomechanics performed the best for all clinical parameters including AFO and GOLD stage. All feature sets together were also used for analysis and their performance was almost similar to texture-mechanics combinations. A similar trend was observed by Bodduluri et al. [6] in their analysis on the COPDGene cohort, where they demonstrated the texture, biomechanics, and density features to perform the best when combined.

Table 4. PVSV Results. Adjusted r^2 values (top 4 rows) and AUCs (last 2 rows) for $\mathcal{B}_{\text{PVSV}}$ vs. $\mathcal{S}_{\text{Density}}$, $\mathcal{S}_{\text{PRM}}$, $\mathcal{T}_{\text{RV}}$, and $\mathcal{T}_{\text{TLC}}$. The columns $\{\mathcal{T}_{\text{RV}}, \mathcal{B}_{\text{PVSV}}\}$ and $\{\mathcal{T}_{\text{TLC}}, \mathcal{B}_{\text{PVSV}}\}$ indicate the performance of specified feature sets combined.

Response	$\mathcal{B}_{\text{PVSV}}$	$\mathcal{S}_{\text{Density}}$	$\mathcal{T}_{\text{RV}}$	$\mathcal{T}_{\text{TLC}}$	$\mathcal{S}_{\text{PRM}}$	$\{\mathcal{T}_{\text{RV}}, \mathcal{B}_{\text{PVSV}}\}$	$\{\mathcal{T}_{\text{TLC}}, \mathcal{B}_{\text{PVSV}}\}$	All
FEV$_1$	0.68	0.67	0.72	0.61	0.67	0.79	0.77	0.82
FEV$_1$/ FVC	0.61	0.70	0.76	0.69	0.70	0.78	0.77	0.82
FVC	0.54	0.34	0.43	0.38	0.33	0.56	0.55	0.60
FEF$_{25-75\%}$	0.56	0.47	0.59	0.47	0.47	0.66	0.65	0.71
AFO	0.87	0.88	0.89	0.88	0.89	0.90	0.91	0.90
GOLD Stage	0.79	0.78	0.80	0.77	0.78	0.83	0.83	0.83

5   Conclusion

Biomechanical features derived from J, SRI, and ADI are strongly associated with clinical measures of lung function in COPD. Biomechanical features computed using four different registration methods produced similar results. A combination of biomechanical features and CT texture measures produced the overall best performing models for predicting clinical measures of lung function.

Acknowledgements. This work was supported in part by grant HL142625 from the National Heart, Lung, and Blood Institute (NHLBI) at the National Institutes of Health (NIH) and by a grant from the Roy J. Carver Charitable Trust. SPIROMICS was supported by contracts from the NIH/ NHLBI (HHSN268200900013C, HHSN268200900014C, HHSN268200900015C, HHSN268 200900016C, HHSN268200900017C, HHSN268200900018C, HHSN268200900019 C, HHSN268200900020C), grants from the NIH/NHLBI (U01 HL137880 and U24 HL141762), and supplemented by contributions made through the Foundation for the NIH and the COPD Foundation from AstraZeneca/MedImmune; Bayer; Bellerophon Therapeutics; Boehringer-Ingelheim Pharmaceuticals, Inc.; Chiesi Farmaceutici S.p.A.; Forest Research Institute, Inc.; GlaxoSmithKline; Grifols Therapeutics, Inc.; Ikaria, Inc.; Novartis Pharmaceuticals Corporation; Nycomed GmbH; ProterixBio; Regeneron Pharmaceuticals, Inc.; Sanofi; Sunovio n; Takeda Pharmaceutical Company; and Theravance Biopharma and Mylan.

References

1. Abdi, H.: Bonferroni and Sidák corrections for multiple comparisons. Encyclopedia Measur. Stat. **3**, 103–107 (2007)
2. Amelon, R., Cao, K., Ding, K., Christensen, G.E., Reinhardt, J.M., Raghavan, M.L.: Three-dimensional characterization of regional lung deformation. J. Biomech. **44**(13), 2489–2495 (2011)
3. Beg, M.F., Miller, M.I., Trouvé, A., Younes, L.: Computing large deformation metric mappings via geodesic flows of diffeomorphisms. Int. J. Comput. Vision **61**(2), 139–157 (2005)
4. Beylkin, G., Coifman, R., Rokhlin, V.: Fast wavelet transforms and numerical algorithms I. Commun. Pure Appl. Math. **44**(2), 141–183 (1991)
5. Bodduluri, S., et al.: Biomechanical CT metrics are associated with patient outcomes in COPD. Thorax **72**(5), 409–414 (2017)
6. Bodduluri, S., Newell Jr., J.D., Hoffman, E.A., Reinhardt, J.M.: Registration-based lung mechanical analysis of chronic obstructive pulmonary disease (COPD) using a supervised machine learning framework. Acad. Radiol. **20**(5), 527–536 (2013)
7. Busacker, A., et al.: A multivariate analysis of risk factors for the air-trapping asthmatic phenotype as measured by quantitative CT analysis. Chest **135**(1), 48–56 (2009)
8. Cao, K., Du, K., Ding, K., Reinhardt, J.M., Christensen, G.E.: Regularized non-rigid registration of lung CT images by preserving tissue volume and vesselness measure. Grand Challenges in Medical Image Analysis, pp. 43–54 (2010)
9. Celli, B.R., Wedzicha, J.A.: Update on clinical aspects of chronic obstructive pulmonary disease. N. Engl. J. Med. **381**(13), 1257–1266 (2019)
10. Charon, N., Trouvé, A.: The varifold representation of nonoriented shapes for diffeomorphic registration. SIAM J. Imaging Sci. **6**(4), 2547–2580 (2013)
11. Couper, D., et al.: Design of the subpopulations and intermediate outcomes in COPD study (SPIROMICS). Thorax **69**(5), 492–495 (2014)
12. Craney, T.A., Surles, J.G.: Model-dependent variance inflation factor cutoff values. Qual. Eng. **14**(3), 391–403 (2002)
13. Durrleman, S., et al.: Morphometry of anatomical shape complexes with dense deformations and sparse parameters. NeuroImage **101**, 35–49 (2014)
14. Fortis, S., Eberlein, M., Georgopoulos, D., Comellas, A.P.: Predictive value of prebronchodilator and postbronchodilator spirometry for COPD features and outcomes. BMJ Open Respiratory Res. **4**(1) (2017)
15. Galbán, C.J., et al.: Computed tomography-based biomarker provides unique signature for diagnosis of COPD phenotypes and disease progression. Nat. Med. **18**(11), 1711 (2012)
16. GBD 2015 Chronic Respiratory Disease Collaborators: Global, regional, and national deaths, prevalence, disability-adjusted life years, and years lived with disability for chronic obstructive pulmonary disease and asthma, 1990–2015: a systematic analysis for the global burden of disease study 2015. The Lancet Respiratory Medicine **5**(9), 691 (2017)
17. Gerard, S.E., Herrmann, J., Kaczka, D.W., Musch, G., Fernandez-Bustamante, A., Reinhardt, J.M.: Multi-resolution convolutional neural networks for fully automated segmentation of acutely injured lungs in multiple species. Med. Image Anal. **60**, 101592 (2020)
18. Liaw, A., Wiener, M., et al.: Classification and regression by random forest. R News **2**(3), 18–22 (2002)

19. Miles, J.: R-squared, adjusted R-squared. Wiley Statistics Reference Online (2014)
20. Müller, N.L., Staples, C.A., Miller, R.R., Abboud, R.T.: "Density mask": an objective method to quantitate emphysema using computed tomography. Chest **94**(4), 782–787 (1988)
21. Newman, K.B., Lynch, D.A., Newman, L.S., Ellegood, D., Newell Jr., J.D.: Quantitative computed tomography detects air trapping due to asthma. Chest **106**(1), 105–109 (1994)
22. Pan, Y., et al.: Image-registration measures of lung biomechanics in SPIROMICS: Robustness across four methods (in review)
23. Pan, Y., et al.: Assessment of lung biomechanics in COPD using image registration. In: 2020 IEEE 17th International Symposium on Biomedical Imaging (ISBI), pp. 1891–1895. IEEE (2020)
24. Pan, Y., et al.: Pulmonary blood vessel and lobe surface varifold (PVSV) registration. In: 2020 IEEE 17th ISBI. IEEE (2020)
25. Regan, E.A., et al.: Genetic epidemiology of COPD (COPDGene) study design. COPD: J. Chronic Obstructive Pulm. Dis. **7**(1), 32–43 (2011)
26. Ruxton, G.D.: The unequal variance t-test is an underused alternative to Student's t-test and the Mann-Whitney U test. Behav. Ecol. **17**(4), 688–690 (2006)
27. Sakamoto, Y., Ishiguro, M., Kitagawa, G.: Akaike information criterion statistics. Dordrecht, The Netherlands: D. Reidel 81 (1986)
28. Shao, W.: Improving functional avoidance radiation therapy by image registration. Ph.D. thesis, Department of Electrical and Computer Engineering, The University of Iowa, Iowa City, IA 52242 (Aug 2019)
29. Song, G., Tustison, N., Avants, B., Gee, J.C.: Lung CT image registration using diffeomorphic transformation models. Medical Image Anal. Clinic: Grand Challenge 23–32 (2010)
30. Van Griethuysen, J.J., et al.: Computational radiomics system to decode the radiographic phenotype. Cancer Res. **77**(21), e104–e107 (2017)
31. Vestbo, J., et al.: Global strategy for the diagnosis, management, and prevention of chronic obstructive pulmonary disease: GOLD executive summary. Am. J. Respir. Crit. Care Med. **187**(4), 347–365 (2013)
32. Wallace, D.L.: Simplified beta-approximations to the Kruskal-Wallis H test. J. Am. Stat. Assoc. **54**(285), 225–230 (1959)
33. Zhang, Z.: Variable selection with stepwise and best subset approaches. Ann. Transl. Med. **4**(7) (2016)

Deep Group-Wise Variational Diffeomorphic Image Registration

Tycho F. A. van der Ouderaa[1](✉), Ivana Išgum[2,3], Wouter B. Veldhuis[4],
and Bob D. de Vos[1]

[1] Quantib-U, Utrecht, The Netherlands
t.vanderouderaa@quantib.com
[2] Department of Biomedical Engineering and Physics, Amsterdam University
Medical Center, University of Amsterdam, Amsterdam, The Netherlands
[3] Department of Radiology and Nuclear Medicine, Amsterdam University Medical
Center, University of Amsterdam, Amsterdam, The Netherlands
[4] Department of Radiology, University Medical Center Utrecht,
Utrecht, The Netherlands

Abstract. Deep neural networks are increasingly used for pair-wise image
registration. We propose to extend current learning-based image registration to allow simultaneous registration of multiple images. To achieve this,
we build upon the pair-wise variational and diffeomorphic VoxelMorph
approach and present a general mathematical framework that enables both
registration of multiple images to their geodesic average and registration in
which any of the available images can be used as a fixed image. In addition,
we provide a likelihood based on normalized mutual information, a well-
known image similarity metric in registration, between multiple images,
and a prior that allows for explicit control over the viscous fluid energy
to effectively regularize deformations. We trained and evaluated our approach using intra-patient registration of breast MRI and Thoracic 4DCT
exams acquired over multiple time points. Comparison with Elastix and
VoxelMorph demonstrates competitive quantitative performance of the
proposed method in terms of image similarity and reference landmark distances at significantly faster registration.

Keywords: Deep learning · Variational · Diffeomorphic ·
Group-wise · Image registration

1 Introduction

Image registration, the process of aligning images, is a fundamental problem in
medical image analysis [32]. For example, it can be used to align image volumes in
longitudinal studies [25], or to align images acquired temporally during contrast
enhancement [27].

Electronic supplementary material The online version of this chapter (https://
doi.org/10.1007/978-3-030-62469-9_14) contains supplementary material, which is
available to authorized users.

© Springer Nature Switzerland AG 2020
J. Petersen et al. (Eds.): TIA 2020, LNCS 12502, pp. 155–164, 2020.
https://doi.org/10.1007/978-3-030-62469-9_14

A common way to register images is to apply a transformation, such as an affine transformation, B-splines [28], or a deformation (vector) field [29], and to optimize its parameters using some form of numerical optimization. The objective is to minimize misalignment defined by a loss, such as a squared error, negative normalized cross correlation, or more advanced dissimilarity measures such as negative normalized mutual information [24]. Additionally, unrealistic deformations are mitigated by regularization or by using a constraint family of deformations.

Methods that constrain deformation fields to diffeomorphisms, such as LDDMM [4], Diffeomorphic Demons [31], and SyN [1], guarantee preservation of topology, and have shown to be very effective.

Recently, it has been shown that deep learning models can be trained to perform image registration, leveraging on the increased availability of medical imaging data [2,34]. Once a model is trained, deformation fields can be obtained by inference, which is much faster than aligning images through an iterative optimization process. In [13] and [14], diffeomorphic neural network-based methods were proposed, further bridging the gap between learning-based and classical approaches. Although deep learning methods show great potential, they are restricted to image pairs or require a heuristically constructed template [8].

In this work, we extend learning-based methods to enable fast group-wise image registration. We build upon the variational framework proposed by [14] and stack multiple images along the channel axis of the input and output of the network. In addition, we propose a likelihood based on normalized mutual information and a prior which yields explicit control over the *viscous fluid energy*. We quantitatively evaluate our model and compare it with Elastix [18] and Voxelmorph [3].

2   Method

Let us consider random variables $\mathbf{x}$ and $\mathbf{y}$ each consisting of a collection of image volumes acquired at K different timepoints. We consider $\mathbf{y}$ to be unknown aligned ground-truth and let $\mathbf{z}$ be a latent variable that parameterizes transformations $\phi_{\mathbf{z}}^{-1}$ that describes the formation of $\mathbf{x}$ as a transformation of $\mathbf{y}$ through $\phi_{\mathbf{z}}^{-1} \circ \mathbf{y}$. All variables can be partitioned into different subsets for each timepoint $k \in \{1, ..., K\}$, where $\mathbf{z}_k \in \mathbf{z}$ defines a transformation on 3D voxels $\phi_{\mathbf{z}_k}^{-1} : \mathbb{R}^3 \to \mathbb{R}^3$ that maps the volume $\mathbf{y}_k \in \mathbf{y}$ onto volume $\mathbf{x}_k \in \mathbf{x}$ via $\phi_{\mathbf{z}_k}^{-1} \circ \mathbf{y}_k$.

Depending on the task, we define images that require registration (i.e. moving images) as observations of $\mathbf{x}$ and the target images (i.e. fixed images) as observations of $\mathbf{y}$. We are not restricted to a predefined fixed timepoint and can describe all of our data as observations of $\mathbf{x}$, effectively letting $\mathbf{y}$ be an unobserved latent variable. We will refer to this case as *all-moving* group-wise image registration, and the case where one timepoint is chosen as fixed image as *all-to-one* group-wise image registration. Observe that we can obtain the former from the latter by constraining the deformation $\phi_{\mathbf{z}_p}^{-1} = \mathrm{Id}$ at a fixed timepoint p to be the identity. Moreover, we can view pair-wise registration as a particular $K = 2$ instance in our group-wise framework, where one timepoint is kept fixed and the other one can move.

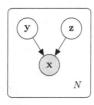

Fig. 1. Graphical model describing misaligned observations $\mathbf{x}$ as noisy observations of unknown aligned images $\mathbf{y}$ that have been transformed via $\phi_{\mathbf{z}}^{-1} \circ \mathbf{y}$.

2.1 Generative Model

We propose a generative model and aim to find the posterior probability of our transformation parameters $p(\mathbf{z}|\mathbf{x},\mathbf{y})$ that govern the deformations $\phi_{\mathbf{z}}$. Because the posterior is intractable we approximate it using *variational inference*.

Prior. We define a multivariate normal prior $\mathbf{z}$ with zero mean and precision matrix $\mathbf{\Lambda}$ as the inverse of the covariance:

$$p(\mathbf{z}) = \mathcal{N}(\mathbf{z} \mid 0, \mathbf{\Lambda}^{-1}), \tag{1}$$

where we choose $\mathbf{\Lambda} = \lambda_v \mathbf{I} + \lambda_u \mathbf{L}$ with identity matrix $\mathbf{I}$ weighted by λ_v and the Laplacian neighbourhood graph $\mathbf{L} = \mathbf{D} - \mathbf{A}$ with degree matrix $\mathbf{D}$ and adjacency matrix $\mathbf{A}$, weighted by λ_u. We treat λ_v and λ_u as hyper-parameters that give control over the norm on the vectors in the field parameterized by $\mathbf{z}$ and the norm on its displacement, respectively. The prior is inspired on the spatial smoothing prior proposed in [13], which can be seen as a particular $\lambda_v = 0$ instance of our prior. If $\mathbf{z}$ describes the deformation field as is done in [3], it penalizes the *linear elastic energy* penalty [22] and in case ϕ is diffeomorphic and $\mathbf{z}$ describes the velocity of the deformation field, the prior is more akin to a fluid-based model and penalizes the *viscous fluid energy* [5,10,30].

Likelihood. It is well known that (normalized) mutual information information is an effective similarity metric for image registration which is robust to varying intensity inhomogeneities [21,33]. Therefore, we model the probability of $\mathbf{x}$ as an exponential distribution of the average normalized mutual information (NMI) across all timepoint permutations:

$$p(\mathbf{x}|\mathbf{y},\mathbf{z}) \propto \exp\left\{ \frac{1}{K(K-1)} \sum_{i\neq j} \text{NMI}(\phi_{\mathbf{z}_i} \circ \mathbf{x}_i, \phi_{\mathbf{z}_j} \circ \mathbf{x}_j) \right\} \tag{2}$$

where we define $\phi_{\mathbf{z}_p} = \text{Id}$ and $\mathbf{x}_p = \mathbf{y}_p$ in case of a fixed timepoint p. Various approaches exist to estimate the probability density functions (both marginal and joint) of the intensity values needed to compute the entropies for the mutual information [24]. In this work, we obtain differentiable estimates of the intensity values using a Gaussian Parzen window estimation [11,21] of the voxel intensities in each mini batch.

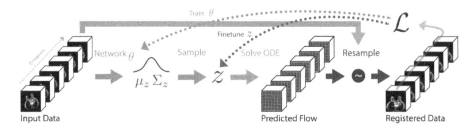

Fig. 2. GroupMorph: A neural network parameterized by θ is trained to output estimates over parameters of velocity fields $\mathbf{z}$ that can be integrated to obtain diffeomorphic flows that align the input images according to some loss $\mathcal{L}$.

2.2 Variational Lower Bound

Since the posterior probability $p(\mathbf{z}|\mathbf{x}, \mathbf{y})$ is intractable, we cannot directly obtain MAP estimates of $\mathbf{z}$. Instead, we estimate the true posterior with a variational approximating posterior by minimizing the negative evidence lower bound $\mathcal{L}(\theta|\mathbf{x}, \mathbf{y})$ which can be derived using the fact that the KL-divergence is non-negative [17]:

$$\log p_\theta(\mathbf{x}, \mathbf{y}) = \mathrm{KL}(q_\theta(\mathbf{z}|\mathbf{x}, \mathbf{y}) \,\|\, p(\mathbf{z}|\mathbf{x}, \mathbf{y})) - \mathcal{L}(\theta|\mathbf{x}, \mathbf{y}) \tag{3}$$

$$\geq -\mathcal{L}(\theta|\mathbf{x}, \mathbf{y}) = -\mathbb{E}_q\left[-\log q_\theta(\mathbf{z}|\mathbf{x}, \mathbf{y}) + \log p(\mathbf{x}, \mathbf{y}, \mathbf{z}) \right] \tag{4}$$

$$= -\mathbb{E}_q\left[\log p(\mathbf{x}|\mathbf{y}, \mathbf{z})\right] + \mathrm{KL}(q_\theta(\mathbf{z}|\mathbf{x}, \mathbf{y}) \,\|\, p(\mathbf{z})) + \mathrm{const}. \tag{5}$$

We let our variational approximate posterior [17] be a multivariate Gaussian:

$$\log q_\theta(\mathbf{z}|\mathbf{x}, \mathbf{y}) = \log \mathcal{N}(\mathbf{z}|\boldsymbol{\mu}_\mathbf{z}, \boldsymbol{\Sigma}_\mathbf{z}), \tag{6}$$

where mean $\boldsymbol{\mu}_\mathbf{z}$ and covariance matrix $\boldsymbol{\Sigma}_\mathbf{z}$ of the approximate posterior $q_\theta(\mathbf{z}|\mathbf{x}, \mathbf{y})$ are outputted by a neural network with parameters θ. To avoid differentiating through a random variable, we obtain the sample $\mathbf{z}$ using the *re-parameterization trick* [17] $\mathbf{z} = \boldsymbol{\mu}_\mathbf{z} + \boldsymbol{\Sigma}_\mathbf{z}\boldsymbol{\Sigma}_\mathbf{z}^T e$ where $e \sim \mathcal{N}(0, \mathbf{I})$ is normally distributed.

2.3 Resulting Loss

We find the resulting loss for a single Monte Carlo sample from q:

$$\mathcal{L}(\theta|\mathbf{x}, \mathbf{y}) = \underbrace{-\mathbb{E}_q[\log p(\mathbf{x}|\mathbf{y}, \mathbf{z})]}_{\text{Reconstruction Error}} + \underbrace{\mathrm{KL}[q_\theta(\mathbf{z}|\mathbf{x}, \mathbf{y})\|p(\mathbf{z})]}_{\text{Regularization}} \tag{7}$$

$$\simeq \frac{1}{K(K-1)}\sum_{i \neq j} -\mathrm{NMI}(\phi_{\mathbf{z}_i} \circ \mathbf{x}_i, \phi_{\mathbf{z}_j} \circ \mathbf{x}_j) + \frac{1}{2}\left[\mathrm{tr}((\lambda_u \mathbf{D} + \lambda_v)\boldsymbol{\Sigma}_\mathbf{z} - \log \boldsymbol{\Sigma}_\mathbf{z}) + \boldsymbol{\mu}_\mathbf{z}^T \boldsymbol{\Lambda}^{-1} \boldsymbol{\mu}_\mathbf{z}\right] + \mathrm{const}.$$

where we define $\phi_{\mathbf{z}_p} = \mathrm{Id}$ and $\mathbf{x}_p = \mathbf{y}_p$ in case of a fixed timepoint p and where we can expand the last term $\boldsymbol{\mu}_\mathbf{z}^T \boldsymbol{\Lambda}^{-1}\boldsymbol{\mu}_\mathbf{z} = \lambda_u \frac{1}{2}\sum_i \sum_{j \in N(i)}(\boldsymbol{\mu}[i] - \boldsymbol{\mu}[j])^2 + \lambda_v \sum_i \boldsymbol{\mu}[i]^2$ where $N(i)$ are the neighbors of voxel i.

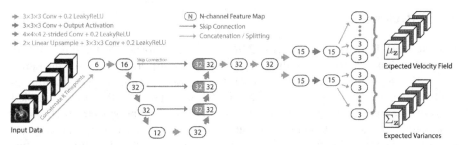

Fig. 3. Illustration of the 3D U-Net architecture used to output mean $\mu_{\mathbf{z}}$ and variance $\Sigma_{\mathbf{z}}$ of distribution over velocity fields $q_\theta(\mathbf{z}|\mathbf{x}, \mathbf{y})$ used for diffeomorphic image registration.

2.4 Diffeomorphic Transformations

Diffeomorphic deformation fields are invertible (ϕ^{-1} exists) and have found to be very valuable in image registration as they preserve topology, by design. For diffeomorphic GroupMorph, we follow [3] and describe transformations $\phi_{\mathbf{z}_k}$ for each timepoints k as an ordinary differential equation (ODE):

$$\frac{\partial \phi_{\mathbf{z}_k}^{(t)}}{\partial t} = v_{\mathbf{z}_k}\left(\phi_{\mathbf{z}_k}^{(t)}\right) \tag{8}$$

where $\phi_{\mathbf{z}_k}^{(0)} = \mathrm{Id}$ is the identity transformation and t is time. For every timepoint k, we let $\mathbf{z}_k$ parameterize the vectors of the velocity field $v_{\mathbf{z}_k}$ and solve deformation field $\phi_{\mathbf{z}_k}^{(1)}$ using the *scaling and squaring* solver, proposed by [13] in the context of neural-based diffeomorphic image registration. For non-diffeomorphic models, we let $\mathbf{z}_k$ parameterize the vectors of the deformation field $\phi_{\mathbf{z}_k}$ directly.

3   Implementation

We let a 3D U-net [2,3,26], output the parameters $\mu_{\mathbf{z}}$ and $\Sigma_{\mathbf{z}}$ of the approximate posterior $q_\theta(\mathbf{z}|\mathbf{x}, \mathbf{y})$, as illustrated in Fig. 2. Fixed and moving image volumes are concatenated along the channel dimension and form the input of the network. Figure 3 gives a more detailed description of the network architecture, including filter sizes and channel counts. All layers are followed by a Leaky ReLU [20] with 0.2 slope, except for the $\mu_{\mathbf{z}}$ and $\Sigma_{\mathbf{z}}$ heads which are respectively followed by a hyperbolic tangent scaled with $\alpha = 15$ that limits the output to $[-\alpha, \alpha]$ voxels and a Softplus[1] activation to ensure positive variances.

We train for 100k iterations using Adam [16] with a batch size of 1 and a learning rate of $1e^{-5}$ ($\beta_1 = 0.9, \beta_2 = 0.999$) decayed with cosine annealing [19]. Inputs are normalized using 1–99 percentile normalization [23] and training samples consist of $96 \times 96 \times 96$ patches for all timepoints at a randomly sampled location. For the hyperparameters we choose $\lambda_u = 1$ and $\lambda_v = 0.01$.

---

[1] Softplus$(x) = \log(\exp(x) + 1)$.

4 Datasets

Breast MR Dataset The *Breast MR* dataset comprises 270 training and 68 evaluation dynamic contrast enhancement series of subjects with extremely dense breast tissue (Volpara Density Grade 4). Each series contains DCE-MRI images ($384 \times 384 \times 60$ voxels with spacing $0.966 \times 0.966 \times 3.000$ mm resampled to 1mm^3) acquired on a 3.0T Achieva or Ingenia Philips system at $K = 6$ timepoints in the axial plane with bilateral anatomic coverage. The interval between timepoints between the first two timepoints is 90 s in which a 0.1 mL dose of gadobutrol per kilogram of body weight is injected at a rate of 1 mL/s and 1 min for the other timepoints.

DIR-Lab 4DCT This set contains 4D chest CT scans of 10 different patients that have been acquired as part of the radiotherapy planning process for the treatment of thoracic malignancies. For each patient 3D CT volumes have been acquired at $K = 6$ timepoints during the expiratory phase with an average voxel spacing of $1.04 \times 1.04 \times 2.5$. A detailed description of the data acquisition can be found in [7] and [6]. The dataset is a subset of the publicly available *DIR-Lab 4DCT* dataset [7] and contains 75 landmark reference points for all timepoints. The volumes have been cropped in-plane to 256×256 voxels in such a way that all reference points are present. We report performance on the first scan ('Patient 1') and used the others for training.

5 Experiments and Results

Using the proposed GroupMorph model, we have performed intra-patient registration of multiple 3D scans acquired at different timepoints in two different ways. First, we performed *all-to-one* registration where the scan acquired at the first time point was used as fixed image and all other scans of the same patient as moving images. Thereafter, we performed *all-moving* registration, where we compute deformation fields for all images and the register to a geodesic average.

To compare performance of the proposed GroupMorph model with state-of-the-art conventional and neural-based methods, we performed registration using Elastix [18] and VoxelMorph [3,14] . For registration with Elastix we use configuration described for registration of DCE-MRI described in [15]. For fair comparison with VoxelMorph, we use the same loss, network architecture and hyper-parameters in VoxelMorph and GroupMorph. We only vary the channels in the first and last layers to match required dimensions and set $\lambda_v = 0$ for VoxelMorph.

Experiments were performed using both breast MRI and chest CT scans. For breast MR scans no landmarks were available, hence evaluation was performed with root mean square error (RMSE) and NMI. For chest CT, a set of 75 landmarks was provided at all timepoints within DIR-Lab, hence performance was evaluated by measuring the average distance between the landmarks after registration and over all timepoint combinations. Moreover, for both sets we report percentages of negative Jacobian determinants $(\% \ |J_\phi| \ < \ 0)$ that indicate undesirable folding. Additionally, we evaluate the speed of registrations. Results are listed in Table 1 [2]. They show that the group-wise models perform better in terms of RMSE and NMI on both sets, especially in the *all-moving* case. We find that diffeomorphic registration models (indicated with '-diff') lead to lower amount of negative Jacobian determinants, which means that less folding occurs and indicates that the fields are smoother than those of non-diffeomorphic counterpart. Average registration times

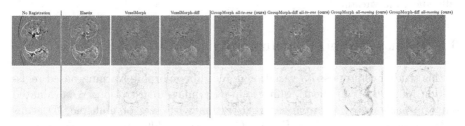

Fig. 4. Qualitative evaluation of first patient of *DIR-Lab 4DCT* dataset after applying different registration models. TOP: Axial slice of average timepoint after subtracting the first timepoint. BOTTOM: Axial slice of the Jacobian determinant field averaged over all timepoints.

Table 1. Quantitative performance using different registration methods. LEFT: Models and average registration time per serie. CENTER: RMSE and NMI on *Breast MR*. RIGHT: RMSE, NMI and average displacment on *DIR-Lab 4DCT* evaluation set.

Model	Time (s)	Breast MR			DIR-Lab 4DCT			
	-	RMSE	NMI	$\% \ |J_\phi| < 0$	RMSE	NMI	Avg Displacement (mm)	$\% \ |J_\phi| < 0$
No Registration (Identity)	-	24.15	0.24	-	63.39	0.47	1.83 ± 2.24	-
Elastix	652	23.42	0.25	0	36.84	0.49	1.09 ± 1.30	0
VoxelMorph	5	22.43	0.26	3.31e-2	28.42	0.50	1.18 ± 1.33	4.32e-6
VoxelMorph-diff	5	22.12	0.26	1.55e-4	25.37	0.51	1.12 ± 1.33	7.79e-7
All-to-one GroupMorph (ours)	2	21.97	0.28	4.20e-5	27.11	0.51	1.16 ± 1.36	3.05e-5
All-to-one GroupMorph-diff (ours)	2	22.00	0.27	1.60e-5	25.26	0.51	**1.08 ± 1.35**	2.60e-7
All-moving GroupMorph (ours)	2	**21.47**	**0.32**	2.00e-4	23.15	0.53	1.39 ± 1.32	4.98e-6
All-moving GroupMorph-diff (ours)	2	21.57	**0.32**	1.90e-4	**22.09**	**0.54**	1.52 ± 1.34	9.74e-7

---

[2] We measured time to calculate all required deformation fields for Elastix on two 10-core Intel Xeon Silver 4114 2.20 GHz CPUs and of the neural-based methods on a NVIDIA GeForce RTX 2080 GPU.

per series (Table 1) show that registration times of the GroupMorph model are significantly lower than the registration times of the baselines, especially compared with Elastix.

Figure 4 illustrates the axial slices of the first volume in the *DIR-Lab* dataset. Subtraction images illustrate improved alignment for all registration models, especially at borders and in particular for *all-moving* group-wise models. From the Jacobian determinant fields, we can observe particularly strong local expansions and compression in the *all-moving* models and most notably in the non-diffeomorphic variant.

6   Discussion and Conclusion

In this study, we proposed a variational and diffeomorphic learning-based registration method for application in group-wise image registration. We evaluated our approach using intra-patient registration with sets of multiple 3D scans of two different modalities (MR and CT) showing different anatomies (breast and chest). In addition, we provided a likelihood based on normalized mutual information, a well-performing image similarity metric in registration, between multiple images and a prior that allows for explicit control over the viscous fluid energy to effectively control regularization of deformation fields.

In spite of using diffeomorphic transformations, we observed some negative Jacobian determinants likely resulting from approximation errors. Hence, future work could investigate options for further improvements. It can be expected that training with more data, further tuning of the network architecture and hyper-parameters will lead to higher performance. Other potential advancements include a 4D network [9] to more explicitly model the temporal component, fine tuning of z after inference (see dotted grey arrow in Fig. 2), time-dependent velocity fields to allow more flexible diffeomorphic transformations, and a bi-directional cost [12] and non-diagonal covariance [14] to further improve smoothness of the deformation fields.

To conclude, we found that our GroupMorph model can simultaneously register multiple scans with performance similar to conventional registration with Elastix and learning-based VoxelMorph, enabling close to real-time group-wise registration without delaying clinical reading.

Acknowledgements. Authors would like to thank Jorrit Glastra, Tim Henke and Rob Hesselink for insightful discussions and support.

References

1. Avants, B.B., Epstein, C.L., Grossman, M., Gee, J.C.: Symmetric diffeomorphic image registration with cross-correlation: evaluating automated labeling of elderly and neurodegenerative brain. Med. Image Anal. **12**(1), 26–41 (2008)

2. Balakrishnan, G., Zhao, A., Sabuncu, M.R., Guttag, J., Dalca, A.V.: An unsupervised learning model for deformable medical image registration. In: Proceedings of the IEEE Conference on Computer Vision and Pattern Recognition, pp. 9252–9260 (2018)
3. Balakrishnan, G., Zhao, A., Sabuncu, M.R., Guttag, J., Dalca, A.V.: Voxelmorph: a learning framework for deformable medical image registration. IEEE Trans. Med. Imaging **38**(8), 1788–1800 (2019)
4. Beg, M.F., Miller, M.I., Trouvé, A., Younes, L.: Computing large deformation metric mappings via geodesic flows of diffeomorphisms. Int. J. Comput. Vision **61**(2), 139–157 (2005). https://doi.org/10.1023/B:VISI.0000043755.93987.aa
5. Bro-Nielsen, M., Gramkow, C.: Fast fluid registration of medical images. In: Höhne, K.H., Kikinis, R. (eds.) VBC 1996. LNCS, vol. 1131, pp. 265–276. Springer, Heidelberg (1996). https://doi.org/10.1007/BFb0046964
6. Castillo, E., Castillo, R., Martinez, J., Shenoy, M., Guerrero, T.: Four-dimensional deformable image registration using trajectory modeling. Phys. Med. Biol. **55**(1), 305 (2009)
7. Castillo, R., et al.: A framework for evaluation of deformable image registration spatial accuracy using large landmark point sets. Phys. Med. Biol. **54**(7), 1849 (2009)
8. Che, T., et al.: Deep group-wise registration for multi-spectral images from fundus images. IEEE Access **7**, 27650–27661 (2019)
9. Choy, C., Gwak, J., Savarese, S.: 4d spatio-temporal convnets: minkowski convolutional neural networks. In: Proceedings of the IEEE Conference on Computer Vision and Pattern Recognition, pp. 3075–3084 (2019)
10. Christensen, G.E.: Deformable shape models for anatomy (1994)
11. Collignon, A., Maes, F., Delaere, D., Vandermeulen, D., Suetens, P., Marchal, G.: Automated multi-modality image registration based on information theory. In: Information Processing in Medical Imaging, vol. 3, pp. 263–274. Citeseer (1995)
12. Dalca, A.V., Balakrishnan, G., Guttag, J., Sabuncu, M.R.: Improved probabilistic diffeomorphic registration with cnns (2018)
13. Dalca, A.V., Balakrishnan, G., Guttag, J., Sabuncu, M.R.: Unsupervised learning for fast probabilistic diffeomorphic registration. In: Frangi, A.F., Schnabel, J.A., Davatzikos, C., Alberola-López, C., Fichtinger, G. (eds.) MICCAI 2018. LNCS, vol. 11070, pp. 729–738. Springer, Cham (2018). https://doi.org/10.1007/978-3-030-00928-1_82
14. Dalca, A.V., Balakrishnan, G., Guttag, J., Sabuncu, M.R.: Unsupervised learning of probabilistic diffeomorphic registration for images and surfaces. Med. Image Anal. **57**, 226–236 (2019)
15. Gubern-Mérida, A., et al.: Automated localization of breast cancer in DCE-MRI. Med. Image Anal. **20**(1), 265–274 (2015)
16. Kingma, D.P., Ba, J.: Adam: a method for stochastic optimization. arXiv preprint arXiv:1412.6980 (2014)
17. Kingma, D.P., Welling, M.: Auto-encoding variational bayes. arXiv preprint arXiv:1312.6114 (2013)
18. Klein, S., Staring, M., Murphy, K., Viergever, M.A., Pluim, J.P.: Elastix: a toolbox for intensity-based medical image registration. IEEE Trans. Med. Imaging **29**(1), 196–205 (2009)
19. Loshchilov, I., Hutter, F.: Sgdr: Stochastic gradient descent with warm restarts. arXiv preprint arXiv:1608.03983 (2016)
20. Maas, A.L., Hannun, A.Y., Ng, A.Y.: Rectifier nonlinearities improve neural network acoustic models. In: Proceedings of ICML, vol. 30, p. 3 (2013)

21. Maes, F., Collignon, A., Vandermeulen, D., Marchal, G., Suetens, P.: Multimodality image registration by maximization of mutual information. IEEE Trans. Med. Imaging **16**(2), 187–198 (1997)
22. Miller, M.I., Christensen, G.E., Amit, Y., Grenander, U.: Mathematical textbook of deformable neuroanatomies. Proc. Nat. Acad. Sci. **90**(24), 11944–11948 (1993)
23. Patrice, D., et al.: Image Processing and Analysis: A Primer, vol. 3. World Scientific, London (2018)
24. Pluim, J.P., Maintz, J.A., Viergever, M.A.: Mutual-information-based registration of medical images: a survey. IEEE Trans. Med. Imaging **22**(8), 986–1004 (2003)
25. Reuter, M., Fischl, B.: Avoiding asymmetry-induced bias in longitudinal image processing. Neuroimage **57**(1), 19–21 (2011)
26. Ronneberger, O., Fischer, P., Brox, T.: U-net: convolutional networks for biomedical image segmentation. In: Navab, N., Hornegger, J., Wells, W.M., Frangi, A.F. (eds.) MICCAI 2015. LNCS, vol. 9351, pp. 234–241. Springer, Cham (2015). https://doi.org/10.1007/978-3-319-24574-4_28
27. Rueckert, D., Hayes, C., Studholme, C., Summers, P., Leach, M., Hawkes, D.J.: Non-rigid registration of breast MR images using mutual information. In: Wells, William M., Colchester, Alan, Delp, Scott (eds.) MICCAI 1998. LNCS, vol. 1496, pp. 1144–1152. Springer, Heidelberg (1998). https://doi.org/10.1007/BFb0056304
28. Rueckert, D., Sonoda, L.I., Hayes, C., Hill, D.L., Leach, M.O., Hawkes, D.J.: Non-rigid registration using free-form deformations: application to breast MR images. IEEE Trans. Med. Imaging **18**(8), 712–721 (1999)
29. Sotiras, A., Davatzikos, C., Paragios, N.: Deformable medical image registration: a survey. IEEE Trans. Med. Imaging **32**(7), 1153–1190 (2013)
30. Tian, J.: Molecular Imaging: Fundamentals and applications. Springer Science & Business Media, Dordrecht (2013)
31. Vercauteren, T., Pennec, X., Perchant, A., Ayache, N.: Diffeomorphic demons: efficient non-parametric image registration. NeuroImage **45**(1), S61–S72 (2009)
32. Viergever, M.A., Maintz, J.A., Klein, S., Murphy, K., Staring, M., Pluim, J.P.: A survey of medical image registration-under review (2016)
33. Viola, P., Wells III, W.M.: Alignment by maximization of mutual information. Int. J. Comput. Vision **24**(2), 137–154 (1997)
34. de Vos, B.D., Berendsen, F.F., Viergever, M.A., Sokooti, H., Staring, M., Išgum, I.: A deep learning framework for unsupervised affine and deformable image registration. Med. Image Anal. **52**, 128–143 (2019)

Author Index

Printed in the United States
By Bookmasters